Once Bitten, Twice Fined

Who exactly is going to read your book?
Anon

Once Bitten,
Twice Fined

Graeme Pagan

Birlinn

First published in 2004
by Birlinn Limited
West Newington House
10 Newington Road
Edinburgh EH9 1QS

www.birlinn.co.uk

ISBN 10: 1 84158 307 3
ISBN 13: 978 1 84158 307 5

British Library Cataloguing-in-Publication Data
A catalogue record of this book is available from the British Library

Typeset in Garamond by Koinonia, Manchester
Printed and bound by MPG Books Limited, Bodmin

Contents

	Foreword	vii
	Acknowledgements	ix
	Introduction	xi
1	Highland Exhilarations	1
2	From the Beaches of Tiree to the Nightspots of Nairn	24
3	'Damn and blast you to hell . . .'	34
4	'Try a redhead next time'	41
5	For Justice and Decency	52
6	In Every Court in the Land	69
7	The Power of the Fiscal	83
8	Dad Would Have Laughed	105
9	Never a Lost Cause	125
10	'We know what's best for them'	144
11	'We had a dream'	162
12	Mysteries of the Air	181
13	'Death is not extinguishing the light . . .'	190
14	After 300 Years – One Minute Late	205
15	Through Life's Changes	218

Foreword

Most lawyers' memoirs are mince. I know; I've written mine. Yet now and again you come across a stunner. Graeme Pagan's is such a book. Try this test. Open the book at random and start reading. I guarantee that ten minutes later you'll still be reading, maybe with a glance over your shoulder in case the sales assistant thinks you're in a for a freebie. Whether it's skill or a knack I don't know. With the merest twist of a sentence, the author can create a character and bring him to stand talking beside you. This is not a quaint book full of teuchters. The people in it are real people. The dialogue is real. The situations are real. The questions people ask are real. The whole book reeks of experience, legal and otherwise. You are entitled to ask how a country solicitor, in a small practice, in a small town can manage such things, but he has. When I hear he was writing a book I groaned. When I was asked to write a foreword I broke into a sweat. I've read judges' books and laughed at judges' stories, but all from sycophancy. Don't listen to judges' jokes and don't buy their books; buy this one.

The author is something of an oddity. He is a small fish in a small pool but his powers of observation are universal. He sees far beyond his own horizons, and now and again speaks for all humanity. His sparse comments on his duties as a Fiscal give us an insight into how such a job must be animated by a passion for justice. Above all he excels at bringing ordinary people to life and making them noble. He fails only when he tries to do this with his Liberal party colleagues. Mary Shelley herself would have found breathing life into Liberals harder than creating Frankenstein's monster. From this remark you will see that I don't share the author's politics. Nor am I a particular friend. I am quite disinterested when I say this is a fine book.

When I first spoke to Mr Pagan it was to tap him for a fiver. He refused. I have waited with exasperated affection for thirty-one years to write this next sentence. Graeme Pagan is a miserly bastard, but he has written a cracker of a book.

Ian Hamilton
March 2004

Acknowledgements

I am very grateful to those who first inspired me to write this and to those who encouraged me to keep going during the inevitable periods of self-doubt. I also acknowledge with thanks those who have allowed me to pass on their own experiences.

Special gratitude is due to Elsie Miller for the hours she spent typing this manuscript and even more hours dealing with the numerous changes as I tried to put everything together. Her enthusiasm and reassurances were a great help.

Introduction

M any people have said to many over the years, 'You should write a book.' During my nearly fifty years' experience of practising law, almost all of it in a small community and dealing with all sorts of people, and because of my involvement in many other things, people have often said the same thing to me. It was when three separate ladies, in a space of ten days towards the end of 2001, said it to me that I thought I must do something. Particularly so when I realized that none of the ladies knew each other and that their ages were very different – one was in her eighties, one in her sixties and one in her forties. When the younger one added, 'before it is too late', I was really spurred into action.

I am not sure exactly what she meant but if she was thinking of a failing memory as the years went by, she was right. I have not kept diaries and although I have access to some papers and to my own scrapbook, most of this book is from memory. I hope I shall be forgiven for any historical inaccuracies or confusions with names which will inevitably have crept in. Many of my experiences have been amusing, many sad and many interesting, but I have always believed in trying to make people laugh and I hope that will help this book to be entertaining. I also think it is important to pass on to others some of the experiences I have been privileged to have been part of and experiences which others may never encounter. Some of the sadder occasions may help most of us to realize how lucky we are. Some of them will also, I hope, help people to cope a bit better if they are having to face similar difficulties.

I once read a very inspiring book called *The Good Women of China*.

Xinran had had many harrowing experiences in helping women subjected to violence, abuse and general deprivation in many parts of China and she passed on what someone had once said to her about writing things down. 'Writing is a kind of repository and can help create a space for the accommodation of new thoughts and feelings. If you don't write these stories down, your heart will be filled up and broken by them.' There is something of that here as well.

Everything that is in this book is true and a lot of names are real, but obviously for reasons of professional and personal confidentiality, I have sometimes had to change names and on one or two occasions to disguise the stories altogether. Some of the experiences go back several decades and some of the episodes reflect attitudes and ways of life which are no longer appropriate. But I have no wish to disguise the way things used to be. A lady I knew, who herself had been a victim of the country's appalling housing situation, told me that she was very glad to hear that I was writing a book. 'People should not be allowed to forget how things used to be,' were her words.

I have been lucky and privileged in many ways and I hope my experiences can help or entertain others, perhaps both. I think it would be a waste to take those experiences to my grave. I have never believed they were intended only for me.

Finally, I gladly acknowledge the debt I owe to Heather and the rest of my supportive family – present and future.

I

Highland Exhilarations

A police torch was flashed into my eyes. It was 3 o'clock in the morning and there was a pause as I sat at the wheel of my car before hearing the very welcome words, 'Och! It's yourself – carry on home.' Where else, I wondered, could someone be 37 miles from home and get such a welcome from the local police. It was all the more surprising because, at the time, I had only been living in Oban for two weeks. It was no wonder that when I again passed through Tyndrum at the same sort of time two weeks later, I felt a warm glow on seeing the Argyll sign at the roadside. 'I'm home,' I felt with a secure and satisfied emotion.

Despite the security of my upbringing, I was in a sense a bit of a nomad, having been at boarding school since the age of eight and then at school in England and then, after that, going on to university in Edinburgh. I had not really had the chance to put my roots down in my original home patch of Cupar.

It was one of life's happy coincidences which had brought me to Oban and the Highlands in the first place. With hindsight it was clearly something which had been mapped out for me. In the late 1920s, when my father was himself studying law at Edinburgh University, he was aware of a fellow student but it was some time before they ever spoke to each other. For a while they had simply acknowledged one another by raising their bowler hats as they passed each other in Charlotte Square, which they did regularly. However, at last, they found themselves sitting next to each other in a barber's shop at which coffee was served and magazines provided while they were waiting their turn for the chair. The other man was looking through the *Punch* magazine when, without even looking at Dad, he suddenly said, 'No relation of mine, unfortunately.'

Dad looked across at the magazine the other man was reading and saw an advert for John Harvey's Bristol Cream Sherry.

'I presume by that, that you are introducing yourself to me as Harvey.'

'Not only Harvey, also John,' he said, thereby inviting Dad to go onto Christian name terms immediately, which was not usual in those days. From that there began a family friendship which lasted near enough seventy years.

John Harvey, in fact, became virtually part of the family because he married comparatively late in life. Typically, having been Dad's best man, he chose the same date for his own wedding twenty-seven years later. We therefore had his company at home on many occasions during my childhood, including New Year and other holidays. By another happy chance, in the summer of 1957, John, who by then was the senior partner of the solicitor's firm Hosack & Sutherland in Oban, was spending the weekend at my parents' home immediately after my graduation. I told him that I had two weeks' holiday with nothing particular to do for the first time in many years and asked if he had any suggestions.

'Why don't you come back with me to Oban,' he said, and I did. In the Highlands I immediately found great peace of mind, which I had never experienced anywhere else. I felt totally at home and in five days, with John's help, I got a real taste of the area. On one memorable trip I managed to see the islands of Mull, Coll, Tiree, Barra, South Uist, Canna, Rum, Eigg and Muck before arriving, with just a single boat change, at Mallaig, having set out from Oban twenty-four hours before. I also managed a crossing from Mallaig to the spectacular Lochs Scavaig and Coruisk on Skye, where, almost thirty years later, I returned with my family for a memorable holiday at Elgol. My 1957 Highlands and Islands visit was enough to decide me where my future would be. Three years later I joined John Harvey's legal practice in Oban.

I had been more than ready for my Highland holiday, not just because it marked the end of what had been, for me, years of very hard studying, but because of a balls-up I had made at my graduation ceremony, which had caused embarrassment to some – not least to my poor parents who were watching from the balcony. The ceremony was pretty straightforward. Students had simply to walk up six steps, bow, be tapped on the head by part of John Knox's breeks, receive their parchment scrolls, go back down the steps and resume their seats. Never a man for formalities and ceremonies, I managed to get it wrong. Instead of going back down the steps, I turned immediately right and found myself in a very tight space, clambering over the knees of many professors and other dignitaries. 'Excuse me.' 'Excuse me.' 'Excuse me.' Halfway along, I wondered about turning back, but that would have drawn even more attention to myself. I decided, not for the first time in my life, to put a bold face on my stupidity. Then I panicked at the thought that there might be no steps at the far end of the platform and that I might have to jump, using my gown as a sort of parachute. Fortunately, I was spared at least that self-imposed humiliation.

A few hours later, I found myself at the graduation ball. I had threatened to boycott it when they refused to sell me a single ticket; the situation was saved by one of my friends. Hearing of my predicament, he produced his diary, which had names and useful details of a number of possible ladies. Eventually he fitted me up with a very nice student nurse, who was desperate to outscore her own friends by being invited to the graduation ball. After all, it was not immediately necessary for her to admit that her partner was going to be a boring lawyer and not a glamorous doctor.

At the ball I encountered two entirely different reactions to my morning performance at the graduation ceremony – 'Excuse me.' 'Excuse me.' 'Excuse me.' They both occurred while Hilary and I were standing in the buffet queue. First there was a loud pukka Edinburgh voice: 'There's that stupid idiot who got it all wrong this morning' – words hardly designed to impress my new date. I cowered away for a few minutes until there was a much more welcome encounter with a different voice: 'There's this morning's hero. Well done, well done. May I shake your hand. You were the only one among the 300 of us who had the guts to do your own thing. All the rest of us slavishly followed orders like gormless sheep.'

I decided not to enlighten him by confessing that I had not been at all brave, just stupid. But I learned something useful from that experience, which is that you cannot always tell what people are thinking or how they will react to anything. More often than not I have been in a minority, but when I have had the courage to speak out about something important – which does not always happen – someone has often come up to me afterwards saying something like: 'I'm so glad you said what you did because that's how I feel but I thought I would be alone.' We would all do well to remember a saying passed on to me by one of my friends from the Carmelite Monastery which is, sadly, no longer in Oban: 'We would worry less about what people thought of us if we realized how seldom they do.'

I obviously made a big impression on Hilary because she very quickly got engaged to someone else. Sadly, I heard thirty-five years later that the friend who had introduced us had died of alcoholism while living on a Scottish island.

Forty-five years after my graduation, as I was writing this, I opened another financial appeal from The University of Edinburgh which began: 'As an Edinburgh graduate, you will have your own memory of graduation day in the historic McEwan Hall.' 'Little do you know how right you are,' I thought to myself.

John Harvey was an outstanding character – very knowledgeable, courteous, old worldly and apparently unruffled by anything. Most important to us as solicitors, were his complete integrity and high standards, both in his personal and professional life. His character is perhaps best summed up by an incident which was referred to in his obituary. At one time he had been a keen sailor, but during a storm his boat sank to the bottom of Oban Bay. The following morning someone commiserated with him in his loss.

'I was thinking of giving it up anyway,' came his philosophical reply.
The boat is believed to be still there.

It was an interesting commentary on the times that when I joined John Harvey's business in 1960 there were two ladies there who had begun working for the firm forty-two years earlier, at the time when the First World War was about to start. They were both examples of the catastrophic effects of that ghastly war, which wiped out huge numbers of the young men of this country – and many other countries as well, of course. I am sure that is why the two ladies who became my colleagues never married. They continued with me for several years after I arrived, before finally retiring. They had never had any other full-time employment and I am also sure that they were never out of the country – maybe even never out of Argyll. Now, young ladies go on holiday for two weeks to Cyprus and come back having visited the pyramids in Egypt. How refreshingly different it all is. Unfortunately, it has not yet led to world peace and unification, but if we give the youth of today the chance, it just might.

The other partner in the Oban legal firm I joined was Bill Liddell, who had come to Oban fourteen years before me in 1946, immediately after the end of the Second World War. He had been on active service, being awarded an MC for bravery. I am not sure exactly what the events were which led to the award as he was usually too modest to discuss things like that. In a tribute to Bill after his death, a former army colleague recalled how, when medals had to be worn, Bill always arranged the MC in such a way that it slipped behind the lapel of his jacket 'to be seen no more'. I did once ask if he had been a prisoner of war.

'Yes,' he replied, 'for about an hour and a half.'

Apparently he and his sergeant had gone on a reconnaissance and had reccied too far, whereupon they found themselves surrounded by the enemy. Not long afterwards, as darkness fell, they were sitting as prisoners at the roadside, when Bill's sergeant suddenly gave him a knowing nod, leapt to his feet and kicked the guarding sentry in the balls as hard as he could.

'After that,' said Bill, 'I just had to run as fast as I could and luckily we found ourselves back in our own lines.'

Not long after I arrived in Oban, one of Bill's elderly lady clients asked him to take her transistor radio into safe custody while she spent the summer holidaying on the Isle of Mull. I used to collide with Bill as we ran in and out of the large store room, which we kept visiting to get the latest cricket test score. I hope we remembered to deduct the cost of two batteries from her next legal bill!

When I joined the legal practice it had the position as Secretary to the Oban Playhouse Company which ran two cinemas in the town. Each to his own, of course, but I certainly found reading film previews a bit more entertaining than studying title conditions from nineteenth-century documents. It was not uncommon for these to contain conditions against erections on the back green without the prior consent of the superiors. I always thought that might be rather difficult to detect and even more difficult to enforce.

When I came to Oban, I was given two separate bits of useful advice. The first came from Dr George Bain, who passed on to me something that had been said to him when he had arrived in the area: 'Don't try changing the Highlands or the Highlander, for as sure as hell they will end up changing you.' The other bit of advice was from Tommy MacDonald, also from Taynuilt. He advised me that, if I wanted to achieve anything here, I would have to kick myself along very hard. He explained that most people found the Highland atmosphere very soporific and that I should try having less sleep than I might think I needed. My friends would claim that that is why I often zizz off at wrong moments, but fewer hours' sleep is nothing to do with that. I can drop off even after a long and apparently good sleep. I have to admit that my slightly unusual weakness can cause embarrassment. On one occasion, I was chairing a meeting when I fell asleep with the speaker still in full flow. It did serve him right, because he had said that he would not speak for long and after twenty minutes talking about the Financial Services Act, I had had more than enough. I would probably have fallen asleep even without my weakness. The problem was that he suddenly turned round, looked at me and said, 'Am I going on too long?' It was time for a desperate gamble. 'No, but I think what we really would like to hear you talk about is the styles of client agreements.' It was sheer chance that he had not already been talking about that for at least the last fifteen minutes.

On another occasion, during a blood-donating session, I dozed off and was vaguely aware of the nurse saying in a rather anxious voice, 'Is he alright doctor, is he alright?'

'No, I think he is dead, but I wouldn't worry about him because he wasn't anybody very important.'

At another blood-donating session, I became very impatient

(another of my weaknesses) with all the questions that were being asked and, when asked if I had any tattoos, decided to adopt an outraged attitude: 'Certainly not. And if I had, I would not show you.' Back came the brilliant reply: 'Oh! But you would have to. It is the only perk I get in this job.'

There are of course millions of Highland anecdotes on all sorts of different circumstances and I find it difficult to pick out from them a common theme to describe what the characteristics of a Highlander are. But Highlanders never allow themselves to be outwitted by anybody, particularly an incomer. They have a way of bringing people back down to earth from any pretence of high station, very often without their victim realizing what has happened. I once witnessed a posh gentleman with an expensive car trying to serve himself petrol at a very old-fashioned pump, which required a handle to be moved back and forward in quick succession before any petrol would flow. Clearly the motorist had lost his temper and was abusing the handle in all sorts of ways. The garage proprietor watched for a long time without saying anything. Eventually, he wandered over to the motorist and said in a quiet, calm, Highland voice, 'Just hang on a minute and I'll get you a screwdriver.'

'What good would that do?' was the irate reply.

'You are trying to take the handle off, aren't you?'

One good example of Highland humour and its ability to gently mock the pompous or self-important came from a local shopkeeper on the day of the Argyllshire Gathering's Annual Ball. On that day, a special floor is laid for the benefit of the guests and no doubt to cover up the parts that us ordinary mortals are allowed to walk on during the rest of the year. On one such morning I went into the newspaper shop as usual to collect my paper, the business being run by a Mr Douglas and his son with no other help. As I entered I was aware of some hammering above the main shop.

'Is this you extending your premises, Mr Douglas?' asked the customer ahead of me.

'No,' said Mr Douglas, 'just laying the floor for the staff ball tonight.'

Sometimes it appears that the Highlander is unwilling to intervene, which can be very annoying when he is right and you are wrong. There was a story of two Department of Agriculture officials who had recently arrived in Oban and were due to visit Islay. From their office in Cameron House they could see the pier, so they would know exactly when they had to leave for the boat. But they got caught up in something else and suddenly found themselves having to make a last minute dash for it. Arriving on the pier, they found to their consternation that the boat was a foot or two away from the pier.

'Can we jump? Can we jump?' they anxiously called out.

'Aye, you can if you want.' There was a suitable pause before the skipper added, 'But we're on our way in.'

There is the classic story of a legendary MacBrayne's skipper who was in the Minch after leaving Stornoway one morning when he came across a yacht, which was obviously in some kind of trouble. He decided to take the ferry alongside and see if his help was needed.

'It's a fine morning,' he called out from the bridge to the frantic yachtsman who, by that time, was jumping up and down, waving his handkerchief for attention.

'I'm sinking; I'm sinking.'

To which he received the worrying response, 'And what would you be sinking about?'

I was myself put in my place by a local plumber after a house that was being built for me was finished – or nearly so. For far too long, to my mind, I had been waiting for a bath panel to finally complete a very nice bathroom, but my constant phone calls and nagging of the plumber produced no results. I decided it was time for strong measures and stormed into his workshop, demanding that he got on to his supplier at once to give me a satisfactory answer.

'I couldn't be doing that.'

'Why on earth not, man? I don't care what offence you cause your supplier, I just want my bath panel.'

'So you keep saying, but I can't get on to the supplier.'

'For heaven's sake, why not?'

'Because I have forgotten who I ordered it from.'

I was sure he hadn't but it was the best way to deflate me and I left his premises with my tail between my legs.

Another encounter I had with a tradesman during the building of my home concerned some railings I needed at the front door. Local blacksmith, Angie Neill, had agreed to do the necessary if I would explain exactly what I wanted. I decided to do a tour round the town and eventually found exactly what I liked. I went to see Angie again and mentioned the house where I had seen the desired railings. He was very noncommittal.

'Have you a minute to jump into my car just now and I'll be able to show you,' I suggested. Five minutes later we were outside the house. I pointed to the railings. Angie said nothing.

'Well,' I asked, 'do you think you could manage something like that?'

There was a very long pause.

'Well, do you think you could?'

Another pause.

'Should manage. I did those railings thirty years ago.'

On another occasion, when I was Procurator Fiscal, I was prosecuting a straightforward case of breach of the peace in a Tiree bar. The local policeman had given evidence about seeing the aftermath of what appeared to have been a near riot, with tables and chairs broken and bottles smashed all over the place, but I needed another witness for corroboration. One islander had been in the bar throughout and I asked him to describe what had happened.

'I could not be telling you that.'

'But you have to. You are on oath and you are duty bound to give evidence and to tell the truth about what you saw.'

'Not a thing did I hear, not a thing did I see.'

'But you must have seen something. We have heard that there was a huge disturbance and you cannot have been unaware of it. Now tell the court what you witnessed.'

'Not a thing did I hear, not a thing did I see.'

'For goodness sake man, are you blind or something?'

'Not totally, Mr Fiscal, but I do have this glass eye.'

'No further questions, my Lord.' I was sure that my unhelpful witness had no impairment of vision but I also knew that he was quite capable of producing something from his pocket and decided that it was safer not to put the matter to the test. The smiling triumph on his face as I gave up and sat down totally convinced me that he was 'at it'.

Highlanders have a way of taking the mickey out of authority. I was once in court when a Fiscal from outside the area was prosecuting a large local farmer for a drink-driving offence. It was pre-breathalyser days and it was necessary for a prosecution to prove – beyond all reasonable doubt, of course – that the farmer had at the time been pretty well drunk. The cross-examination went something like this.

'It is true, is it not, Mr MacCallum, that you had had a good drink on the night in question?'

'I wouldn't say that at all, Mr Jones.'

'But you enjoy a good drink, do you not?'

'That depends on what you would call a good drink.'

'Well, then, what is a good drink to you?'

'That would depend entirely on the circumstances of the occasion.'

'Let us explore that more fully. A half bottle of whisky. Is that a good drink?'

'Good heavens no, man.' Pause. 'That's just a good start.'

The farmer was duly convicted.

The legal definition at the time was that, for an offence to have been committed, the driver's 'judgement was impaired by drink'. In one case I had, my client did little to help himself or me with his defence. The doctor called in by the police to assess him was my friend Ronnie Frew. Apparently, when Ronnie went into the examination room, my client rose to his feet, saluted and fell over. After picking himself up he asked, 'Are you Dr Adamson?'

'No,' said Ronnie, 'I'm Dr Frew.'

'That's a pity,' replied my client, 'Dr Adamson's the best bloody doctor in the town.'

Ronnie later commented, 'I had no hesitation in certifying your client. His judgement was clearly impaired.'

Fortunately for the safety of other road users, my client was disqualified for a very long time because of other misdemeanours as well.

A dentist's receptionist had her own way of keeping patients in their place. Leaving Hamish Isaac's room on one occasion, I breezed over to the reception desk for another appointment.

'Hamish wants to see me again. Nice to be popular isn't it?'

The receptionist gave me a steely look and an instant reply: 'Here's the estimate for your next treatment.'

One visit I had to make to my dentist was with more than the usual trepidation. A day or two before, I had had to fill up a questionnaire of personal details to help the dentists with their computerization – name, age, sex – and I answered the last question by saying: 'Why not? It will give me something to do while waiting for the injection to take effect.' The irreverent form filling was probably inspired by the lady accused who filled up a plea of guilty form when I was the local prosecutor. The Civil Service form demanded that she state her sex, place and date of birth, eliciting the brilliant reply: 'I was born in Motherwell on 3rd May 1942 and have been of the female sex ever since.'

It was my valuable office colleague, Mairi MacRae, who is from Mull, who coined a memorable phrase on one occasion when the Law Society's Inspectors arrived for their spot checking of our books and finances. I was making my usual unnecessary light comments: 'How long are you going to be here? The last guy was here for half a day.'

The Inspectors stared at me before replying. 'We are planning to be here for five days.'

This led Mairi to comment later: 'It brought a sudden silence to Pagan's face.' It was a typical Highland remark.

My wife Heather and I once made a marvellous visit to Mull, mainly to see the magnificent puffins and other bird life on the island of Lunga. Returning to Ulva Ferry, I decided to take a photo of Mairi's home from the boat and checked with the boatman: 'That is the MacRae cottage isn't it?'

'Yes,' said the boatman, 'Do you know Mairi?'

'We work together,' I explained.

'Is that where she goes every Monday morning?'

By that time Mairi had worked with me for 27 years.

Former Oban solicitor, Robin Banks, tells of a client who was owed money by a military man of high rank, living on Mull. All attempts by

Robin to get any response from the colonel failed and Robin's client asked him if he would mind if he himself were to write again to the colonel, which he then did. Two weeks later, Robin met his client in the street.

'I got my money,' he said triumphantly.

'How on earth did you manage that?' asked Robin.

'I just wrote to him addressing him as Lance Corporal. He wrote a furious letter back immediately. But he also sent a cheque.'

Robin, I am sure, would have enjoyed that because on one occasion he was asked to become Treasurer of the Soldiers, Sailors and Air Force Men's Benevolent Association.

'Did you do National Service?'

'Yes.'

'Excellent. Excellent. What rank did you attain?'

'Lance Corporal.'

'Oh dear, I think we'll just have to call you Mr Banks.'

On one occasion when I was travelling with Robin Banks, we were driving through Glencoe in the early hours of a winter's morning with the moon shining impressively above the mountains. Suddenly he tooted his horn but there was nothing in sight – not even a deer.

'What on earth did you do that for?' I asked.

'We were just passing my uncle's croft and I always hoot as I go by to let him know that I have not forgotten him.'

It may be that some of the Highlander's characteristics come from the severe hardships they have had to experience over many centuries, coupled with a condescending attitude to them from those who should know better but often don't. Only recently I read in *The Herald* a report from 150 years previously, which quoted a letter from the Agent deputed by the Emigration Commissioners to act with the Highland and Islands Emigration Society at Portree, Skye.

I am much pleased with the selection I have been enabled to make. I believe the Highlanders will prove a most useful class of servants and labourers in Australia and that their removal will prove beneficial to the Colonies. Their faithfulness to their superiors and masters render them, in my opinion, most suitable persons for the service of Australia.

It is not too much to say that many of the swine in England are better fed and housed than are the poor of this island.

With those facts and with that attitude it is no wonder that Highlanders have invented a way of protecting themselves and warding off unwelcome meddlesome intrusions. Usually it is laced with humour, not always appreciated or recognized by incomers.

Once I was in the local store in Lochinver on a beautiful, hot, sunny summer's day, which would have done justice to a continental holiday resort. The radio was on: 'And in the Highlands of Scotland it will be extremely wet and blustery.'

'I'm glad the English have got it right as usual,' retorted the shopkeeper.

It is a common misconception that because Oban is in the Highlands it must have terrible weather. It probably has to be admitted that it can be wetter than some other parts of the country but, being where it is, even the bad weather can be enjoyable, except perhaps when there are gales. It is very rare for snow to lie for long and, despite having lived at the highest spot in the town for forty years, I have never been snowed in and unable to get down to the town. There have been fewer than twenty days in all when I was unable to get the car up the road leading to the top of the hill where I live.

We could, however, do without the gales. So could an elderly, somewhat disabled client of mine who is well into her nineties. Travelling home alone late one very stormy night, she found that Loch Feochan, just south of Oban, had overswelled its banks and, before she could do anything about it, her car was washed out towards the middle of the loch. Somehow she managed to get out of the car and swim about half a mile to dry land, but even then she was not safe. Because of her disabilities, it was easier for her to swim than to walk. Fortunately, two young men in a lorry saw her coming out of the loch and went to her rescue, taking her back to her own home in their lorry. Once there, she said she was going straight into a hot bath but invited the two men, whom she did not know, to help themselves from her drinks cabinet. Minutes later, as she was languishing in a much-needed hot bath, there came a knock on the unlocked bathroom door, which then slowly opened. Looking up, all she could see was a hand passing in a glass of whisky: 'You'll be needing this.'

The difficulties of Highland life were illustrated by an urgent problem which arose in 1962. At the time, I was doing a lot of court work in the area on behalf of a legal firm in Glasgow and they once instructed me, very much at the last minute, to raise a court action against a fisherman on the island of Islay. The incident had to do with a salvage claim and there was a strict time limit, which was about to expire. In the short time available it was necessary not only for the court writ to be correctly drafted, but for court authority to be obtained and then for proper intimation to be given to the defender – all within a matter of days.

Because it was Islay, I had to bring in colleagues from Campbeltown to do what was needed and they set about the thing with all speed, sending the court writ to the Islay fisherman by registered post, as was the form in those days. Unfortunately, two days later, with only a few hours left, the court writ was returned to them by the Post Office marked: 'gone away – gone fishing'. I doubted whether that really was the case and gave a thought to at least the possibility that the wise islander knew the writ was coming and had decided to keep well out of the way.

Nonetheless, it meant that we had to have the writ served on the fisherman personally, which required getting a Sheriff Officer to go to the island and actually hand the court document over to him. Unfortunately there was no Sheriff Officer on Islay and, although there was one in Oban, ferry timetables did not fit in with what he was able to do. When discussing the problem with my Glasgow colleague, he sensibly remembered that there was a plane from Glasgow to Islay and that he could try to arrange for a Glasgow Sheriff Officer to fly to the island. However, I had to point out that the court papers were still in Campbeltown and it was necessary for the Sheriff Officer to have them with him. Suddenly, one of us remembered that the plane touched down at Machrihanish, near Campbeltown, on its way to Islay. Eventually, the arrangement was set up that my Campbeltown colleague would go to the airport at Machrihanish the next morning in order to hand over the papers to the Glasgow Sheriff Officer when the plane touched down for a matter of minutes, and all would be well. However, as luck would have it, it was a very misty day and the plane was unable to land at Machrihanish, flying straight on to Islay, with my Campbeltown colleague standing on the tarmac below, frantically waving the papers at the plane. But there was no way of getting them to it.

I then got a phone call telling me exactly what had happened and how we would now have to accept defeat; then suddenly the Campbeltown solicitor said, 'Hold on a minute, what day is it? Tuesday. I'm off, there is a ferry from West Loch Tarbert in an hour.' The phone went dead. Two hours later, I got a phone call to say that he had managed to get to West Loch Tarbert just as the ferry was about to sail. He had given the court papers to a co-operative boatman, perhaps with a bit of a backhander, and told him to hand them over to the Sheriff Officer, who would by that time have landed on Islay. He would have no difficulty in recognizing him. He would be wandering around in a daze, looking totally lost. Eventually all went well, and although the Islay fisherman could still not be found, it was sufficient for the court writ to be pinned to the door of his house, thereby enabling the court action to begin. After all that, I was particularly glad that a successful settlement was achieved – no doubt after a lot of the hassle which goes with most court actions.

On another occasion, the same Glasgow solicitor phoned me.

'Am I speaking to the most famous solicitor in Scotland?'

'What on earth are you talking about?'

'Have you not read today's *Express*?'

'No. Why?'

He then explained that among the court actions I had recently raised on his instruction had been a number of cases by Harrods for payments of sums due to them. One of them had been against a Viscountess somebody-or-other, which didn't mean anything to me. I certainly did not remember paying any more attention to that debt than to the host of other cases. Nevertheless, when the press got hold of it they judged it as something newsworthy and of public interest. Harrods then panicked about damaging the goodwill of their other so-called elite customers – they seemed to remain elite even if they had no money. Harrods instructed that the action be cancelled immediately.

Out of curiosity, I looked back at my papers to see what it was that the Viscountess had not paid for and to my amazement saw the debt was in respect of 'one waistcoat and one Dinky toy'. I had a vision of her lying on the cold, stone floor of her baronial mansion, wearing a waistcoat and playing with the toy car. The mind boggles.

Highlanders are, of course, famous for their lack of concern about the time, on the basis that when the Good Lord created time he made plenty of it. One classic case was a rather unusual local laird who, on his marriage, was invited by another landed estate owner to come to dinner to introduce his bride. These people have a habit of keeping in with their own private magic circles, despite the known eccentricities of many of them. This particular laird and his bride agreed that 7.30 for 8 p.m. would be perfect timing for the party being arranged in their honour. Seven thirty came and went; 8 p.m. came and went; 9 p.m. came and went and still no laird and bride. Eventually the party sat down to dinner without them. Halfway through it, the laird and his bride arrived. The hostess remonstrated angrily with them. 'You are terribly late. We agreed 7.30 for 8 p.m.'

'That's right,' said the laird, 'it's only just on 8 p.m. now.'

'Nonsense,' retorted the hostess, 'your watch must be wrong.'

'Not at all,' responded the laird, 'my watch keeps excellent time but you may not understand how we live. You see, what we do when we get up in the morning is to set our watches for 9 a.m., no matter what time it is and we live the rest of the day through on that basis.'

I have always considered myself so lucky to have arrived in the Highlands and to have been (I hope) welcome here. But it took a long time for some to accept me. After I had been here twelve years, a friend overheard this conversation as I was crossing the street.

'Who's that man?'

'That's that new-fangled solicitor that Hosacks have just got hold of.'

Oban Bay must be one of the most beautiful in the world and would be interesting to look at, even if nothing ever happened on it. The changing scenery of the Mull and Morvern mountains and the different colourings of the water – not to mention the different size of the waves depending on the winds – would be more than enough to justify hours of standing admiring the view. The fact is, as others have commented before, that something is happening all the time. The bay certainly seems to become more active and have more different and interesting boats almost every day – liners, ferries, fishing boats, naval boats, commercial boats, pleasure boats – everything.

There can be few more inspiring or invigorating starts to a working day than walking along Oban's front, looking across to the magnificent mountains and watching the activity in the bay, both from a miscellany of boats and from the seabirds and other wildlife. Sadly, the very pressures of work have often meant that there has not been time to take advantage of what is on my own doorstep. My office is on the first floor of a very impressive, Victorian building on the front. Many have commented favourably on the old-fashioned atmosphere of the office, from which they take a feeling of security and reliability, although some would prefer a more modern, open-plan type office with synthetic stuff. Not me. Change is needed in many things but only if change brings improvement.

I have been lucky enough to have enjoyed from the bay window of my own office the brilliance of Oban Bay and the distant views beyond. Separate from that, one of the benefits of my room is that it is ideally placed to enjoy and share one of the great moments every year, which is just before Christmas and New Year. Not only young students but older people too return from other parts of the country and from abroad to be back where they belong at celebration time. The excited buzz permeates upward from the streets below, as trendily dressed and colourful young people and others come home, sometimes after being away for the first time, to meet up again with friends and people of older generations; it is a delightful scene to watch.

There was a similar experience in October 2003 when the 100th Royal National Mod was celebrated in Oban. I had occasion to walk along the front when the Mod was in full swing, on one of the hottest days, despite it being October. There was an animated buzz from many groups of middle-aged to elderly people, gathered together and laughing away like school children as many met up for the first time for a year or more. In some cases it was the first meeting since school days. The Millennium New Year was, of course, celebrated all over the

world. Oban's celebrations had what seemed to be its whole population taking over the town centre beside the magnificent bay and
meeting up with a huge number of people whom they all knew. The
generation gap did not exist and, personally, I was more than glad to
come across, as the new century began, the younger members of my
own family, who had set out from home a few hours earlier to go to
different functions.

It was in the *Sunday Post* well over fifty years ago that I read a
column called 'The Honest Truth', in which Jack Harkness, of foot-
balling fame, was asked where he would like to retire. 'Anywhere that
has a view of Oban Bay. There is so much happening there, I could
never get bored.' I wonder what he would say if he saw it now with all
the increased activity.

Sometimes when I go to work in the morning I detect the ominous
presence in the bay of a Customs or Navy protection vessel, perhaps
indicating the arrest of a foreign boat for illegal fishing. One unfortunate Oban solicitor had to represent in court the French skipper of
one such boat, who had been charged not just with fishing in the
wrong place, but with trying to escape from the British Naval boat and
ignoring all orders to stop. The solicitor did his best, explaining that
the French boat's radar had malfunctioned, which was why it was
fishing within our protected area. As for failing to stop, it had all been
a huge misunderstanding caused by language difficulties. When he
finished, the Sheriff interjected saying that he wanted to be absolutely
sure that the Frenchman understood the court proceedings. He
addressed the skipper accordingly and to the consternation of the
Oban solicitor, got the reply, 'I understand perfectly. We zee the boat
coming. We get the hell out.'

I was also extremely fortunate when another lucky coincidence led to
the building of my home on an idyllic spot overlooking Oban Bay and
Kerrera, with views towards Mull, Lismore, Morvern, Ben Lora,
Glencoe and numerous mountains. It occurred when I bumped into
local architect, Bill Crerar, one Saturday when I was out wandering in
the town. Like me, he had only been in Oban for a year or two. 'Have
you seen my dog?' he asked; 'He has disappeared again and I am

concerned in case he is up the hill among the sheep.' I was doing nothing special and offered to go with him in search of the errant Afghan hound. I can't remember whether we found the dog that night but what we did find was the site for my house, for which we were not even looking. It all happened so simply.

'What a wonderful spot this would be for a house.'

'I'll design one for you.'

'I'm sure you could, but I couldn't possibly afford one.'

'I could do something for you for about £4,500.'

This he proceeded to do, and it was just within my limit with a bit of extra borrowing and also with the fact that the new Oban Sheriff, John Peterson, had recently arrived in Oban and was looking for a site to build on. We were therefore able to share the cost of the private road, drains, water and everything else that had to be provided from scratch. I will never forget that fortuitous moment of bumping into Bill Crerar and have been glad to have seen how his business has flourished nationwide since then.

Among many of the Highlanders I have been honoured to know was the late Iain Crichton Smith, a literary giant and genius in both English and Gaelic. At the same time, he was full of humour, often at his own expense, because there was no side to him. I once met him coming out of a Sale of Work.

'I don't like going to this kind of function.'

'Why not?'

'Because I find too many of my books on the second-hand bookstall.'

Out of respect for him, I attended a dinner in his honour, at which a number of other Scottish literary figures were present. I mistakenly thought it would be a serious and highbrow evening. I could not have been more wrong. It was more entertaining even than many rugby dinners I have attended. Iain Crichton Smith thanked the various guests for having the kindness to attend this dinner in his honour, then commented, 'I don't really think I deserve this. I never thought I was that good, although I might be the best poet in Combie Street.'

Later on, I think it was Norman McCaig who commented that Iain would often go down to Edinburgh to meet with him, book into a bed and breakfast, then go out on the town, which would lead to literary discussions lasting through the night. 'Iain is the only man I know who pays for bed and breakfast for a suitcase,' he added. When I attended Iain's funeral service, I was pleased that reference was made to the old-fashioned typewriter which he had used. The comment was made that one always knew when a communication was from Iain without even reading it, because when the envelope was opened confetti-like pieces of paper fell to the ground, punched out by his old fashioned, sharp typeface. I was glad of that reference because I can remember seeing the typewriter when I first visited Iain in Combie Street, and staring at it in awe at the realisation that it was from that that all these great works were created. It was at Iain's dinner that someone told the story about another leading Scottish poet, speaking at a primary school and being asked by a wee girl, 'Excuse me sir. When did you write your first poem?'

'Good gracious, lassie, it was years and years ago. I cannot possibly remember.'

'What was it that made you decide to continue?'

Oban has generally been extremely well served by its medical people. One of the most memorable was Kenny Lipp. Many people have a favourite story of Kenny. There was always something different and something very memorable about him and a whole chapter could be written simply about him and his basic, down-to-earth humour. He spoke with a serious Aberdeen accent, which not everybody could fully understand and it was typical of his humour that, once when I called to see him, he was on the phone, commenting in his broad Aberdeen accent as he put the receiver down: 'That was a woman from London. Couldnae understand a word she was saying.'

Once, when I was Fiscal, an irate lady came into my office because she had been cited as a witness and said that she would not be going. I explained to her that if she didn't, she could be arrested and probably held in contempt of court and that the only way out was to obtain a medical certificate. Triumphantly, she called in the next day, shouting that she had the certificate and throwing it on my desk. Wisely, I told her to wait until I had read it. It read:

I certify on soul and conscience that Mrs Jemima Bartholomew does not wish to give evidence. I further certify that she is perfectly fit and capable of doing so and that there is no medical reason for her to be absent from the court.
Dr K.L. Lipp

Kenny once commented to Hamish Hoey, a joiner and undertaker, when the latter was working in his house, that either Kenny would end up signing Hamish's death certificate or that Hamish would end up burying him. Kenny was a very matter-of-fact character, concerned about other people, but he did not believe in making a fuss about anything. Nor did he believe in being messed about unnecessarily. On one occasion, he got sweet revenge after he had been called out wholly unnecessarily in the middle of the night. By chance, he happened to be passing the same door at about 4.30 one morning when he was out on another call and decided that it was a good moment to ring the doorbell and enquire how the patient was getting on. He did not get a good welcome – not that that would have bothered him.

Anyone walking up Ben Lora will find, not too far from the top, a welcome seat, donated in Kenny's memory. It is good to pause there for a while and recall some of the happy stories.

During the 1979 Referendum Campaign for a Scottish Parliament something occurred on another car journey, which could not have happened in any other part of Britain. I was acting as chauffeur for the Nationalist MP, Iain McCormick, a man of great charisma, and we were on a visit to Lochaline via Mull. The journey home had to be made entirely by road as we left quite late after the meeting, by which time the two ferries were off. After his excellent speech, I could not complain that Iain fell asleep in the car on the way back. However, I woke him after three hours' driving to comment that something had happened that would not happen anywhere else that I could think of. I had just had to dip my lights for an oncoming car for the first time on that journey, which, in one way, sums up my love of the Highlands – the space as well as the beauty.

Another incident which could only happen in the Highlands or very small communities, concerned my mother-in-law's purchase of a birthday card for my son. She was rightly proud of her choice, which was particularly appropriate, until she went to pay for it. 'You can't buy that one. His mother bought the same card for him ten minutes ago.'

A wonderfully amusing example of Highland life came from my friend, Stewart Fairlie. At his newspaper desk one morning, word filtered through of a plane crash in a remote part of Scotland. There was no one they could think of to phone for verification and details of the story. Eventually, after much scratching of heads, one of his colleagues suddenly remembered that she had an elderly aunt who ran a post office in the area. Somehow they managed to find a number. They phoned. It was obviously a call box and it was answered by a passer-by.

'Hello! I have heard that there has been a plane crash of some kind. Can you tell me anything about it?'

'I certainly can. I am the pilot and I am trying to phone for help.'

One of many benefits I have had from being involved in political and charitable campaigns has been that I have seen far more of the Highlands than I would have done without them. Many people make these journeys for their holidays and I was fortunate in being able to campaign in such marvellous surroundings. Our campaigning had to take in car journeys from Oban to the main centres of Dunoon, Campbeltown, Lochgilphead and Rothesay (which also involved a ferry crossing), not to mention numerous smaller and lovely places such as Inveraray, Arrochar and Carradale. Journeys would take two to three hours and often we had to come back very late at night. Then of course there were numerous ferry crossings to various islands; some of these visits would mean being away from Oban for a couple of days or more.

Looking through an unused cupboard in my legal office one day, I came across a letter from almost 50 years ago, addressed to my former senior partner. It read as follows:

Dear Harvey
I took you to see the old Post Office at Lochavich, now occupied by Mr Charles Lovestock. I want to put it on written record that, if the

Almighty in his wisdom should promote me to another sphere, I do not want Lovestock disturbed in his occupancy of that house. He has helped me a lot at different times. But there is another reason. I have been permitted the great privilege of spending the last seventeen years amid some of the most beautiful scenery in the world. I am very grateful. You cannot do much to show gratitude to the good Lord: you cannot give him anything, but you can in return show some kindness to one of his human beings . . .

You had better file this letter.

Yours sincerely

I do not think I ever met the writer of that letter but I share his sentiments totally, especially since, in my case, the years now extend to forty-three.

2

From the Beaches of Tiree to the Nightspots of Nairn

Bank managers have in the past played an important and influential part in rural communities and Oban was no exception. Over many decades we have had a number of characters and, on a personal basis, many of them not only influenced but expanded my own life. David MacRitchie came to Oban in about 1965 to manage the Royal Bank, where my own firm had most of its business. He was dead straight and honourable and one of the most forthright people I ever met. Everybody knew what he thought, especially his head office. When I was first introduced to him, I asked innocently, 'Do you think you will enjoy yourself here, Mr MacRitchie?' getting the immediate reply, 'There are too many bloody overdrafts in the branch and I am going to get rid of most of them.'

'Help!' I thought. 'We are definitely one of them.' I didn't know then that David would turn out to be one of the most loyal and helpful supporters my business ever had.

Later on, as changes came in and obsessive control of local branches was introduced from head office, David lamented the old freedoms and the power of the local manager to make the right decisions for the benefit of the community, while at the same time protecting the bank's interests. He particularly railed against the result of the merger between the Royal Bank and the National Commercial, which had left the town with three branches. The Edinburgh decision makers, having looked at the situation on the map, decided that the best thing to do was to close down the middle branch, although it was by far the most impressive building. Despite all David's protestations, the bank did get rid of that great building, leaving two far less imposing buildings to carry on the bank's business, even although one of them was only a door or two away from the one they insisted in closing.

I remember another great character, Angus MacIntyre, who managed a bank in Tobermory and who obviously thought his prime duty was to make sure that the islanders received as much support as possible from his bank. In fact, it became apparent to me that, whenever I threatened to sue anybody from the island of Mull for debt, I almost invariably got a friendly phone call from Angus which went something like this: 'I see you are wanting some money from Roddy. How much do you want and will there be any court expenses?' A bank cheque would arrive on my desk the following day, thereby saving a lot of trouble and expense, particularly for the debtors. When Angus retired, I was glad I was not the manager that had to take over from him, but the support he gave was vital for the island community and the bank could well afford the small amounts that Angus was lending. Certainly that bank is still in existence so I don't see why it should complain. In any event, it would give the bank something to do. Peter MacLeod, who managed the other bank in Tobermory told me that he once went to close the doors at the end of the business day and found that he had never opened them. Peter was renowned as a great after-dinner speaker and a leading Burns authority. He even went to Moscow to speak at the Burns Supper there, which seemed terribly far away at that time.

I was glad it was Peter that was going to Moscow and not John Stevenson, another good Highland solicitor, whom I succeeded as the part-time Procurator Fiscal in Oban in 1970. John told a classic story of setting out to speak at a Burns' Supper in Tobermory and ending up buying an overcoat in Sauchiehall Street, Glasgow. What happened was that, while he normally caught the boat to Mull early in the morning, on that particular occasion, because he had had some function the night before, he decided to board and sleep on the boat overnight. He had done the journey thousands of times and got a terrible fright when he woke up, because he recognised instantly that the boat was not manoeuvring in the normal way for the Oban to Tobermory run. In fact he had slept in and the boat was well on its way to Tiree by the time John realised it. There would be another two hours' sailing before John would reach dry land. He duly landed on Tiree and made all kinds of efforts to get a lift back with a friendly fisherman or boat hirer from Tiree to Tobermory in time for the dinner, at which he was to be the main speaker. A catalogue of Highland misfortunes stood in the way of that objective and eventually John decided that the only thing to do was to cut his losses and catch the plane to Glasgow.

Of course, in the 1960s the whole attitude to banking was far more relaxed than it is now. The Royal Bank, which was immediately below my own offices (and which now houses Ottaker's book shop), had a communicating door which made life very easy for me and my colleagues as it remained unlocked virtually all the time and we could wander in and out whenever we had some business to transact with them. Our close contact with them was often very useful.

A sports shop in Oban was run by a man who had emblazoned above his shop: 'Founded in the reign of Queen Elizabeth.' What he really meant was that he had been in existence for a matter of months. It did not take him long to realise that paying the bank for what he had borrowed to set up his business and keep it afloat was far more expensive than letting his creditors wait and sue for their money. He was often able to get interest-free credit for periods well in excess of a year – sometimes two – the court expenses which he would eventually have to pay being far less then the bank interest. I received a large number of letters from English solicitors on behalf of his suppliers, asking me to take the necessary action in the local Sheriff Court, which I did to begin with. Later I realised that it was an awful waste of my time as well as a waste of the sports man's money, so I did a deal with him. Whenever I was asked to raise a court action against him, I would phone him and he would come round immediately with a cheque in settlement.

For some reason, perhaps increasingly reduced funds, our deal did not last too long and eventually I had to raise the court action and wait for the cheque, which would eventually arrive. But a large number of them, of course, bounced. We then arranged for our bank colleagues to phone up whenever he was in the queue with his pay-ins, whereupon we ran down with the previously bouncing cheques, stood behind him in the queue, and paid them in immediately.

Willie Melville was another Royal Bank manager ideally suited for this area with his passion for the sea, the hills and the mountains. I learned a lot about outdoor life from him without ever acquiring his range of knowledge or skills. To my shame, I had been in Oban almost ten years before Willie educated me by showing me an oyster catcher. It is never a good thing to be as tied up with work as I was at the time; it prevented me from seeing or noticing even things which were on my own doorstep. But I had two partners who were considerably older than me and one day I would somehow have to find the money to pay them out of the business. I knew they would be patient but they would still have to be paid. My other difficulty was that, being a newcomer to a small community, it was not always easy to find new clients, particularly as there were two solicitors, slightly older than me, who had been born and brought up in Oban. It would inevitably take a long time to build my own reputation.

It was while we were on one of Tiree's marvellously large and beautiful beaches that Willie introduced me to oyster catchers. There was not another soul in sight despite it being a beautiful August day. Actually, there was another soul but he was asleep in his pram, the beach being firm enough to make pram-pushing easy. 'One thing about oyster catchers,' Willie pointed out, 'is that they always go around in pairs.' I have since spent over thirty years trying unsuccessfully to prove Willie wrong by counting oyster catchers whenever I see them together, but the number always seems to be divisible by two.

There was one salutary experience I had with Willie when we and a few others set off to reach the top of The Cobbler near Arrochar, a well-known and relatively easy mountain climb which Willie knew extremely well. In fact, it is so easy that you can walk up as an ordinary hill walk on one side, but need ropes if you are attacking another side of it. I only realised this when we reached the top and decided that for safety I should take my dog Sam back down from the summit and wait for the party to rejoin me a few minutes later. When the group got back to me about a quarter of an hour later, I was alarmed when one of them asked, 'Where's Willie?'

'He's with you,' I answered.

'No, he's not. He came down about ten minutes ago to join you.'

Fortunately, with Willie's knowledge of the mountain, there was no danger and he caught up with us shortly after but neither of us could believe that he had walked within a few feet of me and Sam without either of us realising it. Mountains are obviously not to be trifled with.

Willie was with the group on one memorable occasion when we were a short distance from the top of the Pap in Glencoe. One of our companions, Marnie Clark, suddenly shouted to Jimmy Finlay, another nature expert, 'Look Jimmy, weasel droppings.'

Jimmy hardly paused to look before replying, 'No, Marnie, grouse shit.'

'I am sure it's weasel droppings,' Marnie persisted.

'Grouse shit,' came the only reply.

'How can you be so sure?'

'Because,' answered Jimmy with the authority of an Oxford professor, 'no weasel in its right mind would climb 2,000 feet to have a crap.'

In the 1970s there was a frequent problem of telephones having crossed lines. Another bank manager, Hugh Mackay, had invented a way out of this difficulty, at least so far as he was concerned. I was with him one morning when he picked up the phone to make a call on a matter of mutual importance and found the line crossed. It was obvious from hearing one side of the conversation that there was an argument between him and the other person as to who should hang up. I think the other person was maintaining that he should hang up because she had been on the line first.

'Oh!' replied Hugh, 'it is not as simple as that. What is your number?'

'2503' came the reply.

'Ah!' said Hugh, 'That means it's you that has to hang up, because if you add all your numbers together they come to less than mine and it is always the lower number that has to hang up, otherwise the lines can remain crossed indefinitely and we will have to get an engineer out.'

'I didn't realise that,' said the other caller.

'No,' replied Hugh innocently, 'Not many people do.'

On another occasion Hugh told me about a dilemma he had once found himself in when, on getting out of a train at Haymarket and putting his coat on, he had knocked his lit cigarette out of his mouth and it had rolled on to the seat opposite, between the legs of a rather large man who was sound asleep. To begin with he thought he would take the cowardly way out and leave the man to burn, but his principles of decency got the better of him and he decided to try to retrieve the cigarette with the inevitable consequence that the man woke up and hit him. I have often envisaged that scene: Hugh standing there on the train wondering what was the best thing to do.

Another banking friend told me of a bizarre experience on his first day as manager at a new branch. A rather strange customer was shown into the managerial room and my friend had some difficulty in understanding what the man was wanting. Eventually, to my friend's relief, he got up to go.

'Could I ask a favour of you. Could I take your photograph?'

'What for?'

'Because I have photos of all your predecessors and I would like to complete my collection.'

'Very well then,' said Iain preening himself and patting his hair into place as one does. After the photo was duly taken, he escorted the customer from the premises. Before returning to his own room, he said to one of the more experienced bank ladies. 'Wasn't that nice. That funny old man took a photo of me for his album.'

'Not really,' came the disconcerting reply, 'he never has any film in his camera.'

Iain is a kind guy and said he felt sorry for the eccentric old man.

'It's you I feel sorry for,' I replied, 'I can see him going home to his wife and saying "I got another bank manager today", and his wife replying, "You really must stop teasing them like that".'

Yet another Royal Bank manager, Cameron Sommerville, has been over the years one of my closest and most loyal of friends. It was through him that I eventually developed a great love for jazz, which has given me hours of enjoyment and relaxation and also some bizarre experiences. On one occasion, when Cameron and I were at the Edinburgh Jazz Festival, we had attended a lunchtime bash which was perhaps more liquid than it should have been. As we left the Platform One restaurant of the Caledonian Hotel, we decided to leave by a different door than the one we had entered. We found ourselves in a garden with a gazebo and, beyond, some French windows, which was obviously the way to go out. Beyond the glass windows were a number of seated ladies, who I assumed were resting or sleeping after their lunch. When we went in, with me leading, I found to my horror that there was a fashion parade going on and Cameron and I were on the catwalk. I got out of the way quite quickly but Cameron remained on a collision course with the model while the compere continued unperturbed with her commentary: 'And as you can see ladies, the colour mauve is very much in vogue this season.' Cameron, as well as walking with slightly less elegance than the model was also wearing a scarlet polo neck jumper.

As we left, Cameron claimed that that was the most embarrassing experience of his life, but that he was looking forward to the session later that afternoon at the George Hotel. Unfortunately, on arriving there, there was a HOUSE FULL notice.

'That's a pity,' said Cameron, who is one of those characters who never let the misfortunes of life knock him back too far.

'Never mind,' said I, 'I sussed this place out yesterday and I think I can get us in.' A few minutes later we were in the basement of the hotel, one floor below the venue for the next jazz bash and two floors below the ticket office.

The afternoon became very convivial, in the course of which we had the fun of chatting to two elderly jazz musicians who had been around almost from the beginning of jazz – Benny Waters and Al Casey. A few years later I acquired an excellent bit of jazz recorded by Benny on his ninety-first birthday! Towards the end of the afternoon, I found myself saying to Cameron, 'Watch out, something extraordinary is about to happen.' He looked puzzled. At that, a man of our kind of age, carrying drinks, sat down near to us. I shouted out, 'You always were a mean bastard Mick. Where's my drink?'

He turned and looked at me in amazement. It was my best man

from my first wedding, who had fallen out with me when the marriage broke up eleven years before and whom I had not seen since. There in the very venue where I had had my first wedding reception, I introduced the first best man to my second best man – Cameron. Eventually it came to the end of an enjoyable but bizarre afternoon and, on going upstairs and passing the ticket office, I had a pang of conscience. I went up to the desk and asked for a ticket for the afternoon session.

'You mean the evening session. The afternoon session has just finished.'

'I know, I have just left it.'

'Then why do you want to pay for it?'

'Because I got in without paying and I now wish to pay – it was a good afternoon.'

'How very honourable of you. It is not often we meet people as honest as you. What a pleasure.'

Pause. The mood changed.

'But wait a minute, how did you get in without paying?'

'I am not going to tell you. I may want to do the same thing again tomorrow.'

'We can't have this kind of behaviour. I will not allow it.'

'Do you want my money or don't you?' said I before slamming some coins onto the desk rather ungraciously and storming off, only to find that I had left my programme behind and would have to buy another one. Serve me right.

A lot of people, of course, don't enjoy jazz, but often that is because they misjudge it. Like most things, there are all different kinds and I certainly don't like all of it. When my mother was eighty-five, she happened to hear me listening to a lovely bit of jazz by trombonist, Dan Barrett. 'If I had known jazz could be as nice as that, I might have paid it more attention,' she commented.

One of the many nice things about jazz people is that there is no side to most of them, rather like the Highlander, and they are usually very happy to chat, even to strangers if they share their love of the music. One day I came across Dan Barrett and passed on that compliment from an elderly lady, which greatly pleased him.

The annual Jazz Festival in Nairn which Heather and I attend as often as work allows is ample proof of the friendliness of so many jazz performers. The organisers have no difficulty in attracting many of the leading players to Nairn, most of whom seem to thoroughly enjoy the Highland surrounding and relaxed hospitality.

My greatest jazz hero is the legendary cornet player Bix Beiderbecke, who really aroused my passion for the music and who is one of the most legendary figures in the history of jazz. Strangely, he shared the same birthday – 10 March – as my grandmother, but their life spans were very different. My grandmother was already twenty-seven when Bix was born in 1903. They then shared twenty-eight years of life before Bix sadly died, mainly through drink and general disillusionment with life, in 1931. My grandmother then went on to survive for a further forty-one years before dying at the age of ninety-six in 1972.

There was a coincidental and happy business connection with Bix in 2001. An old lady client died – and, incidentally, it was the first death certificate I had ever seen which simply gave the cause of death as being 'old age'. A nephew of hers came over from America for the funeral and by chance one evening I passed him on one of my all too infrequent bike rides. Months later, when he phoned me from America to discuss how things were progressing, he asked if I was going to be in Iowa the following month.

'No, why?'

'Because there is a convention of bikers taking place then.'

I explained that I was not that keen on bikes but that if there was one thing that would bring me to Iowa, it would be to celebrate the life of Bix Beiderbecke. My client had never heard of him, but about a week later I got a message from him that he had looked up Bix on the Internet and had been absolutely fascinated by his life. A further week later, my office mail included an envelope from Davenport, Iowa, with a mass of stuff about Bix and a membership card in my name for the Bix Beiderbecke Memorial Society. Not all clients are so appreciative.

I have strayed a bit with my reminiscences about bankers but there are a couple more I'd like to mention. I recall the first week that Stewart Harkess, a Clydesdale Bank manager arrived in Oban. That was when there were masses of building societies, all vying for custom. Cameron told me that there were then seventeen different building societies in Union Street, Aberdeen alone and that he could have had two free meals a day, every day of the month, if he so wished. Oban's feasts came from a number of societies, but the Provincial's area manager was perhaps renowned for producing the most convivial and longest events. The average dinner would last anything up to ten hours. Unfortunately, Stewart was not aware of this and on leaving home, said to his wife Elsie in all innocence, 'I'll not be late dear.'

He staggered home in the early hours, about 3 a.m. and received the understandable greeting from Elsie: 'You said you would not be late', to which came the instant reply, 'I'm not late, I'm the first away.'

But the banker with whom I had most dealings was Angus Simpson. It was on the same night that Stewart came to grief that I first met Angus. Two or three days later, early on a Sunday evening, the phone rang. It was Angus reminding me who he was and where we had met. His words were something like, 'You seem to be involved in a number of things. Is there anything I can help with?' He joined the Shelter Campaign immediately and went on to do a tremendous amount of voluntary work, not just for that but during nearly the whole thirty-year life of the Oban Housing Association and various charitable spin-offs from that as well as many other charities and organisations with which I was not involved. One of life's many mysteries is the way in which, apparently by chance, people are brought together. My encounter with Angus was one example of the coincidences of timing which can play such an important part in all our lives. Even more amazing was the chance encounter, ten years before I was even born, which had brought me to Oban in the first place.

3

'Damn and blast you to hell – you have grossly mishandled my business'

'I want a divorce.'

Another week was coming to an end. It was late on a Friday afternoon and my thoughts had already turned to the weekend ahead. I looked across the desk at the rather imposing military man opposite me and tried to weigh up how to convince him that I would be on his side without giving him full powers over my actions.

I already knew that I would have a hard task with the Brigadier. He had made it clear that it was only because one of the more senior solicitors was unavailable that he even deigned to come into my room. My mind went back to my not too distant university notes and recalled the only six grounds for divorce in those days:

| | Adultery | Cruelty | Desertion |
| | Insanity | Sodomy | Bestiality |

All divorces had to fit strictly into one of those classifications and detailed proof was needed. Already I had formed doubts as to whether public courts with their often aggressive and antagonistic attitudes were the best forum for sensitive matters like divorce and for things as important as child custody and the like. Which of the six would it be, I wondered. At the same time I wondered whether at the end of my career I would have scored, as it were, a double hat-trick, being involved with cases of all six kinds. Perhaps this would be an interesting divorce, I thought.

'Why do you want a divorce?' I asked.

'The bitch has left me,' came the angry reply.

Ah! I thought to myself, with the quick mental agility of solicitors, that seems like desertion. I recalled the strict aspects of desertion, which not only meant that you had to be apart for three years but also that, during those three years, the person wanting the divorce had to prove undying love and determination to get the partner back. The door had to be kept open was the public conception of that strange rule, but not in the depth of winter, as I had on one occasion to reassure a rather unfortunate farm worker who was already living in a cold and remote farm cottage. As soon as the three years were up, of course, you were entitled to think anything you liked about your partner. Sometimes I wondered about the logicality of the divorce strictures. On insanity, for example, I often felt, in a cynical way, that divorce should be awarded to the insane person and not the person who had caused that condition.

I recall a Glasgow solicitor telling me about a husband who had disappeared and it later turned out that he had had a complete memory loss. Eventually he returned to the loving care of the marital home and gradually his memory came back, whereupon he promptly left again. I remember Lake Falconer, a humorous and excellent local solicitor at the time, advising me in a jocularly cynical manner what style of letters might be written to establish the attitude of mind during the three years of desertion. He devised something along these lines:

Dear Madam
My solicitor has advised me to write to you to say that I am desperate for you to return home.
Yours faithfully,
Your husband

At the end of the three years the letter was to read:

Dear Madam
The three years expired at 11. 22pm yesterday evening and I now want rid of you as soon as possible. Please co-operate in a divorce on the grounds of desertion.

I wondered if the Brigadier's three years were up yet.

'When did your wife leave you?' I asked.

'How the hell can I remember? 1933 I think it was.'

That was before I had even been born. Certainly, the three years had passed but I wondered what the Brigadier could prove about his attitude towards getting his wife back during them. I put that question to him.

'Of course I tried. I went round to her lover's house and broke all his windows with my umbrella.'

You can never tell how courts will interpret things and I was not sure if they would regard that as an act of violence or an act of endearment. I explained to the Brigadier that we would have to find out where his wife was so that we could consider starting court proceedings.

'I have no idea. I have not seen the bitch since she left.'

He agreed to make some enquiries among friends and to let me know how he got on. Needless to say, he either forgot or did not manage to make any progress and phoned demanding to know what progress I had managed to make. I reminded him that the ball was in his court so to speak. Unfortunately, in my youthful naivety, I had not immediately appreciated that the reason for all his appointments being at 3.15 p.m. had to do with the fact that the pubs closed at 3 o'clock.

Eventually, after many months of inactivity, I received an excited phone call from the Brigadier, who told me that he had at last traced 'the bitch' and that she was still living with the lover she had taken on way back in the '30s. Not only that, but he told me that they had married as, apparently, they thought the Brigadier had been killed during the Spanish Civil War. I suggested that he should come in so that we could talk fully about the latest developments and arranged an appointment for the inevitable 3.15 p.m. When he came in, no doubt fuelled by the activities of his previous appointment, he was desperate for revenge on not only 'the bitch' but her equally disgraceful lover. I told him that if a divorce was what he really wanted, I should simply write to his wife and ask her to consult her own solicitors with a view to progress in one direction or another. Unfortunately, that was not good enough for the revengeful Brigadier. He demanded that I reported her to the Passport Office for travelling abroad on a false passport because she had assumed her new husband's name, or rather, the man she thought was her husband. I refused to do that for him and advised him just to leave that issue alone but he insisted that was what he wanted to do, which he did, despite my advice. A few weeks later, I opened my morning mail and came across the most surprising letter I think I have ever received in business. It was from a firm of solicitors in London and read like this:

Dear Sirs,
MRS MARY GARDINER
BRIGADIER HAROLD ENSBY
We have reason to believe that your client Brigadier Ensby is proposing to divorce our client, Mrs Mary Gardiner, on the grounds of her alleged desertion from him. We think it is time you were told that our client and your client were never legally married. The facts are that on 17th July 1917 in St Petersburg, Russia, your client went through a ceremony of marriage with a lady called Olga Kaspov and that said marriage persisted at the time of your client's purported marriage to our client in London in 1931. The London marriage was clearly a bigamous one and our client and your client were never legally man and wife. Any divorce action you care to raise will, of course, be vigorously opposed. We trust we will hear no more about this matter.
Yours faithfully

I summoned the Brigadier for another 3.15 p.m. appointment and showed him the letter, demanding an explanation. He read it briefly and said, 'What the hell has that got to do with anything?' I replied, no doubt somewhat pompously, that I thought it had everything to do with everything and asked whether talk of the Russian marriage in 1917 was correct.

'Of course it is correct,' he said. 'It was the time of the Revolution and I and a number of my friends were going in and out of Russia all the time, marrying ladies in danger and taking them back to safety on our passports. There were hundreds of them.'

'But,' I countered, 'you lived with Olga in London for two or three years.'

The Brigadier gave his usual reply: 'What the hell has that got to do with anything?'

I told him that I thought it might make quite a difference. Having received nothing from the Brigadier to nullify the apparent Russian marriage, clearly a lot of re-thinking was going to have to be done. I suggested that we meet again in a week or two.

At the next meeting, I told the Brigadier that I thought everything was stymied, but if he wanted to pursue the matter I would gladly arrange for an opinion from a Scottish QC after putting all the various facts to him. He reluctantly agreed to that course, clearly still thinking it was totally unnecessary, since he persisted in his erroneous belief that he could divorce Mary on the grounds of her desertion. I remember the consultation well. I drove the Brigadier down to Edinburgh, picking him up at Tyndrum. Five miles later, when we reached Crianlarich, he demanded a stop because, he said, 'I want to empty number one tank.' We went into the hotel and I almost had to drag the Brigadier away because he was enraged at the night porter for not having the bar open at 8 o'clock in the morning. Eventually, we made it to Edinburgh for the consultation with learned counsel. It was the only time that I entered counsel's chambers with two people carrying briefcases and one carrying an empty bottle of whisky. It was not surprising that it was empty because he had acquired it by some secretive manner almost as soon as we had arrived in Edinburgh about one hour earlier. The information given to the learned QC was a little bit garbled to say the least, but he took the view that there was no reason to invalidate the Russian marriage. However, he recommended the introduction of a Russian specialist lawyer to advise about the legal status of wedding bureaux in Russia because it was in one such bureau, introduced by the regime of that time, that the Brigadier had tied at least one knot.

I have never forgotten the journey home. The Brigadier had had nothing to eat all day – just masses of whisky – and his condition was inevitable. Going through the Pass of Brander, Loch Awe, he threw his cigarette out of the car window. A mile or two further on I noticed billows of smoke coming from the Brigadier's overcoat, which was lying on the back seat. I stopped the car so we could extinguish the fire and as we resumed our journey the Brigadier said, 'I say, Pagan, that was bloody clever of you to spot the fire.'

Some time after my return to Oban, further enquiries through the Russian experts were made, but they led nowhere different. The Brigadier was legally married to Olga. This set us the problem of trying to find out where she was. She was presumably also in desertion. A few weeks later, another interesting letter arrived with the sad news that Olga, after splitting up with the Brigadier, had made her way to Hollywood in search, like many other young ladies, of her fortune. This did not appear to have materialised and she apparently died there in 1959. By chance the Brigadier had already arranged a 3.15p.m. appointment on the same day that the letter arrived and he turned up in the usual slightly aggressive form, demanding to know what progress I had made. I had to commiserate with him and advised him that he was now a widower. He replied in his usual understanding way.

'Damn and blast you to hell man – you have grossly mishandled my business. I do not want to be a bloody widower. I want to divorce the bitch on the grounds of her desertion.'

I explained for the umpteenth time that that was not legally possible and there the matter eventually ended. I am glad to say that I remained on friendly terms with the Brigadier, which I was pleased about, not just because he was a man with a fund of amusing and sometimes disgraceful stories. One of them had to do with an early drink-driving case which, quite properly of course, are not now regarded as a matter for jokes. I suppose in those days, when there were far fewer cars around, there was an air of bravado about the whole thing and few people got hurt. His story concerned an army dinner when, very much the worse for wear, he was being driven back by an army driver who was in no better condition. Not surprisingly, an on-coming car had to leave the road to avoid him. When the driver got out demanding retribution, the Brigadier's driver adopted surprisingly friendly terms, saying gently, 'That was all your fault.'

'How on earth was it my fault? It was entirely your fault, you were on the wrong side of the road, driving like a maniac.'

'No,' the Brigadier's driver insisted, 'It was all your fault. You forgot to dip your lights.'

'There is no law in this country that requires me to dip my lights,' replied the innocent driver.

'No, indeed not, my good man. There is no law in the country that requires you to wipe your arse, but most decent people do.'

The Brigadier enjoyed that example of wit, improved rather than worsened by drink. I saw the Brigadier in his dying days and I am glad that they were peaceful. He was either having a quiet dram or sleeping wrapped in a tartan rug.

4

'Try a redhead next time'

It was unfair of my friend the Brigadier to blame the law for his problems. At the same time, many have legitimate grievances about court cases. The delays and expense caused by cumbersome procedures can lead to dissatisfaction and not only amongst the public. The fact that I believe the English system to be infinitely worse is not a reason to be complacent. I have always objected to the system in England where, for example, coroners' courts hold public enquiries into suicides and private death, which have nothing to do with anybody else. They cause unnecessary additional grief. And then, the English criminal system is unnecessarily long-winded and confusing. At one time, they used to have two criminal trials for each crime: one to see if it was worth having a trial at all. If the answer was yes, you ended up with witnesses having to give evidence twice on the same matter and huge amounts of time being unnecessarily wasted. That seems to have gone now, but English criminal cases still begin with opening addresses from counsel for the two different sides, which can last for several days, each of them trying to predict what the witnesses might say when their time comes to give evidence. How, at the end of the day, a jury is meant to differentiate between what they were told the witness might say and what the witness actually said, I cannot begin to understand.

Scotland too has had a large number of miscarriages of justice and possibly, proportionately, just as many as there are in England. Huge improvements are still needed. I recall one particular divorce case which had both moments of humour and moments of tragedy. It had to do with an island case where the wife claimed, probably with some justification, that her husband frequently drank to excess and that that amounted to cruelty. My client, Donald, was not always an easy man to get hold of and late one evening, after a particularly difficult day in the office, I tried for about the tenth time to get him on the phone, going, as one had to in those days, through the operator. On failing yet again to get an answer, I exploded somewhere along the lines of 'Oh, bugger it, he is out again', which brought an intervention from the operator, who asked helpfully, 'Would it be Donald you would be wanting?' On receiving my confirmation, I was advised that Donald was in the pub, but if I tried after 10 o'clock I would probably be able to get him. On another occasion, my temper over the phone caused me even more embarrassment when I said after three days of trying to get hold of a Sheriff Officer from a different area, 'That bastard's never at home.' I did not know that the people at the other end who had just answered were still on the line and was mortified by the reply, 'I'll give Dad your message when he comes in.'

The particularly tragic part of Donald's case was the fact that he was separated from his children as well, pending the divorce, and his wife and the young children moved to Callander. It was there that Donald and I stopped for a bit of relief on our way to a consultation in Edinburgh – all divorces in those days having to be in the Court of Session there. While we were in the public toilet at Callander, Donald's two young boys came in, which was the first time he had seen them for several months. I thought then that there had to be a better way of a father exercising contact with his own children. Fortunately with family mediation and so on, things are improving but there is a long way to go yet.

Sadly for me personally, it was at that same toilet twelve years later that I stopped on the journey home from Edinburgh after a futile and, no doubt, pathetic attempt to save my own rapidly deteriorating marriage. My two children then were both under three and I wondered if I would ever see them again as a normal father. I would not find it easy to adapt to becoming a father who only sees his children on occasional visits to Edinburgh to walk round zoos, museums and parks. But that is another story.

Despite the dreadful sadness of Donald and his children, I remember a few amusing bits from his divorce proof, which had to do with whether Donald did or did not drink to excess and whether he had any reason for that. On one occasion, the local village policeman, who had been brought by the wife's lawyers, no doubt to give evidence about Donald's excesses, was asked the straight question, 'Have you ever seen Donald drunk?' to which the policeman replied, 'No never.'

'Good for us,' I thought, 'I wonder why they bothered to bring him as a witness.'

Unfortunately, the policemen then added, 'But I have frequently seen him under the influence of drink.' This exasperated the judge, who was having difficulty in coming to terms with the realities of island life.

'I'm sorry Constable, I simply do not understand your evidence. You say that you have never seen him drunk but frequently under the influence. I do not understand the difference.'

'Well, my Lord,' clarified the policeman for the benefit of the out-of-touch judge, 'I have never seen him lying in a roadside ditch.'

Later, when Donald's turn came to give evidence, it was very apparent that his Lordship had made up his mind that he was a drunken rogue and his wife was the purest thing that ever walked the island. When Donald tried to explain that he suspected that his wife was having an affair with a neighbour, evidence of such an unfounded suspicion was demanded by the judge, who clearly gave the impression that he would not believe what he was told anyway. Donald replied that on one occasion in the early hours of the morning, he had gone downstairs into the kitchen and found this particular neighbour with his wife in some sort of degree of close friendship. The judge demanded to know what on earth was wrong with that. Donald responded to the effect that the explanation he was given simply increased his grounds for suspicion, the neighbour having apparently claimed that he was there because he had kindly taken some sheep out of Donald's garden.

'That could be perfectly true, couldn't it?' asked the irate judge, to which he got the excellent reply, 'My Lord, I do not keep sheep in my kitchen.'

Donald's wife got the divorce shortly after and I will leave out the more intimate parts of the judgement, but reading them again after more than three decades reminded me how appallingly public divorces once were. But there was some consolation for Donald in part of the judgement:

> The one redeeming feature in this unhappy case is that both parties have a deep affection for the two children and it is clear that neither had allowed their personal dispute to influence them in their regard for the welfare of the children. Both speak highly of the other as a parent. The children now reside with the Pursuer who is employed as a resident cook/housekeeper in a private house . . .

I noticed recently in the correspondence of that divorce that the wife's wages as the live-in cook/housekeeper amounted to £5 per week! I have no idea what happened over the years about Donald's relationship with his children. So far as I can remember, I have not seen him since. I can only hope that things worked out as well for him as they eventually did for me.

In all my many dealings with separated parents where children were involved, I tried to ensure that the circumstances would reflect what had been contained in that part of the judgement. A quarter of a century later, I was proud of the fact that I and my partners were founder members of the Family Law Association, which was set up by some solicitors in Scotland. The association had the main objective of trying to persuade all lawyers to act sensitively and not aggressively, not just where children were involved but also in any husband and wife dispute. Someone said that the three main traumas of life are bereavement, divorce and moving home. As solicitors have to be closely involved in all three, it is no wonder that we are sometimes not the most popular of people. No one, unless they have been through a divorce themselves, can wholly understand what is involved. It can entail all the different emotions imaginable.

I remember one case in particular. I will call my client 'Jean' as she will no doubt be able to recognise herself, which means that others will as well. What was special was the way she recovered from the total depression and defeatism which assailed her when she discovered what her husband had been up to for a number of years, quite unknown to her. Later, by sheer determination, she transformed herself into a confident and attractive person. So much so that, having lifted herself out of her difficulties and depression, she agreed to offer help to any other of my clients who were similarly knocked out by their husband's behaviour. An attractive young lady once said to me that there was only one way to get over a man.

'What's that?' I enquired with interest.

'Get under another one,' was the unabashed reply.

It is always good to see a recovery like Jean's and often, at the top of my stairs, when I say goodbye to a client who has been through the agonies of a divorce, I wish them luck and demand that they let me know if they get married again. This has often brought the reply, 'I am never going to look at another man in my life.' I have, on occasions, placed a bet with such people which I often waive as an easy way out of buying a wedding present when I have proved my point.

The other unusual thing about Jean's divorce was advising her on New Year's Eve that it had at last gone through. For reasons of convenience and finance, the divorce was eventually raised under the more civilised modern procedures by her husband and by chance I met the other solicitor – another local one – when we were both taking advantage of the early holiday to look at some books in what was then Menzies shop. He was able to take me to one side and tell me that the divorce had been granted. I had trouble getting through to Jean to give her the news and didn't in fact manage until just before the bells. After advising her I said, 'You will be going out for two celebrations now.'

'I don't think so,' came the reply. 'I think I'll just stay at home and read a book.'

I could understand why, on hearing of her divorce that New Year's Eve, Jean decided not to go out. Something which begins with such love and commitment and optimism and which ends with such sadness and disappointment and often with such bitterness and hatred can never be a cause for celebration.

One trouble with relationships can be that emotions do not always coincide and when one partner is feeling particularly strong in love, the other can be feeling a bit the other way. And I have never heard of a case where, on telling a partner that you are no longer in love and want to leave, the response was, 'That's wonderful; so do I.' There is nearly always one partner being hurt, often both, no matter how much they may pretend otherwise. I have heard of the apparently wronged partner inventing an affair of their own, presumably for what they see as their own self-esteem.

I think it was one of my first ever divorce experiences in about 1958 that quickly sickened me of the whole procedure and made me realise how inappropriate the court setting was. That case involved two young people who shared everything – especially a very deep religious belief and commitment. They had clearly been much in love and probably still were even at the time of the horrible court hearing, which lasted in the Edinburgh Court of Session for four or five days. With divorces at that time only being possible in the big court in Edinburgh, it was necessary to involve not only the local solicitor but also an Edinburgh solicitor to actually be responsible for the case and then learned counsel to actually conduct it. Fortunately there were no children involved in that religious divorce. The firm I was working for was acting for the husband in defending an action brought against him by his wife on what seemed very empty grounds. No doubt, however, there was a lot more to it than came out at the divorce hearing but quite enough came out to upset me. With seven or eight lawyers all present, various court officials and the hearing being open to the public, it was I think humiliating to all of us to have some intimate details of their sex life brought out into the open. The case ended in moments of farce because our counsel, who happened to be a personal friend of the unfortunate husband, was not particularly good and whilst it was obvious to all that the wife had not established her grounds for divorce, our counsel made such a mess of his summing up that the Edinburgh and Glasgow solicitors had jointly to pull him down to his seat by his gown before he lost it for us. I often wondered what had been behind that whole very unhappy tale.

Obviously, I was not alone in having concerns about courts being the appropriate way of dealing with family issues. In 1988 I was consulted by a lady who came from Scotland but who had married and was then living in England with her husband and two children aged six and three. It became necessary for her to flee from the family home, taking the children with her, and she returned to Scotland. The court proceedings had, however, to take place in England, where, of course, not only the law but various other things are very different. With all the cross-border and other difficulties, it was well over a year before everything went through the way it was thought best for the benefit and stability of the children. It must have been an extremely stressful time for the mother and children and no doubt the father as well but, over ten years later, I had a nice surprise. By that time I had lost touch with Grace and I had no idea how things were working out for her. But one day I opened my mail and there was a book with a very appreciative card from her as a thank you for the way I had tried to help during such a difficult period of her life. She was one of four joint authors of the book, which was entitled *Absent Fathers?* What had happened was that she had decided to put her experiences to positive use and, while a research student, had joined with others to carry out an investigation into the way divorce was affecting children and fathers. When Grace got in touch with me again, she was a Lecturer in the Department of Social Policy at the University of York and her joint book suggested that the policy-makers needed to understand the emotional and moral turmoil that followed most breakdowns in family relationships.

Perhaps more of us should do what Grace did and use our bad experiences to bring about some good for the benefit of others. Coincidentally, Grace's book arrived not long after I had attended a special conference about children and divorce at Stirling University. One of the contributors was Ann Mitchell, an academic researcher who wrote an excellent book, *Children in the Middle: Living through Divorce*, in which she wrote that children do not necessarily equate parental conflict with an unhappy family life. Many of those interviewed, apparently, would have preferred to remain with an unbroken family where there was at least some hope that their parents would eventually cease their arguments and conflicts. This is contrary to many expressed views that children are better off with a separated family than in an unhappy but unbroken home where the only main problem is the parents' conflict. It is quite common for people to say that it was for the children's benefit that they split up, because it could not have been good for them to have seen so much nasty behaviour. The fact often seems to be that, unless the children have been brought into violence or abuse of some kind, they are quite happy for the whole family to remain together as long as they are not actually involved in what is going wrong. That coincides with my general experiences, but no two people are the same. Ann Mitchell's findings do, however, suggest that sometimes when parents say that their separation is what the children wanted, that may in many cases simply be an attempt by the adults to salve their consciences.

I was in my late sixties before I met, personally, someone who had been abused as a child. I had read, as most of us have, about the terrible effects of such treatment on people when they are young and often for the rest of their lives. I believed it without really understanding it. My encounter with an eighteen-year-old friend was a real eye opener and it was only then, from what she told me, that I could begin to understand how people really do have their lives destroyed because of early physical and emotional damage.

My friend's agonies were worsened by feelings of guilt, which are very common in all kinds of victims, despite the fact that they can rarely, if ever, be blamed in any way for the ill treatment dealt out to them. My friend was only eight at the time when her abuse began and she said nothing about it to anybody. Part of this may have been shame, but she also thought that by saying nothing she would be able to protect some young relations who were only three and four from anything happening to them. It was only years later that she discovered that the abuser had turned his attentions to the younger girls as well and my friend wrongly blames herself for that. The other thing that brought her anxieties to a head at the time when I got to know her was that the abuser, who had been away from our small community for a while, suddenly returned to the area and there was talk of a criminal prosecution, with my friend of course being needed as a witness. It was then that she told me the whole story and I have rarely been more upset than I was when listening to her desperately sad tale. Fortunately for me, I was spared the details.

It would be nice to think that we are becoming a bit more civilised about divorce and, with the sadly increasing numbers of people affected, it might be that some children will find things easier to accept. Feeling you are not alone in your misfortune can sometimes make it easier to cope. Also, experiences from others can be helpful and, in my own personal case, I was eventually given two excellent bits of advice, which I wished I had had the sense to think of from the very beginning of the marriage break-up. The first was, so far as possible, to give the children two of everything so that they had as little as possible to pack as they moved from one home to the other. Of course, in most households the finances make that pretty well impossible, but even two toothbrushes is a helpful start. I often wondered how my elder daughter's portable radio cassette survived all the journeys between her parents' different homes. It was always stuffed into the top of her already full bag and fell out so often it was well bashed and cracked, but it still played!

The other advice was for the parents to avoid handing over the children direct to the other or collecting them direct from the other. In other words, where possible, when the time came for the children to move back to the other home, one parent would take them to school and the other would collect at the end of the day. With children's increasing activities as they get older, that advice can often be followed with different parents taking them to and collecting them from swimming, music classes, football, basketball, discos, Guides, Cubs, Kung fu, ballet, visits to friends, pictures . . . Certainly, in the experiences of many, the tensest moments are when one part of the family is waiting for the other parent to arrive and take the children away. But, as we know, we are not all the same. I recently came across a case where an only child liked to be collected direct from one parent by the other. He appeared to take comfort from seeing them both at the same time.

I remember once commiserating with the parents of a boy of the same age as my own son when that other boy had gone temporarily off the rails, and saying something like, 'It's not always easy being a parent'. To which the other father replied, 'And they don't even give you any training.' If that is true, it is certainly the case that you do not get any training in advance to help you understand how to cope with a separation, if that unfortunate happening confronts you. There may be a bit more understanding now, but well into the new century Bob Geldof was on record as saying that not enough emphasis and support are given to a father when a marriage breaks down. He wrote graphically about the agonies of being separated from his children.

In the 1950s, the easiest way to obtain a divorce was often to set up a pantomime of spending a night with somebody in a hotel and arrange for two enquiry agents to pay a surprise and wholly unexpected visit at a prearranged time. It was a total charade, but the legal presumption seemed to be that if a man and a woman were alone together after midnight, they had to be up to something naughty. One of the clients I came across in the 1950s while I was still an apprentice, was an aristocratic landowner who was wanting a divorce as he was playing the field – probably literally. His wife eventually agreed to co-operate with raising a divorce action against him on the grounds of adultery and this had to be set up so that the proper evidence could be produced at the court. Two attempts at the charade failed for the simple reason that all the women he seemed to fancy looked very much like his own wife and no detective was able to say that it wasn't her. He wrote an angry letter to my Apprentice Master pointing out that his advice had failed at least twice and he demanded better and further legal advice, to which he was given the fairly obvious reply: 'Try a redhead next time.' Eventually he got his divorce.

Nothing had improved almost twenty years later when I had to adopt the same charade to establish grounds for my divorce. Fortunately, it was not necessary to actually do anything and I remember taking my very friendly Dalmatian dog with me. I also recall that the two enquiring agents were not unduly impressed when my dog put his dirty paws all over their white raincoats. The worry I had, of course, was whether the detectives might fail to arrive as I would have had difficulty finding the money to re-enact the ludicrous scene. It was a very expensive hotel!

Fortunately, in 1976, a more civilised way of divorce was introduced ending a lot of these charades and other unfortunate experiences for many people. Obviously, divorce is an emotive issue and those who are not in favour of divorce on any grounds have every right to their views. But the fact is that marriages often do break up, and if there are going to be divorces of any kind the whole thing has to be arranged in a civilised fashion.

But some of us, inevitably, cope better than others. One lady I represented had a husband who had a reputation for bizarre behaviour. It was claimed that he was the first (I hope the last) man ever to do a ton on a motorbike in George Street, Oban. On one occasion, apparently, on leaving a dinner dance with his wife, very much the worse for wear, he decided to prove his undying love for her by throwing himself into the bay.

'Good heavens,' I said, 'What did you do?'

'Nothing,' she replied, 'I knew that the tide was out so I just waited for the silly bugger to come back up the ladder.'

5

For Justice and Decency

Like many others, no doubt, I entered the legal profession with romantic and idealistic notions of securing justice and righting wrongs. At that time, the principles of Scottish law seemed to be, quite simply, common sense and fair play. Now, of course, everything has become much more complicated and regulatory with a frightening amount of centralised control, not just from government, but from big business. As an interesting experiment, one of my solicitor colleagues, Irene Reid, and I compared the number of Acts of Parliament in the twenty years after 1979 with the twenty years before that. What we did was to put all the pre-1979 Acts of Parliament on the left-hand side of my desk and all the Acts since 1979 on the right-hand side of my desk. The right-hand side was about five times higher and the desk must have been in danger of toppling. Another change was much more welcome. When I graduated in 1957, there were 32 graduates along with me, only four of whom were ladies. Thirty-one years later in 1988, when Irene herself was admitted as a solicitor, the ladies outnumbered the men by 38 to 34. It was Irene who told me the classic story of the dyslexic, agnostic insomniac, who lay awake all night wondering if there really was a dog.

An example of how, in the early days, advice could often be relatively easy, is the case of a young lady who was being threatened with eviction from her cottage on the estate of a wealthy landlord. I explained that, without special grounds, she might be secure in her tenancy and enquired on what grounds attempts were being made to get rid of her.

'Because of insolence,' was the reply. It did not need too much legal knowledge to be able to reassure my client. However, I recently read of a case from the early nineteenth century where a man had been locked up in Greenock Prison, not just for leaving his job without permission but, far worse than that apparently, he had treated his employer 'with a lack of respect'. So perhaps my young lady client was wise to check the law after all.

It was not long into my practice before I found it was not going to be a simple case of discovering injustices and putting them right. For a start, in the day-to-day sort of cases that I was involved in, there were, at least as far as I could detect, hardly any wrong convictions. I remember my solicitor father telling me that he had once asked a Sheriff Clerk in Cupar how many miscarriages of justice he had seen in his long experience of the courts. The reply from the Sheriff Clerk was that he had seen no wrongful convictions but a lot of wrongful acquittals. Another interesting conversation which my father passed on to me was a discussion he had had with the local Procurator Fiscal at Cupar, when he asked how difficult it was for him to decide on prosecutions when he might know or even be related to the people accused. The answer was a simple one, the Procurator Fiscal explaining that he never looked at the names of the accused on the Police Reports before reading the papers and deciding whether there should be a prosecution or not.

I usually adopted the same idea when I became the Fiscal at Oban in 1970. On one occasion I had to prosecute a close friend, fortunately only on a small speeding matter, but what was unfortunate was that it was I who had caused him to speed in the first place. We had together been organising a charitable function and I asked him to rush along to the other end of the town to collect something vital for the afternoon's event, as a result of which he was stopped by the police. A day or two after he got notice of the prosecution, he phoned in a manner which suggested that our friendship might be under strain.

Another thing that militated against a solicitor like me being able to spend his whole time searching for and putting right wrongful decisions was simply time and money. Obviously I could not afford to give up too much of my time to speculative investigations, which could involve huge travelling distances round this Highland area. I hope I never did ignore an injustice but the fact is, however, that it was usually the more serious cases like child murders and terrorist actions, with which I did not normally get involved personally, that produced the major injustices.

As a young man, the first serious miscarriage of justice I was aware of was the Oscar Slater case, which concerned the murder of an old lady in her Glasgow flat in 1908. Although my own father was only a year old at the time, it was he who brought home to me the appalling iniquity of that case. The major aspect, at the time I first heard about it, was the judge's summing up, when he had implied to the jury that because Oscar Slater was a small-time criminal and also a bit of a pimp, the normal principle of being innocent until proved guilty did not apply to him. Strangely enough, it was the father of the solicitor under whom I served my own apprenticeship who had the thankless task of defending Oscar Slater.

Oscar Slater spent twenty years in prison before he was properly released, but at least it did the rest of us some good because it led directly to the introduction of the first Criminal Appeal Court in Scotland. More recently, a book has been published which suggests that it was not just the trial irregularities which were at fault, but that Oscar Slater was the victim of a stitch-up, the murder having actually, so it is claimed, been carried out by a member of the old lady's family for financial gain. It is also now being claimed that the family was friendly with leading members of the legal establishment, who helped to cover up the actions of the real murderer.

Ninety years after the murder, I visited the tenement with a member of my family and a friend and it was very eerie indeed because the door directly leading into the flat where the murder was committed was obviously the same as it had been all those years before. The old lady had, apparently, been very frightened of being burgled and had a number of different locks fitted on the door to try to protect her. They were still there when I paid my visit one dark winter's night and I was glad to get out of the tenement quickly.

In the early '60s James Hanratty was convicted of a murder and the attempted murder and rape of the victim's girlfriend. Many people have been very unhappy about that conviction, which resulted in

James Hanratty being hanged in Bedford prison, only a few yards from where I spent five years at a privileged English public school. My other tenuous connection with the James Hanratty case was that, unknown to me until afterwards, I had been in correspondence with his solicitor on a, by comparison, wholly trivial debt collection matter involving a rather shady character who lived at Barcaldine and I could not understand why the correspondence had suddenly dried up. It was only when I read the Sunday papers the day after James Hanratty's conviction that I well understood why the solicitor had stopped writing to me. It is interesting to recall that the *Sunday Observer*, the day after the verdict, reported that the defence solicitor was obviously distressed at the verdict and, even at that early stage, it mentioned that many had serious misgivings about the outcome of the trial. The family's fight for justice still continues all these years later.

As a student in 1957, I had seen a man sentenced to death in the High Court in Edinburgh. Some fellow students and I managed to get out of a lecture early and rush to the court just in time before the jury delivered its verdict. It was a moving and nasty experience, with the judge having to go through the ritual of producing a black cap of some sort from under his bench and holding it over his own wigged head as he pronounced the words of doom. The murderer had killed a night watchman in Leith, battering him over the head with a torch. The drama in the court was of course enhanced by the various productions, including the torch, which sat there in all their apparent innocence.

The murderer, a man by the name of Alexander Forbes, was reprieved shortly before the death sentence was due to be carried out and, after a reasonable time in prison, was released, whereupon he committed another murder. He was quite often in the news because, not long after his reprieve, he had married in prison, which is the type of story that some sections of the press seem to think is important. By the time Alexander Forbes committed his second murder, the death penalty had been abolished and, inevitably, there were loud cries from those in favour of the death penalty that it should never have been abolished and that Alexander Forbes was one person who should certainly have been executed.

Very nearly half a century later I was at a seminar when I suddenly realised that one of the speakers, by then himself a judge, was the son of the judge who had imposed the death sentence when I had been present. I told the then Lord Wheatley of my remote encounter with his father and his demeanour changed as he recalled those days. He told me that his father, who was well known to be very much against the death penalty, changed a lot in his behaviour in the three weeks between imposing a death sentence and the sentence actually being carried out. Apparently, he did not talk much during that anxious period, did not eat much and, quite simply, was not himself. It is not generally known nowadays the terrible effect that the death penalty could have even on people remotely involved in the particular case. For example, there were instances of witnesses who had only been at the very periphery of a murder trial having nervous breakdowns as a result of the death penalty being passed on the person at whose trial they had given evidence. It is good that those barbaric days are behind us.

At least my conversation with the younger Lord Wheatley ended on a more cheerful note when I told him that I had had one other encounter with his father. That was on the cricket field, when I had been playing for the Solicitors in their annual match against the Bench and Bar. Lord Wheatley Senior had been out first ball and the Solicitors had been mean enough not to offer him another chance.

The death penalty is not something that I could ever support. It is wrong on Christian and moral grounds and it has proved time and time again to be no deterrent. Even if you were to disregard those aspects, there are, and will continue to be, far too many miscarriages of justice for it ever to be safe to put someone to death. The mistakenly convicted Guildford and Birmingham bombers alone are examples of ten lives which would have been wrongly taken had there been a death penalty at the time.

One of Scotland's worst miscarriages of justice of more recent times concerned Patrick Meehan, described in Ludovic Kennedy's book *In Bed with an Elephant* as 'an incompetent Gorbals safe blower'. Certainly he had been involved in a lot of dishonesty and burglaries but he was not a man of violence. Despite that, because he happened to be travelling between Glasgow and Stranraer on the night that an elderly lady was murdered in her home in Ayr, the authorities decided that it had to be him. In fact, when it later turned out that it wasn't him at all, the official enquiry set up to establish the truth added a ridiculous accusation seemingly from thin air that, while it was then admitted that two other people had been responsible for the murder, nevertheless 'Meehan must have been standing outside the house waiting for the proceeds.' The only thing which could possibly have given rise to such a conclusion was that Patrick Meehan's companion on the night in question, when they were on another activity altogether, had, so it is claimed, some papers planted in his pocket which linked forensically to something found in the murder victim's house. The police claimed that the papers were discovered in a pocket of the companion's overcoat when they were searching his house. But no one explained why an overcoat was being worn on a warm summer's evening. Patrick Meehan was eventually granted a free pardon after serving seven years of a life sentence for murder and received compensation of £50,000.

Among those who constantly campaigned for justice for him were Ludovic Kennedy and one of Scotland's most flamboyant and quick-witted lawyers, Nicholas Fairbairn. Nicholas graduated from Edinburgh University at the same time as me and one of my favourite stories of him concerns a time when he was cross-examining a fisherman and asked him whether he was surprised about something that had happened. 'Surprised?' came the answer, 'I'll say I was. You could have buggered me through my oilskins.'

'What did the witness say, Mr Fairbairn?' asked the astonished judge.

'The witness replied that he had been taken aback, my Lord.'

Nicholas Fairbairn had a very chequered career, being an outstanding artist and politician who served in Margaret Thatcher's cabinet as well as being a leading member of the Scottish legal profession. Sadly, he died far too young.

Hamish McColl, a minister in Oban in the 1960s and '70s was a great campaigner for justice and decency and played a major role as Chairman of the Oban Shelter Group and a member of the successful Oban Housing Association. He was instrumental in the setting up of both and when he later moved to Johnstone, he became a leader of the campaign to right what was probably one of Scotland's greatest ever miscarriages of justice. By one of life's many extraordinary coincidences, Hamish told me many years later that he had very nearly had to serve on the Hanratty jury but instead was picked for the case either immediately before or immediately after Hanratty's – he could not remember which. Could that have been the difference between life and death for James Hanratty, I wondered.

Raymond Gilmour was already being helped by Hamish when a fifteen-year-old girl was brutally murdered in the Johnstone area, which eventually led to Gilmour being charged and convicted of her murder. Hamish was by no means alone in believing in Gilmour's innocence. At Liberal conferences I have heard MP and QC Menzies Campbell mention the case as an example of the law getting it wrong. Among the main concerns about the conviction were the lack of forensic evidence and an alleged confession while in police custody by Gilmour, who was described as 'an easily suggestible and emotionally immature young man.'

I do not know the details of the Johnstone case but have long held the view that the greater the atrocity, the more there is likely to be a miscarriage of justice because of the pressure put on the police by the public – even if they themselves are often not nearly as helpful to the police as they should be. Understandably perhaps, the police often feel that they simply have to get a result. Gilmour was nineteen at the time of his arrest. Twenty-one years later, aged forty, he was still in prison with no pardon, no release and no parole – another victim of the regulation which refuses parole unless the person will admit the crime. Like many others, Gilmour has said, 'I will not confess to something I did not do.' It was, of course, a similar principled stand but in wholly different circumstances and in a different country, which kept Nelson Mandela in jail for twenty-seven years, both men choosing to remain in prison rather than to betray their principles.

Many miscarriages of justice occur as a result of wrong identification. This is not necessarily deliberate, but simply because it is often difficult for people to recognize others. This is yet another of my failings and the family were highly amused one day when we arrived early in Aviemore. We went into one place looking for breakfast for the five of us, only to be told that they did not do breakfast there but the place next door did. We moved on to the other premises and a waitress came forward to greet us. I explained that we had been sent to her restaurant by someone next door because we could get breakfast in her premises. I could not understand why the family was laughing until they pointed out to me that the second waitress was in fact the same as the first one. It was she I had been speaking to just two seconds earlier.

I am not alone in my failings and I was impressed by a television programme on injustices which showed the reconstruction of a video with the alleged robber standing in a bank queue, on the strength of which video the man was convicted. However, the digital enhancing with regard to sizings and other forensic science showed that the identification of that man as the bank robber could not possibly have been correct because he was not nearly tall enough to fit in with other accepted evidence.

There was one brilliant court tale told to me by my former neighbour, Sheriff John Peterson, when he was taking a case in Glasgow. It concerned three shoplifters who had been observed by the store detective. She was a wee lady who, on seeing them leave, chased after all of them but was only able to apprehend one. The captured shoplifter duly appeared in court, pleading not guilty, and the brave detective gave her evidence, explaining how she had observed the three men together but that she had only managed to arrest one of them.

'Do you see in court today the man you did manage to apprehend?' asked the Fiscal.

'Yes. That's him there,' she said, identifying the man in the dock.

'Oh! And there's the other two of them,' she said, pointing to the public gallery, where the two accomplices were sitting calmly in support of their friend. The Sheriff paused the proceedings to allow two policemen to rush up to the public gallery and achieve what the lady detective had been unable to do on her own. I hope she was right in her identification. Fortunately, however, in Scotland corroboration of some kind is always needed and no-one can – or should – be convicted on the evidence of one person alone.

It may surprise some people when I say that it was perhaps in my job as Procurator Fiscal that I was able to achieve most to ensure that justice was done. The Fiscal's decision on a prosecution in the average case is his alone and he has a duty to act as a sort of arbiter between the police and the public. A lot of factors come into the reckoning when a decision is taken about a prosecution and it is not just a question of whether legally a crime has been committed. You also have to consider whether it is in the public interest to take a case to court and whether the expense is justified. The effect on a victim has also to be considered and also the fact that there should always be hesitation before someone is branded as a criminal for the first time, unless of course the matter is especially serious.

I remember one report being given to me by the police concerning a fairly routine breach of the peace by a man in his forties. To my surprise, when I read the papers, I saw that he had no previous convictions, which was unusual. The next time I had occasion to speak to the Chief Inspector about anything, I raised the case and asked if there was a background to the man's behaviour.

'Do you not remember Hamish Walsh? He was the father of that young girl who drowned in the Awe last year.'

I told the Chief Inspector to get a message to the tragic father that I would sit on the Police Report for six months and then throw it out, unless there was any trouble in the meantime.

On another occasion my compassion, if that's what it was, was misplaced. It concerned the case of a Tiree crofter who was reported by the Department of Agriculture for not completing his agricultural return in time. I will not say exactly what went through my mind when I first read the report but I certainly did not regard it as the most ghastly crime I had ever heard of. In fact, I suggested to Chief Inspector Angus Munn that the local constable should visit the crofter some time and see if there was a reason for the failure to complete the form apart from Highland inactivity.

The young constable called and got a very warm and appreciative welcome from the crofter who said, 'Thank goodness you have come to see me, laddie. This agricultural form has been fair worrying me and I haven't slept for months since they started writing to me about it.

You see, the problem is I cannae read and I cannae write and I have been worrying myself sick about it.' The young constable took immediate pity on the crofter and offered on another visit to make time to drop in and help get the form completed. The constable reported back to his Chief Inspector, obviously expecting praise for carrying out some good community policing. Instead the Inspector looked at him with a furled brow and said, 'What did you say this man's name is?'

'Peter McGillivray.'

'The b . . .' exclaimed the Chief Inspector, 'Peter was in school with me and was ahead of me in every class.'

The young constable could not wait to get back to the croft to tell the crofter what he thought of his taking advantage of his common decency.

'Oh damn!' said the crofter, 'I had forgotten that they had moved Angus to Oban.'

To my mind, Amnesty International and the Medical Foundation Against Torture are two of the more important organisations in the world. Amnesty International was started by English lawyer Peter Benenson. How it came about was that he was enraged to read in 1960 about two students in Portugal who had just been jailed for seven years for singing songs taking the mickey out of their government. Peter Benenson decided that he could not just sit back and do nothing and instead wrote a letter of protest to the Portuguese government. At the same time he told the *Observer* newspaper of what he was doing and asked their readers to do the same. From there Amnesty spread all over the country and all over the world and has been instrumental in protecting some from torture and in having other prisoners released. A large number of people who would otherwise have been languishing in jail if they had not already been killed have reason to be thankful to Amnesty International.

On a lighter note, a friend of mine was once asked to do a live interview on television about the work of Amnesty International. It was suggested that she could bring along a freed political prisoner so that he or she could describe what had been involved and why the work of Amnesty International was so vital. She explained that there were not very many such people living in Glasgow and that most of them were in London but she would see what she could do. A few days before the broadcast, she was put in touch with a man called Felix, who had been detained by one of the more oppressive regimes in the world but fortunately later released. On being contacted, he immediately agreed to appear on the programme. My friend and he arranged to meet half an hour beforehand so that they could have a general chat before they went out live on television. Unfortunately, as soon as my friend asked Felix which Amnesty group had managed to support him and get him released, he replied, 'Oh, it was nothing to do with Amnesty. I do not think they had ever heard of me.'

There was nothing for it but for the interview to go ahead and all went well until the BBC interviewer asked, 'One last question, Felix. How did it feel when you were languishing in prison and all those wonderful people from Amnesty International were sending letters and campaigning on your behalf?'

'Here we go,' thought my friend, whereupon she was greatly relieved to hear Felix say, 'It was simply magneefeecent.'

While in Edinburgh in the late 1950s, I was lucky enough to come across David Arthur, who was in the process of establishing the first telephone Samaritans organisation in Scotland, which he achieved very successfully. I remember an occasion when David was none too pleased with me. Returning to my digs after a student night out, I found a message on the table: 'David Arthur phoned – says it's not important.'

'Nonsense,' I thought, 'Samaritans, must be urgent.'

So, notwithstanding the fact that it was the early hours of the morning, I phoned immediately, only to hear a sleepy David saying, 'The message should have said it wasn't at all urgent. I was only wondering if you could play cricket for my XI on Sunday.'

One Friday night I was manning the hotline in the Samaritans office when I got a very distressed call from an Edinburgh tram driver who had just blown the family's whole weekly income on a horse that failed to come in. He was utterly ashamed and felt totally worthless and he couldn't face going home to his wife and children. He thought he should end it all but we managed to get together for a chat and after an hour or two, he went home to face the music and the difficulties. A few weeks later I saw him at an Edinburgh bus stop. I pretended not to recognise him (not too difficult a feat for me) but he came up to me saying something like 'You'll never realise how much you did for me that night. It's OK now.' I did nothing really, just listened. Maybe I said something but I had no magic words or supernatural advice. And that is very often all that is needed.

The Samaritans all began in 1953 when the Rev. Chad Varrah was running a youth club to give young people something to do and to offer guidance from time to time. One day he was horrified to hear that a twelve-year-old member of the club had killed herself. When he enquired about the circumstances he discovered that the poor girl had just started her first period and had imagined that the loss of so much blood internally must have meant that she was seriously ill. So, in fear, she took her own life. How pathetically sad. How unnecessary. And how wrong that she had never been told about the facts of life.

Chad Varrah then decided to extend his club into giving advice on anything he could and, quite correctly, sex information featured. The cheap press vilified him, accusing him of all sorts of ulterior motives and giving him the name of the sexy priest or something equally wrong and unjustified. Fortunately, Chad Varrah was not at all deterred and carried on, knowing that people have to do what is right, no matter how unpopular they become with the ignorant. He soon recognised that adults equally needed help from time to time and that talking in confidence to an anonymous friend could be hugely helpful. Most of us have dark secrets, which we do not want family or friends to know about. It is not therefore surprising that the Samaritans have become such a vital organisation, not just in saving lives but in helping people through difficulties which they cannot discuss with anyone else.

In the 1970s there was a television series called *Sutherland's Law*. It was based on the life of a Procurator Fiscal in a small town in Scotland, widely recognised as Oban. The writer, Lindsay Galloway, in fact lived not far from Oban and apparently got his ideas from various visits to the Oban Court, at the time when I happened to be Fiscal. When the series finally finished in August 1976, it was described as the best free advertising that Oban's tourist industry had ever received; the programme was as associated with Oban as *Dr Finlay's Casebook* was with Callander. By coincidence, my own legal firm is called Hosack & Sutherland but I denied any suggestions that I had bribed the BBC to use the name 'Sutherland' as a publicity stunt for my business. Our real Sutherland (John) had been in the practice in the early part of the last century, before leaving to become the first full-time legal adviser to the Forestry Commission in Scotland. There is a forest walk named after him at Barcaldine, ten miles north of Oban.

By another of life's weird coincidences, sixty-five years after Sir John left the firm, one of my then partners, during his year as President of the Law Society, used in Edinburgh the same room that Sir John used to carry out his duties, the Forestry Commission offices having by that time been acquired by the Law Society.

The *Sutherland's Law* series was really quite good with the Fiscal's part being excellently portrayed by Iain Cuthbertson. Iain was a very good man who helped Oban in a lot of ways during the time he was associated with it through the series. On one occasion I remember, he drove from Edinburgh to Oban on a Sunday morning simply to lead off the High School children's sponsored walk in aid of a local youth club. His whole part in the thing took about ten minutes but he was nevertheless willing to travel 250 miles just to give support. Similarly, he gave up a Saturday just to publicise one of Oban Housing Association's new developments, driving a JCB to lay down the foundations. The new homes were much in demand by young married and many other people in Oban. Sadly, Iain later had a stroke, which meant that he had to re-learn how to talk before continuing his excellent career.

Iain had a good sense of humour and on one occasion an English Sunday newspaper photographer came to Oban to get a photograph of him as the TV Fiscal and me as the real one. They were having trouble with my lack of photogenicity (if there is such a word) and, despite the beautiful outlook from the top of Pulpit Hill, looking over the bay and well beyond to mountains and islands, they were trying to get me to put on a facial expression which I couldn't quite manage.

'Make him sit on that spiked fence over there. That will put an expression on his face,' said Iain. Looking at the photograph today, I see that is exactly what they did.

Willie Melville has one of my favourite photo stories, which comes from his early days in the National Commercial Bank in Oban. At that time there was a street photographer who wandered around with a pet monkey, presumably to attract the children. His pitch was sometimes right outside Willie's bank and the monkey would often walk back and forward along the ledge immediately outside Willie's window. On one occasion Willie had in his room a very boozy client, who must have been nearing the DT stage. The monkey chose that moment to put in another appearance on the ledge, which absolutely terrified the customer, who almost fell off his chair. Willie decided to play it along a bit.

'Is something the matter, Mr MacEwan? Did you think you had seen something?'

'No, no. I didn't see anything. Nothing wrong.'

This happened a few times and, of course, each time Willie looked behind him, the monkey had jumped off the ledge back on to the street. Eventually Willie asked his customer, 'Did you think you had seen a monkey?'

'Why should I have seen a monkey?' asked Mr MacEwan defensively, after which Willie put him out of his misery. The relief was obvious.

The legal adviser to the *Sutherland's Law* series was my predecessor as Oban's Fiscal, John Stevenson, and there were two particular cases which I am sure were based on John's inherent sense of justice. One fictional case concerned an unfortunate crofter from one of the outer isles who unwisely produced a shotgun when Sheriff Officers were sent to evict him from his croft. In serious criminal cases, after an accused has been found guilty, it is necessary for the prosecutor to rise to his feet and to move for sentence before the judge or sheriff has any power to do anything. In a brilliant bit of drama, Fiscal Sutherland remained seated after this poor crofter was convicted, with the result that the Sheriff was unable to impose any sentence and the crofter had to be released back to the peace of his own croft. Another episode dealt with the tragedy of suicide and attempts by an insurance company to avoid paying out the policy money, which was desperately needed to support the widow and young family. Iain Cuthbertson's portrayal of an obstinate Fiscal who refused to be browbeaten by a large organisation was masterly.

The abuse of power is something that we have all got to watch out for and fight against. It does not matter if it is abuse of power by an oppressive, dictatorial regime in another part of the world or an individual incident of domestic violence close to home. The link between the two should be obvious because, once any act of violence goes unchecked, it will only grow.

It is now beginning to be recognised that there is a huge amount of abuse and harassment, not just in the home but at work. Neither is now tolerated but that is not to say that it does not happen. There was one restaurateur in the Dunoon area who was notorious for sexually harassing his female staff and whom, by sheer chance, I had heard of from a friend living there. One day I was talking to a lady who was seeing me about the housing difficulties that she and her young child were having. I knew that she had been working at that same restaurant and I asked if she was still there.

'No,' she said, 'I have left.'

'Don't tell me he was having a go at you as well.'

'What do you mean?' she said with wide-eyed surprise.

'You know what I mean.'

'Yes I do, but how did you know?'

I told her that it appeared to be pretty common knowledge and that I had simply put two and two together. I asked her why she and others affected had not banded together to report him.

'What is the point?' she asked. 'He is friendly with the local Sheriff, the local Procurator Fiscal, local councillors, local police – all those in authority in the area. They all wine and dine in his restaurant. Who is going to believe our word against his?'

I could well understand her reason for that defeatist attitude. In the same way I can understand why someone like a minister's wife or a judge's wife would have terrific difficulty in getting anyone to believe that they were victims of domestic violence, but they can be as well.

In March 2001, in recognition of National Friendship Week, some frightening statistics were produced. For example, nearly 60% of the entire world's wealth is owned by six people, all from America; only twenty out of a hundred people have a decent home; half of the whole population of the world suffer from malnutrition. It doesn't have to be that way and it shouldn't be. Also, if you have money in your purse, some coins in a dish at home and save money in the bank, you are among the top 8% of the world's wealthy. That includes me and probably some or many of those who read this. I'm not sure whether that fact makes me feel better or worse!

Just as I was writing this, I saw an excellent programme on television about two Church of Scotland ministers, the Rev. Willie McPherson and the Rev. Eddie McKenna, one of them being from Bo'ness. They acquired a former Royal Navy ship, had it renovated, and went out to Peru to help street children living in appalling conditions of poverty and abuse. There was one street kid who had been abused by both his father and another man and, not unlike those subjected to domestic violence and other children sexually abused, he for some reason blamed himself for what had happened. That did not stop him from feeling great urges to revenge himself on his two oppressors, both of whom he was determined to kill. The Bo'ness minister was able to involve him in some of the work that was going on, with the result that he felt much more worthy within himself. He then blamed himself less for the abuse he had suffered, which reduced his feeling of violent vengeance. There are important messages within that short tale for a number of people.

Another of the street children interviewed spoke of going to a factory in search of work and being told that he would be taken on but on one condition – he had to hand over one of his kidneys, which obviously had a marketable value. I had heard of people having to provide sexual favours to get a job but I had not heard of anything of that sort before. Perhaps the most distressing story on that programme concerned a mother with two girls, aged six and four, who had been playing together in the park when the girls went missing. The mother panicked, looked all over for them and eventually decided to go home in case for some extraordinary reason they had gone there themselves.

There she found a note on her door which read: 'If you go to the Police you will never see your girls again. We will be in touch later.' Four days later, there was another note on the door which read: If you want your girls back, be at the park on Sunday, same time, same bench.' She went there, overjoyed to find her daughters, but when they turned round to look at her, they were both blind and would be for life. Their corneas had been removed for sale and they would never see again. How can any of us ignore that? How can that 'not be our business'?

However, there are courageous individuals who want to reduce suffering. One man I greatly admire is Magnus MacFarlane-Barrow from Dalmally, twenty-odd miles from Oban. He gave up his job for six months at the height of the horrors in Bosnia in order to take some supplies out there to give at least a token of relief. He never went back to his job. Instead he formed a charity named Scottish International Relief and now, over ten years later, he has carried on the good work to such an extent that well over £10 million-worth of aid has been delivered to many countries and marvellous projects carried out in them as well. I think especially of Romanian children with Aids written off by the authorities along with other children who were regarded as permanently handicapped because of perceived mental difficulties. Magnus and his volunteers found them chained to their beds and virtually abandoned in some kind of orphanage. Thankfully they are now being revived, thanks to loving care and attention, in a purpose-built home – appropriately called Iona House. It was to be followed by two more such homes and often the workers at the homes found that at least some of the children were not backward at all. They were simply suffering from neglect and the love and care given to them brought them out as normal kids.

When I think of Magnus and all the dangers and discomforts that he must encounter when he continually goes abroad with more and more supplies of help, I feel somewhat ashamed at the luxury of my own home and office where I spend most if not nearly all of my time. But I hope that it is true that there is a role for all of us.

6

In Every Court in the Land

Nervously I rose to my feet as the Court Officer Gibby Morrison, shouted 'Court' and the Sheriff took his place on the bench. It was to be my first ever court appearance and I had been landed with it very much at the last minute, owing to the sudden illness of a more experienced solicitor who dealt with all our court cases. The papers I was holding were shaking along with me when Grace Fraser, the extremely helpful Sheriff Clerk, lent across the court table, grabbed them from me and said in a low whisper, 'These have to be lodged with the Sheriff Clerk twenty-four hours before the court sits.' I thought, with her help, the court experience might not be too bad after all and, as well as that, Sheriff Kermack, who was well into his seventies, was a very kind, benign man. Twenty years later, shortly before his death, I visited him and his cheerful wife at their home in Connel and as she opened the door, I announced who I was. 'How good of you to say who you are,' she said. 'I can't see a thing and Stuart can't hear a thing, but you are very welcome. Do come in.'

Actually, before that Oban Sheriff Court occasion, I had, as an apprentice, appeared in the Small Debt Court in Edinburgh, but that hardly counted. A fellow apprentice, Norman Mair, had been instructed by our bosses to attend the court and to take me with him so that, between us, we could try and get the thing right. Norman and I agreed that he would make the speech, which consisted of two words – 'Pursuer satisfied' – and that I would remember the case number which was 169. I recall the room was filled to capacity with a large number of people, most of whom were standing, and it looked more like a textile auction from the 1880s than a court. However, between us, Norman and I made no mistakes and as we left the court he remarked that the words he had had to use would have been more fitting for a marriage agency than for a court.

Norman was a keen sportsman and a double Scottish Internationalist at rugby and cricket. He went on to become a very authoritative sports writer, especially on rugby and golf. He was a good man to be with in Edinburgh in those days and one of the most amusing and witty men I ever met – when in good form. Our visits to the various coffeehouses, which were welcome interruptions to our apprenticeships, involved my meeting some of my sporting heroes, which really pleased me, until their attractive hangers-on became of more interest.

The President of the Scottish Rugby Union at the time was John Bannerman, with whom Norman constantly fell out on matters of rugby tactics. I was not of course to know then that twenty years later, in Oban, I was to form a long, happy and successful political partnership with John Bannerman's daughter, Ray Michie. I never met John Bannerman but, very much later on, I read his book and he and I seemed to have a lot in common. Nor was I to know when I made that first proper court appearance in Oban how many memorable incidents I would experience in that place – often tense and dramatic, sometimes very sad and sometimes of course with great moments of humour. All I was aware of when I first took my court place was the ticking of the clock and my own heart-beat.

In those days, there was no legal aid for the accused in criminal matters but there was the Poor's Law System. Two local solicitors were appointed on an annual basis to represent all accused who could not afford to pay for their solicitor, receiving from the state a half-yearly payment of £15 for all the work that was involved. While it could be interesting, it often got in the way of important and more lucrative business. However, it was a duty we were usually happy to carry out, although I could well understand a very busy colleague of mine who, on hearing that someone had been arrested for murder, decided that the prudent thing to do was to beat a hasty retreat out of Oban and take to the hills. He could ill afford the time that would have been involved in fully investigating the circumstances and being responsible for the person's legal representation in the numerous and lengthy court proceedings which were likely to follow.

Of course that has all changed now and, by contrast, the criminal legal aid system, going to quite the opposite extreme from the original Poor's Law System, did at one time lead to a situation where certain solicitors would visit places all over Scotland to poach as much business as they could. Some also abused the system by travelling to Oban from places like Paisley for court appearances, which were no longer or more difficult than Norman's and my Small Debt experience. Usually there was no reason for them not to instruct a local solicitor to do the necessary but the legal aid payment at the time allowed them full travelling expenses plus several hours of fees at the then going rate. Sometimes such unscrupulous solicitors would arrive in Oban in separate cars and enjoy some socialising before returning to where they had come from.

One of the more memorable cases that I had during my time as a Poor's Law Agent was when I was asked by the police to go and represent somebody who was in custody on two charges of assault. I was told that there was another case in progress but that it was likely to finish mid-afternoon and that my client's case would be heard immediately after that. I visited him in the cells and asked for an explanation of what it was all about.

'Promise you won't laugh and I'll tell you.'

'Of course I won't laugh,' said I at my most serious. 'I see nothing funny about someone being on two charges of assault.'

'Well,' he said, 'it was like this. I am working in a forest just now, sleeping in a caravan overnight and on getting up in the middle of last night to answer a call of nature, I was attacked by a ferret, who grabbed the most sensitive part of my anatomy and refused to let go.' He went on: 'A ferret bite is not like a dog bite you know. A dog bites and lets go, a ferret holds on and nibbles away.'

He paused and looked at me. 'You said you wouldn't laugh.'

'I know,' I said, 'but I didn't realise that it was going to be quite like that. In any event, why the assaults?'

'Well, I was so angry that I went and thumped the owner of the ferret. I then went to the doctor with it and he said, "Soap and water every two hours," and then two hours later when I saw the mess that it was in, I went and hit the man again.'

To give him his due, my client saw the funny side of things, despite the pain he must have been in and said that he was sure it was a story I would be dining out on for many years to come. He wondered if he might be entitled to some royalties. He also made the comment that he was glad he was not due home that following weekend as he would have had a lot of explaining to do to his wife. I thought there was a fair statement to be made on my client's behalf in mitigation but my concern was whether I would be able to do that while keeping a straight face. I went up to the court to wait for the end of the previous case and found a large number of people on the spectators' benches. I was mightily relieved when they all left at the end of the case but somebody must have said something because, almost immediately, as the people involved in the previous case were half way down the court stairs, they turned almost as one and went back into court to sit down and hear about my extraordinary case.

The Sheriff was not as understanding as I would have liked and fined my client £10 and £25. The *Oban Times* report on the ferret case had the heading: 'ONCE BITTEN TWICE FINED'. Looking at the *Oban Times* report again, I see that I explained that my client had been in extreme pain at the time and that normally he and the ferret owner were on quite good terms. I remember Alan Cameron, the proprietor of the *Oban Times* telling me that the story had gone down well with readers all over the world and that he had even had a phone call from someone in America saying that it was the funniest thing he had ever read. Also, Angus Shaw from the *Evening Times* wrote to Alan:

Dear Alan,

I must hand it to the *Oban Times* for giving me moral uplift at a time when it was sorely needed!

Your Barcaldine ferret story published in this week's issue gave me the biggest laugh for some time. My son, Gus, whose humour is as perverted as his father's, went into hysterics when he read the story last night; I must confess I was similarly affected. Our condition wasn't improved when we tried to speculate as to my aged aunt's reaction – she is 99 – when the story was read out to her by a spinster neighbour over the weekend!

In future I will treat anyone who possesses a ferret with grave suspicion; I feel like adding a codicil to my last will and testament!

Thanks for brightening up a dull December day.

Yours aye

Angus

To my knowledge, I have never seen my client again but he deserves the thanks of a lot of us.

A year or two after my first court experience, I went up for the weekly court expecting nothing out of the ordinary, but I was to encounter then the man who, more than anyone else, justifies the title to this chapter. One of my cases that day was a simple one of asking for an award of court expenses in a case where I had successfully sued a company, which so far had failed to pay the expenses. I noticed before I sat down a strange character, who was not a solicitor, sitting near the well of the court and on the court table was a briefcase with the initials G.B.R.D. It turned out that the man was Gerard Brian Ramsford-Duncan; he owned a property company and a building company on a nearby island and was well known for enjoying court battles. What he had decided to argue then, for the fun of it, was that court expenses should not be awarded in my case, but that he should be allowed to lodge a counter claim to raise an entirely new matter, which he had not bothered about before. The Sheriff decided to continue the case for a legal debate and I went up to court again about a month later, to find in the solicitors' room, a youngish advocate by the name of Ian Kirkwood, whom I had known slightly in my Edinburgh days.

'What on earth are you doing here?' I asked.

'I've come up for some rather trivial debate.'

'Say no more,' I said, 'I think I'm here for the same case.'

Ian Kirkwood went on to have a pretty distinguished legal career as a QC and judge and was one of the Appeal Court Judges in 2002 after the ghastly Lockerbie plane bombing in 1988 – almost certainly Scotland's most important ever criminal case. Even he, however, could not win the spurious argument for Mr Ramsford-Duncan and I did not really expect to come across the man again, but I was wrong. I was later given an example of Mr Ramsford-Duncan's apparent enjoyment of court cases and of his strange sense of humour. One cross-examination apparently went something like this:

'Have you been telling the truth today, Mr Ramsford-Duncan?'

'Indubitably.'

'Do you always tell the truth, Mr Ramsford-Duncan?'

'Indubitably.'

'Have you ever been to prison, Mr Ramsford-Duncan?'

'Indubitably.'

'What for?'

'Perjury.'

Apparently, he had made an appearance before some Tax Commissioners in England and maintained that, as they did not have a quorum, he was able to tell whatever lies he liked. It does not seem that his argument succeeded any more than usual, but that did not stop him from causing a huge amount of trouble and anxiety to a number of vulnerable people One such person was a client of mine, who was unwise enough to instruct Mr Ramsford-Duncan's building company to renovate a cottage she had recently bought on Mull. The contract price was meant to be somewhere in the region of £5,000 but Mr Ramsford-Duncan, having put some materials on the adjoining ground ready to start work, was demanding a payment to account of something in the region of £4,000 before he had really done anything. Obviously that had to be resisted. It ended up with numerous Court Actions.

Almost as soon as I had taken the necessary steps to terminate the building contract on the basis that he was refusing to do the work without being paid unjustifiable sums of money, three Court Actions were taken against my client by Mr Ramsford-Duncan and his various companies. One was by the building company, which continued to demand further extortionate sums of money; one was from his property company, which owned the adjoining ground and which was attempting to terminate my client's legal right to maintain a private water supply from his ground, and the other was again by his property owning company, which was attempting to charge my client rent for the time that the company's ground had been used by his building company for the storage of the various materials. In yet another Action he tried to maintain that the building works, which he sort of began, were being carried out without his knowledge or consent as the Superior of the land. The man was obviously an outrageous rogue.

In brief summary, this led to one Action in Oban Sheriff Court and two Actions in the Court of Session in Edinburgh. Various appeals were taken whenever the judgement went against Mr Ramsford-Duncan and one eventually ended up in the House of Lords, but again his appeal was thrown out. The water right argument, which was the one which reached the House of Lords, was simply to do with the fact that my client's title deed gave her the right to draw water from a spring; her awkward opponent said it had dried up and she had no right to water from a well in the same spot. The opposing QC somehow managed to speak without interruption – apart from a much needed lunch break – for over four hours. As soon as he stopped, their Lordships rejected his appeal without even asking us to reply. This ludicrous example of legal nonsense brought publicity in the *Scottish Daily Express*, which lauded the fight for the small individual under a story which was headed: 'Springing a Victory.' The story included this passage:

> In 1965 Miss Alexander got an Order forbidding the company to interfere with her water supply. The company appealed and in 1966 they lost.
>
> In 1967 with two Queens Counsel on each side, the fight was carried 400 miles south to the House of Lords. There, yesterday, their Lordships said that so far as her rights were concerned, a stream was as good as a spring and now Miss Alexander could be sure of a permanent supply and Mr Ramsford-Duncan's company will be paying about twice as much in legal costs as Miss Alexander paid for her cottage.

There was one very memorable and indicative moment in the Court of Session case while Mr Ramsford-Duncan was giving his evidence. His Lordship suddenly cottoned on to exactly what was happening and exploded:

'Mr Ramsford-Duncan, do I understand this correctly. What you are trying to do is to use your position as a director of your property company to blackmail this poor defenceless woman into paying money to your building company to which you are in no way entitled?'

'Indeed, my Lord. That is exactly the position and may I congratulate your Lordship on the clarity with which you have expressed the matter.'

I am glad to say that my client's cottage was successfully renovated by another building company, but the matter did not end happily, at least for me. Not long after the ending of the several years' saga with Mr Ramsford-Duncan and his various companies, Miss Alexander was prosecuted in Oban Sheriff Court for allowing her dog to worry some sheep on the island. She insisted on pleading not guilty and I set out to defend her, although the evidence seemed pretty overwhelming. However, she was insistent that I should advance the defence that it was not a dog but a fox which had killed the sheep. In my ignorance I did not realise that there were no foxes on Mull at all. I was sharply reminded of that halfway through the trial when an elderly local solicitor, who represented most of the landed estate people on the island, shouted out that I should have known better. He was obviously there with a view to getting compensation from my client for the lost sheep but I heard no more about it. Despite my high success rate on her behalf with her various cases and the huge amount of attention given to her, she then decided that for reasons best known to herself, she would sack me and take her business to somebody else.

It is not necessary to appear in the highest courts in the land to get cases which are worthwhile or amusing. The Dean of Guild Court no longer exists but it was there to grant building permission to anyone who wanted to build or renovate a property within the burgh boundaries. It was usually quite a relaxed court and there was a classic report in the *Oban Times* one day where it quoted the Dean of Guild Court in Tobermory as saying to one applicant, 'We do not believe in standing on too much ceremony in this court but we do feel that you should show us a bit more respect than to submit your plans on the back of a used envelope.' I liked the emphasis on the 'used', almost implying that if it had been an unused envelope, it would have been acceptable. But I should not give the impression that Dean of Guild Courts were a walk-over.

I recall my senior partner, John Harvey, who was normally a very gentle, tolerant and laid-back character, being enraged by the Burgh Surveyor after one Dean of Guild Court sitting. John had had the sense to discuss the client's plans in advance with the Burgh Surveyor and was assured that there was absolutely nothing wrong with them and that the application would be granted on the nod. John attended the court on that basis and was taken aback when the Burgh Surveyor was asked, as was customary, to comment. 'Yes, your Honours, I have a number of objections to this application. There are a whole range of things which are not right with the plans and I will now point them out to you one by one.'

I can imagine how anybody would have felt in that situation and it was compounded when, on leaving the court, the Burgh Surveyor patted John gently on the back and said, 'If only you had discussed these plans with me in advance, there would have been no difficulty.'

The Burgh Surveyor did have a reputation for having to flannel his way out of various situations, one of which had to do with the pressure of the Oban water supply at a time when the number of tourists was rapidly expanding. This led to various guest houses having inadequate water supplies in the morning when our welcome visitors were attempting to have their showers. Apparently what happened was that if anyone phoned in to complain, he would check which area they were in and reply, 'Ah! Yes, there is a very small leak in that area but it is on the point of being put right. You will get your full supply back within the next ten minutes.' He would then make a phone call to an underling which went like this: 'Turn off Area B's water supply and turn on Area A's.' I was never sure how accurate that anecdote was but certainly a number of people I spoke to at the time had experiences which suggested that the story had at least some grounds for credibility.

The Burgh Police Court dealt with minor criminal cases committed within the burgh and the JP Court dealt similarly with such offences outside the Burgh boundaries. I was Clerk to the local JP Court because John Harvey was Clerk of the Peace for the whole of Argyll, just as my father was Clerk of the Peace for Fife. There was one very memorable case in the JP Court in Oban in the 60s, which resulted from a Highlander in Glencoe choosing his own way of cooling down an irate, demanding English visitor. The Highlander in question was operating the Glencoe ski lift and it was his lunch break when the English skier insisted that he should interrupt his break to send him up the mountain on the ski lift. After a heated argument, the Highlander appeared to give way by going back to the ski lift to set the operation in motion but when it was half-way up the mountain with the skier unable to leave the chair, the operator decided that that would be a good moment to return to finish his lunch, leaving the skier suspended for about an hour. He was charged and convicted of assault and the case brought reporters from as far afield as America.

Another bizarre incident I recall from Glencoe concerned a road accident involving an expensive sports car which was the pride and joy of its owner. He had had to stop very suddenly when a sheep decided to wander across the road in front of him. Unfortunately, as often happens in such cases, the car behind couldn't stop in time and ran straight into the back of the sports car. Its proud owner was enraged and rushed out of his car to the car behind. Tearing open the offside door, he threw a tremendous right hook to the person sitting there – only to discover that it was a left hand drive. To make matters worse, the innocent passenger was simply a hitch-hiker who had only been picked up a mile or two earlier. For once, however, the law got it right and what brought things to the criminal court was a charge of assault against the sports car driver rather than a charge of careless driving against the other driver, who could hardly have been blamed for failing to stop in time.

One of the main functions of the JP Courts was to deal with juvenile offenders. It also dealt with licensing matters and I had a very nasty experience with one such JP. I am sure that it was not at all typical and that most are very honourable people but what happened was at the time of a Licensing Court application. I was in dispute on behalf of a client with the trustees for one of the local estates about the terms of a title deed which was being granted and where, in my and my client's opinions, they were trying to impose conditions which were not justified. Quite improperly and to my surprise, I received a telephone call from one of the trustees which went something like this: 'I understand that your client's dispute with the trustees has not yet been resolved and I think it's time it was.' I pointed out that it was quite wrong that he should be speaking to me at all on the matter because I was dealing with the trustees' solicitors and that was how it had to be handled but he continued: 'I understand all that but I thought I would just give you a chance to come to terms quickly. I see that your client's application for a licence is being heard at the court in two days' time when I shall be sitting and making judgement along with my fellow JPs. It might be as well for you and your client to give up your argument about the title conditions.' I was incensed and would probably have made more of it except for the fact that it would have been to my client's detriment. However, I am glad to say that he stood his ground and eventually he got his licence and we won our way over the conditions.

An amusing story from the Licensing Court concerned one of my own partners, David Preston, who could be very quick-witted on his feet. He was addressing the court in support of his client's application for a licence when he suddenly noticed something from the papers and went on as follows: 'Your Honours, my client was born in Bethlehem on the 25th day of December but, unlike her more illustrious predecessor, she moved to Wishaw at the age of seven.' When I recount that story, I am always asked whether David's client got her licence and one day I must remember to ask him but I presume he did, otherwise he would not have been so proud of his witty statement.

I have not myself dealt very much with Licensing Court matters but there was one memorable occasion in the early '60s after the death of the man who served as Clerk to the Licensing Court in Tobermory. It was not long before the next sitting of the court and it was necessary for me, as one of John Harvey's Depute Clerks of the Peace for Argyll, to act as Clerk when the court assembled in a few days' time. It was in the days before the car ferry went back and forward frequently between Oban and Craignure on the island and it was immediately apparent that by the time the court had finished its business in the middle of the afternoon, there would be no boat to take me back to Oban. Fortunately, local solicitor Robin Banks was also having to attend the court. Having been born and brought up in Oban his knowledge then of the Highland scene was naturally far greater than mine. He therefore arranged to hire a boat, operated by the legendary boatlady Ma Spencer, to sail us back to Oban from Grasspoint late in the afternoon. After an enjoyable evening in the Western Isles Hotel overlooking Tobermory Bay, the court ran smoothly and I remember Robin saying to me as we sailed from Grasspoint, 'Just think of other solicitors in Scotland returning now from Licensing Courts, probably sitting in crowded trains or otherwise fighting their way back to their offices and compare that to the peace all around us.' We had the whole seas to ourselves. But to be honest, I am no seaman and there was to me a bit of a storm blowing, although to a hardened sailor it was probably no more than a gentle breeze. Indeed, Ma Spencer on seeing me holding on to the open boat for dear life, commented quietly, 'Och! He would be no good in a storm!' She continued to stand unmoved in the heaving boat with her arms folded and holding on to nothing.

There was another occasion when I similarly compared life here with solicitors and other workers in different parts of Scotland. My son was then about six and was already keen on biking, so I decided one Friday, after a particularly heavy week, to pack in sharp at five o'clock and go off with our bikes together. Within an hour of leaving the office, we had cycled well into Scammadale Glen without another soul in sight, and were skimming stones on the loch. It was about 6p.m. 'If I worked in Edinburgh,' I thought to myself, 'I would probably still be queuing for a bus to get home or sitting in a car with the engine running and going nowhere very fast – maybe even still trying to get out of a car park and here I am in these beautiful surroundings all to ourselves.' What made that particular jaunt to Scammadale stand out among numerous other visits was that my son's bike was new and he was naturally very proud of it. As we were playing at the lochside, a large Highland cow emerged from somewhere and started licking his saddle with its large, strong tongue, knocking his bike to the ground. My son had to make an emergency dash from the loch to rescue his pride and joy.

I am usually happier when important court cases are handled by trained lawyers and do not at all agree with the English system of lay magistrates presiding over important criminal cases. I once had as a client an English solicitor who, like a lot of English people, assumed that Scottish law was the same as the law prevailing in his country and he was surprised that we did not have the same system of magistrates here. He went on to tell me that he had great fun when addressing these magistrates by saying all sorts of things which totally bamboozled them and pulled the wool over their eyes. I made it clear that we would not be able to get away with such things in this country, where the Sheriff is a trained lawyer who would not tolerate such irrelevancies.

It is not just the old boy network that worries me about lay magistrates, but their lack of legal experience on some occasions. There is one story which concerns a Glasgow magistrate presiding over a court which dealt, fortunately, only with minor cases. The lay magistrate apparently addressed the accused like this: 'Mr MacManus, I find you guilty and I will fine you £10. And I want to add this. If there had been any evidence against you, you would have gone to prison.'

During one memorable year, I appeared in every different type and level of court in the land. My involvement that year with the Criminal High Court concerned a case of attempted murder. A nice but rather inadequate client had consulted me about the fact that his wife was apparently looking for a divorce and he brought her Legal Aid application in for me to see, which indicated that she really meant it. I told him to come back and see me whenever he heard any more and took various bits and pieces of information which might come in useful later if we were going to defend her divorce action, which was what he was bent on doing.

I heard no more from Dugald for over a year, when I received a call from the police to say that he was in custody and that he was asking for me to go and see him to help him out. He said something about attempted murder but I could not believe that of Dugald. He was a sorry figure sitting in the police cells and clearly bewildered about what was happening. I asked him to tell me the whole story but it was clear that he did not remember very much. Graphically, he said, 'All I can remember is waking up in hospital with a very sore head. I went to rub it with my right hand and found I could not move it because it was handcuffed to the bed head so I tried to use my left hand but that was the same. I then noticed that there were two policemen sitting on either side of the bed so I knew I must have done something.'

What had happened was that when he had been drinking in Oban one Saturday lunchtime, someone had mentioned to him that they had met his by then estranged wife and that she had told them that the divorce had gone through. Apparently, Dugald knew nothing of that and got so upset and incensed that he went back to his house, collected a shotgun from somewhere, returned to Oban on the bus where apparently no one noticed what he was carrying, went to the supermarket where his wife was working and produced the gun to everyone's panic and consternation, which was not surprising. Fortunately, one of the shop assistants was in the process of bashing some frozen food items with a heavy hammer and decided very quickly that it was best used on my client's head, which brought the incident to a speedy end.

The public and Dugald's wife were of course fully entitled to protection but you would have needed a hard heart not to have felt sorry for Dugald and his inadequacies. He was absolutely out of his depth and bemused. After he had been in custody for about two months, I went through to the High Court in Edinburgh, when he was put away for eight years. Not surprisingly, the prison sentence did nothing to improve Dugald's life. A few years after his release, he died of exposure one winter's night while he was sleeping rough in Oban.

7
The Power of the Fiscal

It was many years ago and I was attending a legal seminar where I had spotted that there was to be a lecture on the duties of the Procurator Fiscal, a subject in which I had always been interested. The lecturer was one of those highly academic guys who managed to make the subject somewhat boring instead of interesting but there was one bit which stuck in my mind and which I was able to use later. In describing the powers of the Fiscal, the academic emphasised over and over again that it was entirely the Fiscal's decision as to whether a prosecution should be taken. He went on to explain that even after a court case had begun, he had the 'inalienable right' to abandon the proceedings at any time before the Sheriff announced his verdict.

I was glad I remembered that bit because many years later the same academic, by sheer chance, came from Edinburgh to Oban for one day as a temporary Sheriff. The case was not particularly important but the lecturer's ponderous ways were taking up a huge amount of time, which not only was not justified by the importance of the case but was also inconveniencing some witnesses still to be called. He was halfway through yet another of his interruptions, trying to clarify something of no importance which had already been made clear to everybody else in the court when I suddenly remembered his words and rose to my feet.

'My Lord, I am sorry to interrupt but I have decided to abandon these proceedings.'

The lecturer looked decidedly unhappy and started to dispute my decision with me until I was able to quote his own words back at him: 'With respect my Lord, I have it on very good authority that a Fiscal has an inalienable right to abandon proceedings at any time prior to conviction and I am merely exercising that right.' It was only then that I and everybody else was allowed to go away and do something more important.

I think it was the only time I used that power during my reign as Fiscal but there was one other case where I should have used it. Fortunately it was a relatively minor careless driving charge and I had had doubts when I first read the papers as to whether to take the prosecution in the first place, because there appeared to be some doubt as to how the accident had happened and in what way, if any, the accused had been at fault. However, I thought perhaps during the course of the trial with the witnesses and so on present, the scene would become a bit clearer. It did not and I should probably have abandoned the thing once I had finished with the prosecution evidence but maybe I was missing something and I left it to the Sheriff to decide. He duly convicted and I have remained unhappy about it ever since. However, the accused obviously bore me no lasting ill-will because twenty-five years later, one of his family brought his business to me.

The prosecution system works well when those involved carry out their duties impartially, which they usually do. It starts with the police detecting and reporting, the Fiscal then deciding whether there should be a prosecution and, if the accused pleads not guilty, the Sheriff (with a jury in serious matters) deciding whether the evidence has been enough for a conviction. The Sheriff then has the job of sentencing, which is absolutely nothing to do with the Fiscal. His sole role is to bring the case to court and then present the case efficiently, leaving the conviction and sentence to somebody else.

By and large, people did not hold it against me if I had to prosecute them, although I was concerned one day on taking a prosecution involving drink and driving against a man who was at the time thinking of giving me his business. That did not stop him coming to me because he was a very honourable man who realised I was only doing my own job and he allowed me to keep his business for decades to come.

It was not, of course, always like that and I remember being verbally abused in a fish and chip shop queue late on a Friday night about a large fine which had been imposed at a court two days earlier. I did not see the point in arguing that the fine had nothing to do with me. At the time I was a bit embarrassed about the incident and decided not to frequent such places late at night. It was not that much of a sacrifice because I was never that keen on fish and chips.

My first part-time Depute Fiscal, Rowan McCallum, who was also a partner in my continuing private legal business, once had a far more awkward and potentially serious experience. As a member of the Oban Golf Club, he went one Sunday to Machrihanish near Campbeltown for a match, after which one of his team mates got miraculously drunk. Next to the golf club there is, or was, a secret American Air Force base. Somehow Rowan's team mate not only got through the security fence but actually boarded a very large plane which was about to set off for the States. With the confidence of drink, he boarded the plane complete with his golf bag and sat down at the back. Such was his aplomb that no one challenged him. The plane had already taken off and was apparently over the Atlantic before the official military passengers, talking among themselves, realised that no one – but no one – knew who on earth the self-assured passenger at the back was. One of them decided to enquire where the mystery passenger thought he was going and I would love to have seen the enquirer's face when he got the reply, 'Could you just drop me off at Connel.'

The plane about-turned and thereafter there was official silence about the incident, but inevitably the press got hold of the story and contacted Rowan for a comment, both in his position as a Depute Fiscal and as secretary of the Oban Golf Club. His reply was excellent: 'It is true that members of the Oban Golf Club travelled yesterday to play at Machrihanish. It is also true that we are still waiting for one of our members to return.'

Apart from his duties in dealing with all crime in his area (which fortunately in my case did not include Campbeltown), the Fiscal is also responsible for the investigation of all fires and also all sudden deaths. My guidelines into sudden death enquiries were that a post-mortem, which I had the power to instruct, should not be carried out simply because the cause of death was not clear – only if there were suspicious circumstances. On one occasion I fell out with a senior local doctor who could not persuade the family of a holidaymaker to agree to a post-mortem, which he wanted purely for medical research. He phoned urging me strongly to instruct a post-mortem, but I declined on the basis that the feelings of the grieving family should come first when there was nothing suspicious. In England it is, or certainly was, very different. I could not understand why the authorities in London insisted on a post-mortem for my ninety-six-year-old grandmother when, in her dying months, she had fallen and broken her hip, which led to her death within a day or two.

I never envied the police their side of the criminal work. The reason why they sometimes set up road checks at Tyndrum was to keep an eye on burglars and other criminals coming into our area from the central belt in the middle of the night. They would often try to commit their crimes and be back in their own homes before daylight and perhaps before the theft or whatever it was had even been noticed. Of course, such people were often well known to our police officers and encounters would go something like this:

'Hello, Johnny. What brings you to Argyll at this time of night?'

'Nothing special, officer, but you know how much I love the beautiful scenery you have here.'

'That's fine, Johnny, on you go. Enjoy the views.'

Three minutes later Johnny's car would pass again going in the opposite direction back towards Glasgow or somewhere else.

'It's a terrible thing, officer. I've just realised I'm very low in petrol. I'll have to leave the scenery for another time.'

On one occasion I felt particularly for the two policemen checking all vehicles at Tyndrum on a dreadful winter's night during a snow storm. A prisoner had escaped from Oban Police Station at lunchtime that day. He was due in court in the morning, when he was likely to go away for a long time. The force was out in full to make sure that he kept his 10a.m. appointment. They were out all night without success, but the prisoner surrendered himself half an hour before the court sat. What had happened was that, unknown to the police, he had a girlfriend in High Street, only a stone's throw from the police station and the court. So while all the police were outside, all over the wilds of Argyll in freezing conditions, the prisoner was tucked up in a warm bed enjoying some blissful experiences. The only consolation the police could have had was the knowledge that the man would not experience such joy for a long time to come.

I remember thinking at the time that in a properly organised society, the police and the prisoner could surely have done a deal and saved a lot of money and discomfort. After all, criminals are not all bad. Once four prisoners escaped from the cells in Oban and were desperate to get away from the area as quickly as possible. They passed and left untouched my pride and joy – my MG – despite the fact that the keys were hanging from the ignition. My car had been parked in the police pound behind the court with the keys there in case the police had to move it away in an emergency.

The area I was responsible for stretched from Glencoe to Kilmartin (near Lochgilphead) and eastwards to Tyndrum. It also covered many islands including, in no special order, Mull, Lismore, Barra, Colonsay, Tiree, Coll and Staffa. Once I had to make enquiries concerning a death on Staffa, which was unusual because no one had died there for about 200 years. After the usual police enquiries and after studying their report, I was quickly able to conclude that death had been from natural causes as a result of a heart attack. This decision could, of course, only be taken after getting full advice from the doctor who had had to examine the body. The workings between the Fiscal and doctors, local and further afield, worked extremely well.

Grace Fraser, the helpful and cheerful Sheriff Clerk, was once involved in a trivial car accident near Tyndrum. She was mightily relieved when she worked out that the accident had taken place ten yards over the boundary; otherwise, as she put it, 'I might have been prosecuted in my own court.' On another occasion I had to sue someone living near Kilmartin and, not being sure which sheriffdom that was, I took the easy and pleasant option of lifting the phone to speak to Grace. I was bewildered by her reply to what I thought was a simple question: 'Where does he get his water from?' But that was what governed the issue. I decided just to bash on with the case regardless and hope, on the one hand, that the Sheriff did not have a Highers in geography and, on the other hand, that the debtor did not understand the principles of jurisdiction.

A few years later I might have been clearer about the boundary being at Kilmartin because I was being driven in a police car to Cairnbaan for a conference between local Fiscals – in other words those from Oban, Campbeltown and Dunoon – and local doctors. As we passed through Kilmartin, a car was spotted off the road in a ditch. It had obviously been there for a while.

'Should we stop to investigate?' asked the young police driver.

'No need,' replied the experienced Sergeant, 'it's two and a half feet beyond our boundary.'

The conference was addressed by James Imrie, a very knowledge-able forensic pathologist, and we all learned a lot. Inevitably, the question of establishing the time of death cropped up, being a vital part of any investigation. On one occasion James Imrie was proud to announce that the time of death had been 4.17am. Only later did he admit that it had been pretty obvious as that had been when the victim's watch had stopped as he fell to the ground after being shot by his wife.

Ballachulish was the extreme northern end of my Fiscal territory. This had been well illustrated early on in my career. I was told about a nuisance of a man, of no fixed abode, who kept getting into trouble for petty matters in that area. Eventually the police decided that, rather than waste any more time and money on him, they would simply pay his fare on the Ballachulish Ferry and export him to Inverness-shire. But the Inverness police were not daft and it was not long before they were paying his ferry fare to send him back to Argyll.

Death investigations, which are carried out by the police on the Fiscal's behalf, could of course be very harrowing and in certain circumstances the Fiscal has the duty and right to decide whether there should be a public Fatal Accident Inquiry. As far as I was concerned, the main point of these enquiries was to see whether lessons could be learned from the accident leading to a death, which might be avoided in the future. It is interesting to note two traditions which, at one time, marked the inherent decency of Scottish law and practice. One was that solicitors appearing at inquiries wore black ties as a mark of respect. The other was that the Fiscal would formally cite the deceased's nearest relative or relatives as witnesses for the inquiry so that they could have their expenses paid if they wanted to attend. But, at the same time, he would normally send a letter telling them not to turn up unless they wanted to.

In 1972 there was a Fatal Accident Inquiry in Oban Sheriff Court following the death of a school teacher, who fell during a descent from Ossian's Cave on Aonach Dubh in Glencoe when he had been supervising a party of school children. Fortunately none of them was killed but it did raise the whole question of school outings and what protections and standards of safety were needed. Our enquiry had the benefit of hearing the evidence of Hamish MacInnes, from Glencoe, who was one of the world's outstanding mountaineers. I see from the report that when I suggested to him that children had to start by learning somewhere, he gave the sensible reply, 'I do not see why they should have to learn in dangerous places. There are plenty of places where they can learn in pleasure and in safety.' Lessons were learned from that fatality and there were further enquiries about school trips which had gone sadly awry, which led to improved standards. All to be welcomed, no doubt, but we are never going to live in an accident-free world and some of the previously enjoyed freedoms are now being restricted, perhaps unnecessarily.

One of the more successful, if that is the right word, Fatal Accident Inquiries that I conducted was following on a tragedy where a six-year-old boy, while fishing for tadpoles, had fallen into a disused British Rail water tank, which had not been used since steam engine days. The police made it clear to me that there were a lot of such tanks throughout the country still full of water and inviting further similar tragedies. I went to see the unfortunate parents and they generously agreed that the matter should be brought to a public inquiry in the hope of preventing any further similar accidents. The jury of four women and three men had little hesitation in adding to the finding of death another finding that the disused tank should have been covered or drained and filled in. The jury went on to recommend that draining and infilling 'should now be undertaken' for similar tanks. It was therefore very pleasing to read in the papers a day or two after the Oban enquiry that all over the country British Rail officials were starting to empty their disused tanks.

There are two other things that have kept that tragedy in my mind. One was that it was my first ever Fatal Accident Inquiry as Fiscal, the tragedy having occurred only eight days after I took on the job. The other thing was the distress of a young policeman who had a son the same age as the unfortunate tadpole hunter. Although he was the senior investigating officer, I told him that I was quite happy to take evidence from his junior constable and that he would not have to give evidence at the inquiry unless he wanted to, which he clearly did not. It would be good experience for the junior officer anyway, though sad.

Oban's largest tragedy, in number terms, concerned a hotel fire in 1973 when ten people died. It led to a five-day public inquiry where the public benches were well filled and where the front of the court had to be reconstructed to allow for the large number of legal representatives. The Sheriff Principal presided over the inquiry, an Advocate Depute presented it on behalf of the Crown, with me sitting beside him ready to carry the can if anything had not been properly investigated or if any administration went wrong. There was a QC and an Advocate representing the hotel owner, an Advocate representing the relatives of those who had died and an Advocate representing the Fire Brigade Union. Six of these seven lawyers went on to have distinguished careers.

After months of hard work and a huge amount of preparation, the inquiry began with typical Pagan efficiency. Ranald MacLean got to his feet: 'Your Lordship will have before you the names of the 122 witnesses I propose to bring to this inquiry. The first witness … is not on the list. He is Mr Stewart Fairlie, a senior reporter and photographer with the *Oban Times*.' Among the numerous productions were some of Stewart's photos of the ghastly fire. In a criminal case it is necessary to prove the productions but that is not needed in the same way in a Fatal Accident Inquiry. Nevertheless, Ranald MacLean thought it would be useful to hear Stewart's evidence on matters of time, for example. It was only a few minutes before the inquiry was due to begin.

'Do you think he will co-operate at this late stage?' asked Ranald.

'I think so,' I replied, 'He's one of my best friends and I am sure I can persuade him but there will be a condition.'

'What's that?' enquired Ranald.

'That you call him as the first witness. He's here to report the enquiry accurately and fairly for the local paper and the local community and intends to be in court the whole time.'

Ranald smiled. 'I'm sure we can agree to that.'

Unlike in America, apparently, and in some television and film dramas, witnesses in Scotland cannot be in court and hear other witnesses until they have given their own evidence. And so Stewart became the first witness, with the result that, because of the timing, he was named on all the lunchtime radio bulletins. I don't think people always realise when reading newspapers or listening to television and radio news that the stories are not necessarily well balanced but are dictated by the time schedules. The other side to a story is often absent.

Apart from securing justice, my main aim when I was Fiscal was to try to ensure that the court ran smoothly with the minimum of inconvenience to witnesses and others, but it was not always possible. On one occasion, when James Mackay was still the Sheriff Principal, he offered to come to Oban Sheriff Court to help clear some of the backlog. I had four or five trials ready to proceed, none of which demanded James Mackay's great brain. Nevertheless, even when he was told that three of the cases would not after all be going ahead, he was still more than happy to come to Oban and do his public duty. Normally the Sheriff Principal dealt only with appeals and major inquiries but had an overall responsibility for the smooth running of the courts in his area.

Eventually, only one case was to go ahead. Because of a perhaps understandable lack of preparation on my part, it collapsed almost as soon as it began with the result that James Mackay's court time, after coming all the way from Edinburgh, lasted less than a quarter of an hour. The case which collapsed was a simple one of a man being charged with failing to give to the police the name of the person who had been driving his car. What on earth could the defence be, I wondered, and what could go wrong? The policeman reporting the incident came to the witness box to give his evidence.

'Were you on duty on such and such a night?'

'I was, sir.'

'Did you see a man by the name of such and such?'

'I did, sir.'

'Is he the owner of the car registration number such and such?'

'He is, sir.'

'Did he give you the name of the person who was driving the car on the night in question?'

'He did not, sir.'

'Did you ask him?'

'I did not, sir.'

Collapse of prosecution case. I did apologise to James Mackay for wasting his time but he generously accepted my apologies and said he was glad to have helped out in at least one way or another to get some cases cleared off the waiting list.

It was not of course the only time I made a blunder in court when I was prosecuting. On one occasion, being a bit harassed, I rushed up to the court for what was a simple breach of the peace where a man was pleading guilty. I explained to the court that a disturbance had been created at 4 o'clock and that it was not acceptable to create a noise at a time when people were in their beds sleeping. He tried to interrupt but was told in no uncertain terms to be quiet and that he would get his chance to speak later. After my statement of the circumstances, the accused was asked what he wanted to say. He stood up and said: 'I would just like to explain to that joker over there [pointing at me] it was 4 o'clock in the afternoon not 4 o'clock in the morning that this happened.'

On another occasion I had to prosecute a lady on an embezzlement charge where there was a large amount of detail to be produced, but where the evidence taken altogether seemed absolutely overwhelming. She was represented by learned counsel from Edinburgh, who opened the proceedings by trying to get the jury's sympathy straight away. He explained to his Lordship that he knew it would be a huge inconvenience but because of his client's ill health, and the medication that she was on, he would have to ask the court for an adjournment every hour on the hour so that she could take her pills.

Later on, I was taking evidence from a manager from the Leeds Building Society, who had come up from England. Unfortunately, early on in his evidence, it was clear that he himself did not really know anything very much about the case and was relying on what he had been told by somebody else. Every answer I got from the Building Society official resulted in defence counsel leaping to his feet: 'Objection, my Lord. That is clearly hearsay evidence and not something that is within the witness's own knowledge.' After the third or fourth of such correct objections, I was really struggling when suddenly I noticed the time.

'My Lord, unfortunately I see that the hour is up and we are going to have to adjourn. How very unfortunate.'

I sat down, already planning a phone call I would have to make during the adjournment to try to sort out the mess I was in.

'I am greatly obliged to my learned friend for his consideration. Can I consult with my client, my Lord?'

After speaking to his client, Defence Counsel addressed his Lordship again.

'My client asks me to thank the Fiscal for his consideration but on this occasion, she can forgo the adjournment.'

Later on I asked counsel why she did not need the adjournment on that occasion and he said quite simply, 'I told her that you were in trouble and that she was just to sit still.'

I can't remember how I got out of that scrape but I must have done because she was duly convicted. Later I was told that counsel had commented to a friend, long after the case was over, that he had only gone ahead with the 'Not Guilty' plea because he thought that the Fiscal in Oban would not be very capable and that he would be bound to leave some strands of the evidence uncovered. Getting a conviction was not nearly as important as getting a so-called top lawyer from Edinburgh to treat Oban with some respect!

During my time as Fiscal I was heavily dependent on the three different secretaries that I had – all very capable ladies who provided far more than just basic secretarial help. Something I think I have learned is that ladies tend to be better judges of character than men.

For many men, as long as somebody will laugh at their jokes, slap them on the back and buy them a pint, they are good guys. On one occasion, I was prosecuting a case on behalf of the Trading Standards Department where the accused was pleading not guilty. One of the Department's officials, who was to be the main prosecution witness, came to see me shortly before the trial was to begin and I was most impressed. As I passed Elma Stewart, who was busy at her typewriter, I said how impressed I was with this person and that he would make an excellent witness. 'I'll have no problems today,' I said with assurance. Without even looking up from the typewriter, she said, 'The man's a nutter.'

No doubt I made some derogatory comment to Elma and walked confidently up the stairs to the court to start the case. The Trading Standards Officer was my first witness and I asked him one question, whereupon he fainted, and fell to the ground. The court had to be adjourned and I had to retreat back to my office. While tiptoeing past my friend Elma, I clearly heard the comment, 'Great witness, wasn't he?'

Oban had its share of what people would call 'down and outs', but it was interesting from my contact with them as Fiscal to note that they did have standards of decency and often a great sense of humour. One such man, whom I will call Bert, had found it necessary to commit perjury in court when he was giving evidence on behalf of one of his mates. I was not overpleased but was disarmed when he took me aside in the street a few days later.

'I am sorry about all those lies I had to tell in court last week Graeme, but when a friend's in trouble what can you do?'

It reminded me that he was not the only person to have told mistruths in court or elsewhere in business and that some of the more respected offenders had not even had the decency to apologise. One friend, however, did come to my house after his case was all over and gave me a bottle of whisky by way of apology, as it had been very necessary for him not to admit the poaching offence with which he had been charged.

Bert's humour showed itself to the full after his release from a prison sentence for which I was responsible. He had been charged with theft from Low's supermarket when the vigilant police spotted him carrying a box of groceries across Argyll Square.

'What are you doing, Bert?'

'I am doing a good turn for a friend by carrying his box for him.'

'Two problems, Bert,' said the alert policeman. 'First, you don't have any friends. Second, you've never done anyone a good turn. You had better come with us.'

He got out of prison just before New Year and I encountered him in Haddows, where I was filling a box with liquid goodies for the holiday. Bert looked at me and grinned. 'Can I carry your box for you, sir?'

Once I had to prosecute an Oban solicitor, Frank Watt, on a charge of careless driving after the sort of accident which could have happened to any of us. I had no hesitation about bringing the prosecution and Frank pled guilty by letter. The day after the case was over, he telephoned me to apologise for any embarrassment. He thanked me for handling it in the proper manner and for not even mentioning it to him despite the fairly frequent contact I had with him between the time of the accident and the case being in court.

I am sure there are many people who do not realise the impartial and honourable way in which Fiscals do or should behave. Once, driving back from England with two of the family asleep in their children's seats behind me, I was travelling at quite a bit above the permitted speed. The jazz tape was just coming up to one of the great solos by Bix Beiderbecke when it sounded strangely distorted. What I was hearing was a police siren behind me. As we do, I moved into the slow lane, hoping to see it go by, but it did not go too far away before pulling me into the side of the road. I decided that I would certainly not mention that I was Oban's Procurator Fiscal. They took me into the back of the police car and showed me the Vascar device, which I couldn't read because of the sun, but I was later relieved to realise that it was only showing 75 and not 95. I gave my occupation as a solicitor and I thought I could see the hairs on the back of the policeman's neck bristle. He then started to take notes before, in a friendly way, asking, 'Have you seen one of these before?' pointing at the Vascar unit.

Stupidly I said, 'Yes, I had one demonstrated to me once.' 'Why?' I was asked and out came the fact that I was Fiscal at Oban. He threw his hat to the floor of the police car and said 'There is no point in us doing any more; you will just phone up your colleague in Hamilton and tell him to pay no attention when I send him a report.'

I emphasised as strongly as I could that I would do no such thing as, for a start, I did not know which area I was in, having just driven from England and heading straight to Oban and also that I did not know who the Hamilton Fiscal was and would make no attempt to find out. However, he said he was about to go off duty anyway and would just leave it. He had let a lorry driver off a speeding matter so he would just do the same for me. I told him that he should not and he should report it in the normal way but I heard no more.

On another occasion, I had a speeding charge in Glasgow while heading back from a Will Aid interview at the BBC and being in too much of a hurry to get back to my desk. Six months later to the day I realised that there was only an hour or two left for the complaint to be served if I was going to be charged. It was a Saturday morning and on returning home nearer lunchtime, I found a note from the Post Office to say that there was a Recorded Delivery package awaiting me, which I was convinced would be my summons. Reluctantly I went to get it and to my great relief found it was nothing of the sort but a blood donor's badge which the children, having accompanied me to the last donating session, had persuaded me to apply for. I was, with no justification, beginning to feel proud of myself because of the fact that I was approaching 100 blood donations of one pint each when I was taken aback by a newspaper headline: BLOOD DONOR GIVES A TOTAL OF 105 GALLONS. It turned out that the German Red Cross had given publicity to a German aged fifty-eight who had given an estimated 105 gallons of blood and blood plasma over a period of thirty-three years. Even without that hugely superior achievement, I should have realised that my nearly 100 pints was a credit not to me but to my good fortune in normally having good health. Also, I was overlooking the fact that I had once had to take out, or borrow, eight pints for a transfusion thirty years earlier.

I first became aware of blood donating while listening to a radio programme with my parents called *Down Your Way*. It was presented live by Richard, father of the current Dimblebys, and involved him visiting various towns throughout the country and interviewing some prominent and interesting citizens. As one programme came to an end he announced that during the broadcast, while carrying out the interviews, he had managed to donate a pint of blood. That was a great plug for the vital blood donating service and I later discovered that it really was as easy and painless as Dimbleby had made it seem. A few years later, after a student night out, I grandly announced to an intellectual friend that I had decided to change the world single-handed and was going to become a blood donor. 'Is that all?' he asked. I have to admit that when I sobered up by morning, it didn't seem very much at all.

Securing a conviction is, as I have implied, not necessarily the most important part of a Fiscal's job but, like an accused, the prosecution has a right of appeal if they think things have gone legally wrong. There was only one occasion when I did that. The reason I dug my toes in at that time resulted from a careless driving charge where the car had gone off the road and the accused declined to say why. Obviously it is for the prosecution to prove beyond reasonable doubt that an accused has been guilty of a particular offence, but there was no way in which a prosecutor could explain why a driver has driven off the road. It could be drink, it could be carelessness, it could be a deliberate act of bravado, or it could be that he was paying too much attention to his girlfriend. It could be all sorts of things and the law was that it was for the accused to give an explanation as to why his car had gone off the road. If an innocent explanation was accepted, then he was entitled to an acquittal but not otherwise. The Sheriff against whom the appeal was taken was coming to the end of his time anyway and I was going to just forget the thing when the defence solicitor unwisely came up to me and said, 'That was a first class legal decision. The Sheriff was absolutely right.' Eventually, the appeal was taken and the Sheriff was directed to convict. *The Scotsman* reported the advocate who was presenting the appeal on behalf of the prosecution as saying, 'My Lords, I would submit that the primary duty of a motorist is to keep his car on that part of the countryside that is reserved to him – namely the road.'

There was a sequel to that case when I was doing an interview on Radio Shetland promoting the Solicitor's Will Aid Charity, which had been initiated in Oban. As usual, at the start of an interview, they were checking for voice levels and so on and the interviewer said, 'You do realise that we have met before, don't you?'

'No, enlighten me.'

'We met in Oban Sheriff Court years ago.'

'Good heavens, why?'

'You were Fiscal at the time.'

'Oh dear! What happened?'

'You prosecuted me and I was acquitted.'

'Thank goodness, no hard feelings then.'

'Indeed there are, you appealed against my acquittal and I was sent back to be convicted and sentenced. I understand that you v. me has been quoted many times since as legal authority of what constitutes careless driving and yet I haven't had a single penny by way of royalties. I am now looking for my revenge.'

Fortunately, the interview went smoothly and ended with the former accused saying, 'Finally, Mr Pagan, I have to suggest to you that you only prosecuted me because I was a long-haired student with a leather jacket.'

A story that most people enjoy is of the unsuccessful attempt of another of Oban's 'down and outs' to defend himself on a charge of breach of the peace. He arrived very much the worse for wear at the court. After I had produced evidence from the first witness, the accused, who I will call Freddy, was told by the Sheriff that he had the right to cross-examine the witness, which Freddy said he knew all about as he was quite experienced in court matters, which was of course true. Freddy rose rather unsteadily to his feet in the dock, glared at the witness in a way which he had no doubt seen in American court dramas, tilted his head to one side and barked out, 'Tell the truth, sir.'

'I am telling the truth.'

Freddy looked at the witness again, with his head tilted in a different direction and with a different tone of voice said, 'Tell the truth.'

This happened two or three times when the Sheriff interrupted, becoming rather irate.

'If you are not going to ask sensible questions, just sit down.'

'My Lord, I have a lot of very sensible questions for this witness and I want to proceed. Tell the truth.'

This charade went on for a long time with Freddy using every conceivable way of asking the same question.

'Tell the truth, surr.'

'Tell ... the ... truth ... sur.'

'Tell the trrruth.'

It ended with the Sheriff shouting, 'Sit down!' and getting the reply, 'Tell the truth.'

Eventually, after due warning of contempt of court, the Sheriff sent Freddy away for sixty days and Freddy was forcibly removed from court still shouting, 'Tell the truth, sir.' The last I heard of him that day was as he disappeared down the court stairs held upright by two policemen and singing the only words of his cross-examination to the tune of the William Tell overture.

A few weeks later, the police told me that Freddy had been released from prison and asked did I want to resume the trial.

'Not on your life,' I answered, 'I am sure you will get him in for something else before long.'

They did, a few days later, and asked him if he wanted a solicitor to represent him.

'I think I had better,' was Freddy's reply. 'The last time I was in trouble, I defended myself with such vigour that they put me away for contempt of court.'

A very serious thing which a Fiscal may have to do from time to time, is to take what is known as dying Deposition. Obviously, if someone is not likely to survive until a trial date well ahead, it is vital that this evidence is recorded. The Fiscal can take a statement which is later admissible in evidence at the trial. On only one occasion was I in danger of needing to do one. It was after one of Oban Housing Association's openings and my friend Mary Faccenda, who is a Laboratory

Technician and was Secretary of the Association, was at the party as well. It was getting quite late, not much before midnight, and it had been a very good celebration, when I looked out of the window of the flat and saw, not just a police car but Mary's husband Guido. She was wanted at the hospital for blood matching purposes. I was wanted at the police station to stand by to go to the hospital to take a dying Deposition. The victim was a Canadian minister who had been on holiday in Oban and who had been stabbed in a mugging attempt. His life was in serious danger until vital medical attention was given to him by Dr Gordon Murchison.

I have never had to sober up so quickly. It was made clear to me that I could not put off my duty until the morning. Fortunately, it did not need to be done and the minister was well enough to come over from Canada a few months later to give evidence which was very important for Oban. His attacker got a sentence of seven years which, according to his defence counsel, was two or more years in excess of what he would have got for a similar offence in Glasgow but it sent out a clear message in our nice community. The majority of the crimes I had to deal with were relatively minor – breaches of the peace, motoring offences, thefts and assaults. There were a handful of incidents that were not far from becoming rape and murder but, happily, they never quite reached those extreme crimes. However, there were some major incidents of violence and examples of mindless brutality which I had difficulty in understanding.

The young man who scarred his victim's face for life with a knife before blowing him a kiss; the group of young men who battered a down-and-out Irishman to the point of death before going back to pee on him as he lay dying – horrors like these have sadly become more commonplace in recent times, partly, probably, because of the influence of American television and films. But there is almost certainly another explanation. In the mid-1980s, at a Liberal Conference, I heard Russell Johnston speaking of experiences in Europe, where a subclass or down-class of people was beginning to emerge in some larger cities. These were people to whom society had given nothing and who, in consequence, felt they owed no duty to society. No matter in what context, you cannot expect loyalty, decency and service from those who are treated unjustly. Scotland has to rebuild its inherent sense of community.

It is all too easy to make a fool of yourself in court. I heard of a Sheriff in Glasgow who once started to administer the oath in this form: 'Hold up your right hand and repeat the words after me. Our Father, which art in heaven . . .' One unusual Sheriff had a large collection of Dinky car toys which he kept in a sack beneath his bench. During the hearing of any court cases involving car accidents, he would produce the right models so that he could re-enact exactly what had happened. Solicitors round the table below him would snigger as he searched for the appropriate cars in order that the scene immediately in front of him was as accurate as possible. One day he floored his legal colleagues when a witness mentioned a Pickford's removal van which had been in the vicinity.

'Just pause there a minute Mr Johnston. I believe I may have just the van.'

There was then a short delay while he rummaged through the sack before exclaiming, 'Ah! I thought so. I have one here'. Whereupon a Dinky Pickford's van joined the collection on display in front of him. Actually, not at all a stupid thing to do, but definitely unusual.

On one occasion, to the amusement of all those in court at the time, I got the name and details of the witness hopelessly wrong and had the wrong person installed in the witness box. It was on a day when there had been about six or seven identical drugs trials, the only difference being the accused. I had got confused and ended up with a witness who had nothing to do with what I was asking him.

Incidentally, the defence solicitor for that case, rather inevitably, because of his large specialist knowledge of the legal position in relation to drugs, was Keith Bovey, who was one of the most honourable, humane and compassionate of solicitors you could meet. Very early on in the days of television I saw him being interviewed on the subject of Social Security benefits and the fact that lawyers were not fully clued up about the rules and regulations, with the result that people who disputed their benefit entitlements often had nowhere to turn for help. Keith Bovey was a leading Nationalist politician and

Chairman of Scottish CND and under the eyes of the Sheriff, who was almost certainly a Conservative, Keith and I used to swap our Liberal and Nationalist newspapers for common interest.

One of my more embarrassing moments in the court, or rather just outside it, was when I thought I might just have time to go to the loo before a case resumed. I rushed from court into a witness room where I had not expected there to be anybody but found, to my horror, since I had already opened my gown and had already started to unzip, that there were about fifteen people sitting there. Putting a brave face on it, I said, 'I trust the loo is free.'

Lowering his newspaper, one of the fifteen looked at me and said, 'Yes, as you say in your profession, you can have vacant possession.'

I started as Oban's part-time Procurator Fiscal in 1970. Things were quite relaxed in those days and the authorities at the time were more than happy to find another local solicitor willing to take over on a part-time basis from John Stevenson. Naturally, I checked about the prospects for part-time Fiscals and was assured that there was a long-term future for them, that they were part of the future plan and that before long a much better rate of pay and terms would be agreed. When I took on the job, there was simply a basic salary from which I had to pay for my secretary and all the necessary typewriters and other equipment. At least however, they did not charge any rent for the use of the two rooms in the court building. Unfortunately for me, it was not long before the civil servants had a complete change of attitude about part-timers and decided that, presumably for reasons of control, they would do their best to get rid of all part-time Fiscals and employ full-time people in their place. The fact that that would cost a huge amount of extra money in many places, including Oban, did not seem to come into the reckoning at all. Nor was I aware of any complaints from the police or public that the service was not being very well run by me and my colleagues.

My recollection is that I had no increase in the salary allowance at any time during the last seven years I was in the job, despite the fact that the workload increased by a colossal amount and that my secretaries' pay had, quite properly, to be increased regularly. In about 1974, James Hogg, who was the part-time Fiscal in Fort William and who was a friend of the Crown Agent, phoned me to tell me at first hand that the decision had been taken to get rid of all the part-time Fiscals.

'We are to be starved out of existence,' were his words.

No doubt I replied something along the lines of, 'They are going to have to wait a long time. They do not know how obstinate I can be.'

James Hogg resigned more or less immediately and, very sadly, died not long afterwards. In June 1976, the Crown Office Bulletin contained this passage: 'Mr E. Laverock, who has been part-time Procurator Fiscal at Peebles for 27 years, resigned in May. This leaves Mr Pagan, Oban, the sole remaining part-time Procurator Fiscal.' I could imagine what they had left out 'and we'll soon get rid of that little bugger', but it was to be another three years before I finally gave up the battle.

I remember an encounter with the Crown Agent when he came to Oban to look at the scene here and asked me if I had ever thought about becoming a full-time Fiscal. I told him that I was semi-interested but there would have to be one condition and that was that I would have to be guaranteed to remain in Oban for the rest of my working life. He looked at me with hostile bewilderment before answering, 'My Fiscals go where I tell them.'

Before I gave up, questions about the future of Oban's Fiscal service were raised in the House of Commons by our helpful MP at the time, Iain MacCormick. The reply given by the authorities was that Oban would not need a full-time Fiscal and that the service would be run easily from Dumbarton, which was a nonsense and which they knew to be a nonsense. It was March 1979 before I finally gave up, by which time I was forty-three. The authorities were then talking in terms of the Campbeltown Fiscal taking on the Oban job at the same time, but it was the Dumbarton Fiscal who took over my office at the eventual sad end. In a few months, contrary to all that had been said, a full-time Fiscal was appointed for Oban, together with full-time staff. A *Daily Record* headline the day after I gave up read: 'PAGAN'S LAW ENDS IN PAY FREEZE ROW.'

Despite all the unfairness of my treatment and the sad ending, I have never regretted having done the job, which was interesting and important. But shades of the battle with the civil service were to be repeated when, twenty years later, a similar kind of thinking killed off the excellent voluntary work of the Committee of the Oban Housing Association, of which more later.

8

Dad Would Have Laughed

'How are we getting on with bringing Dad home?'

I was on the phone to my younger brother Bill at his solicitor's office in Cupar.

'Not too bad. He's at Turnhouse.'

'That's good, I thought it would have taken much longer than that.'

'But there is a problem with customs. John reckons that Mum has been trying to smuggle home too many duty frees in the coffin.'

That brought back happy memories of holidays abroad with Mum and Dad, when Mum, ever one for a bargain, insisted that we brought back every available duty free that we legally could. She drew up a helpful rota but it was not particularly logical, with me often having to bring back the perfume and others bringing alcohol and the cigarettes. Dad had died three days earlier while on holiday with Mum in Yugoslavia. They had been on holiday there for two weeks and Dad died on the last day of it, leaving Mum with the agony of coming home on the plane without him. Dad would certainly have laughed at John's suggestion. The idea of him coming home in an austere Communist coffin, surrounded by booze and fags and other signs of capitalist decadence would have appealed to his humour. Like all of us, Dad was a mixture of characteristics. How often do we all find that as soon as we say someone was such and such a kind of person, immediately we think of an example to suggest quite the opposite. Dad was a firm believer in the British traditions, the political union of the UK and the overall decency and orderliness of society. Yet, at the same time, he was a believer in reform and he took the greatest delight in publicly knocking all forms of pretentious pomposity. He was also a huge admirer of the separate Scottish legal system, which he regarded as superior to that of our neighbours. He railed at the English domination of the media and on English bank holidays he would object to English newsreaders wishing everybody a happy holiday as he himself set off for work.

Mother's courage was exemplary at all times, especially at the time of Dad's death. She was determined to carry on as normal. On the night of her lonely return we made sure that our phones were open because we knew that she would phone each of us in turn, in age order, just to confirm her safe return, which she duly did. I went to see her the following day and was not really surprised when she said, 'You are remembering that I have got a lunch date so I will have to leave you for a while.' I was not offended that she was going to desert me when I had travelled a distance to see her as I knew what she was going through with the pretence that everything would carry on as normal. Fortunately, I had brought some work with me – I can't remember whether it was office, housing or political – so I had something to do while I stayed in the empty house.

An example of Mother's determination came from a story she told me many years later about what had happened when she had gone to the hospital in Porec, Yugoslavia, to collect Dad and bring him home in a wheelchair, which had been planned as everyone thought he would be alright. On arriving there with the hand luggage and his blazer over her arm, she was given the awful news by the kindly Yugoslavian doctor that Dad had died two hours earlier.

'I don't know what he thought of me,' said Mum later, 'because I found myself saying, "He won't be needing this then, will he?" then folding his blazer and putting it away in the case.'

Another example of her rigid determination to carry on, no matter the circumstances, came a few years later when, well into her eighties, she set out alone by train from Fife to Birmingham to visit my brother John. She fell on the platform at Leuchars and broke her arm before the journey even began but continued on her way, leaving the necessary medical treatment until she arrived in the south. John threatened to sue British Rail for delivering damaged property. Eleven years after Dad's death, just shortly before she herself died, a Health Visitor came to see her and said cheerfully, 'The last time I saw you was just after your husband died. Did you get over it alright?'

'Don't be so stupid. Of course I didn't, but you just have to get on with it.'

One of the difficult decisions you have to make when you lose a loved one is whether to look at the body and take a final farewell. Before deciding what to do in Dad's case, I asked friends but got different advice. Never having had the chance to say goodbye to him properly, I decided that I would look at him and, on balance, was glad I did, and not just because I found that the undertaker had transferred him from the severe steel Communist coffin into something a bit more 'friendly'. When Mum died, I had said goodbye only the day before and had spent some time looking at her unnoticed so I did not feel the need to do so again. But we are all different and my wife, Heather, did go to see her.

Like most lucky children, I have so much to be grateful for from both parents. Among the most important of things was the way that they had prepared me for the inevitability of death by their own attitude to it. They knew there was nothing anyone can do and when you are faced with it, there is no point in collapsing. At the same time, they were marvellous at protecting the family from things which were not inevitable, however threatening they might have been. The war was a classic example and I, three years old when the war broke out, am sure that none of us got any hint from Mum and Dad of the horrible dangers that the country was facing. We had no clues of the fate that would have befallen all of us if an invasion, which was highly likely at the time, had succeeded.

My parents' inevitable fears must have been increased by the fact that Mum's own parents continued to live in London throughout the war even at the height of the bombing. But I never got any indication as each day came to an end that she would be going through agonies that night, wondering about her parents' safety. My principal memory of the war (apart from rationing, which meant hardly any butter and chocolate and no bananas) was the warning that, if the air raid siren went off – which did not happen too often in our part of Fife – we were to rush home immediately. But I do not recall that as being anything we were particularly frightened about. However, on one occasion I and my sister Judy, a year younger, were at the blacksmiths watching some horses being shod when the siren went off, and we said to him, 'You will have to rush home.' When he replied that he would just get on with his work, we thought he must be the bravest man in the country and well worthy of a VC.

My first memory of someone close dying was when I was seven and my grandmother on my father's side moved on. I reacted in a very strange way. At the time I was well into the Brer Rabbit books and had just read how, when his carrots were stolen, he had stamped up and down the garden path waving his paws in the air and shouting, 'Revenge, Revenge'. When mother broke the news to us about Granny, it was fairly early in the morning and I was still in bed. I responded by leaping out of bed and giving an impression of the Brer Rabbit scene as I marched up and down on my bed shouting for revenge. I can still see the astonished look on Mum's face as she rushed out of the bedroom. On another occasion, Dad came home late, having been away at a client's funeral. He came into my room to say goodnight and apparently, I subjected him to a lengthy cross-examination on all aspects of funerals and deaths. At last I paused and Dad, no doubt with some relief, was making for the door when I put my final question: 'And did you see him go up?'

When Dad died he was seventy-eight and I am quite sure that if, when he was born, the good Lord had said to him, 'Right Charles, you have a choice. You can have a guaranteed seventy-eight years or you can take a chance', he would have settled for the seventy-eight. That would have been especially so had Dad known at birth the effect that heavy smoking normally has on health and life expectancy. It was only towards the end of his life that he started to cut down and joined the secret smokers' society. Ronnie Frew has a great memory of when he and his wife, Wilma, and I were staying at Mum and Dad's home at the time of a St Andrews Open Golf Championship. It was after dinner and we had been chatting for a while in the living room when Mum decided to go off to bed. She was just out of the door when Dad dived into his pocket for a fag and lighter. He had hardly started when Mum's footsteps were heard coming back along the hall. Dad was on his feet in an instant and rushed to stand in front of the unlit log fire with his hands behind his back and, as Ronnie described, with this puff of smoke rising as from nowhere out of the top of his head. Mum pretended not to notice.

Dad was not alone. Once I was visiting a generous and wealthy benefactor near Edinburgh, trying to get money for one of our housing projects. While alone with him, I was offered a gin and I asked permission to smoke.

'It's alright with me but not please in front of Jean. She has been a heavy smoker all her life and now she has given up completely. I do so admire her.'

I did not, of course, tell him that on my way up their long driveway, I had passed Jean putting some washing up on the line with a cigarette firmly between her lips.

Thanks to Dad's attitude and the way he had brought me up, I coped relatively well with his death, with not too many tears, although great sadness. Two particular experiences of others, however, warned me that I might suddenly collapse at an inopportune moment. The first had come from Dad himself when he was relating the time of his own father's death. He was in full charge of all the arrangements and took some pleasure from organizing things properly, protecting particularly the female mourners. The undertakers were about to remove his father's body from the house when he realized that they were going to go right past the window where some of the family were still standing. He put the undertakers on hold, rushed back into the house, poured some sherry in a different room and ushered them all through there before allowing the undertakers to complete the removal. Dad told me that it was only after the funeral was over and there was nothing left for him to organize, that the reality of the loss of his father actually sank in.

The other occasion was the tragedy of the death, following a road accident, of the father of a colleague at work. She must have been in total shock and I will never forget the ghastly phone call from the hospital on the Monday morning after the accident with a message for Christine to go straight up there. One of her friends commented afterwards that she did not think that she had taken in what had happened until she saw the hearse driving away after the Free Church funeral service.

Because of those experiences of others, I went into the church alone about an hour before Dad's funeral service and prayed beside the coffin so at least I was prepared for what I would see when I went in with the rest of the family to join the packed congregation. The service was one of the best celebrations of life that I had ever attended, despite the fact that the funeral was on the very day of Dad's birthday. Mum whispered to me as the service was ending, 'I wonder how many people have noticed from the service sheet that this is his birthday?'

And I could hear Dad saying 'That's not a very nice thing to do to a chap – bury him on his birthday.'

The excellent minister got things off to a humorous start. Dad was mad keen on crosswords and on one occasion had phoned the minister saying, 'I am stuck for No. 12 down. It's a biblical quotation and I can't place it. You are the man to give me the answer.'

'I don't immediately recognize it Charles, but I will look it up and phone you back.'

Before he could do so, the phone rang again. It was my father.

'Sorry, old boy, wrong Bible – it was Shakespeare.'

As the huge congregation later filed out of the church, most people, naturally, turned to my two brothers, who were better known in the area, and I was glad when Dave Rollo, a local farmer, shook my hand adding, 'My! He got a rare send off, did he not.' For a time, Dave was Scotland's most capped rugby internationalist, just as Ray Michie's father, John Bannerman, had been four decades earlier. Dad, a keen sportsman on the administrative and officiating side, rather than the playing side, would have enjoyed Dave's comment. By a strange but sad chance, brother Bill's own father-in-law, another Scottish rugby legend, Charlie Drummond, died, totally unexpectedly, forty-eight hours after Dad's funeral. Bill then had another funeral to organize in Cupar exactly a week later. As we left that service, the undertaker who, like surgeons, pathologists and all the rest, have to preserve a sense of humour, whispered, 'Same time next week, Bill?'

The undertaker recalled another story concerning brother Bill when he was very young. He told me that his own father was a down-to-earth man; little upset him and he was well used to strong language. However, on one occasion at my parents' home, father and son had been on their hands and knees fixing part of the stair, when Bill aged four came down to his breakfast in his dressing gown. As he passed the two joiners he said, without even looking at them, 'Get up, you fucker.' The senior undertaker was totally taken aback but there was an explanation: Bill had been on a Fife farm the previous day and had heard that expression being directed towards the horses as they were pulling the ploughs.

Inevitably, in the years afterwards, I shed a number of tears on unexpected occasions at Dad's loss but they were always mingled with some smiles. They usually occurred after something had cropped up which I wanted to share with him, more often than not something amusing or something ridiculous. I would say to myself, 'Dad would have laughed'.

One court story, which I had been able to share with him, concerned an anchor. It was common practice if there was a dispute over a particular article, to raise an action asking for a court order, either for payment of the value of the item or, alternatively, for its delivery. Fellow solicitor David Pender (now Sheriff Pender) embarked on one such case and, having heard nothing at all from the defender, rose confidently to his feet on the appointed day and asked for decree for £1,000 or whatever the value was.

'Hold on a minute,' came a strong and rather aggressive voice from the back of the court. 'That solicitor has asked either for the money or for the anchor and he can't have both. He's certainly not getting my money, so I've brought the anchor to court. It's sitting outside this door here.'

Normally I believe in co-operating with other solicitors when it's appropriate. However, when I saw the size of the anchor as I left the court, I wondered how many men it had needed to get the monstrous thing up the stairs. I therefore decided against offering to help David carry it back to his office, rushing back to my desk as quickly as possible. Dad had to admit that he had never witnessed anything like that in the Sheriff Court at Cupar.

Naturally, Dad and I sometimes compared what sort of day we had each had in our different legal offices. Some time earlier, he had told me of a family dispute about the will of one of the first Pagans in the Cupar firm all those years ago. The suggestion was being made that the old man had gone out of his mind and hadn't known what he was doing when he made his will. His coachman was called to give evidence.

'Did you ever see Mr Pagan evincing any signs of abnormal or bizarre behaviour?'

'Well, yes, there were occasions when he would suddenly leap up in the back of the carriage and start shadow boxing with himself.'

Later, much later, when I enquired how Dad's day had gone, he would sometimes reply, 'Not too good. But I haven't quite reached the shadow boxing stage.'

Classical music was one thing that Dad and I shared before I turned to jazz, but I now find it impossible to listen to Tchaikovsky's Sixth Symphony 'Pathétique' because it brings back the sadness of Dad's loss, as do many other classical pieces we used to share. Dad and I often had classical evening concerts at home on record and we had great fun choosing the programme in advance, which usually consisted of an overture and a symphony. Brother John did not attend our concerts. In the 1950s, a composer of pop music stole a famous theme from a collection of Borodin dances and wrote a tune called 'Take my Hand, I'm a Stranger in Paradise'. On one occasion when Dad and I were listening to the original Borodin, John came into the room and listened for a few moments before walking out muttering, 'Bloody copycat'.

I remember Dad explaining to me that Brahms' Academic Festival Overture was made up of a conglomeration of student songs. What a huge coincidence it was when, ten years after Dad died, my son set off for Strathclyde University. It was one of the most emotional days of my life and I remember sitting in the car in Oban waiting for him to come back from a friend's house where, inevitably at the last minute, he had had to go to return a video. For something to do, I turned on the car radio, which is not something I usually bother with, and instantly recognized the music as Brahms' Academic Festival Overture. Dad was obviously present.

Mum also had a very sensible attitude towards the inevitability of death and we were able to see her a few times in the last two or three weeks of her life, which were spent in Ninewells Hospital, Dundee. On the final Sunday that we saw her, we all knew that it was going to be the last time and that she had decided that she had had enough. Twenty-four hours later, with a little help no doubt from the hospital, in accordance with her directions and after discussion with us, she set off on her next journey. She was never late.

I remember feeling sorry for one of the patients in Mother's ward for being embarrassed about something she had said but didn't exactly mean. We have all done that! On the second last Sunday of Mum's life she asked me to repay that patient for a copy of the *Sunday Post* which she had got – despite the fact that Mum was English, that was the only Sunday paper she ever read. On handing the money over, the patient said to me, 'Oh there was no hurry but I suppose your mother wanted to pay before it was too late.' It was not exactly how she meant to put it and she was quite upset in case she had upset me but, as Mother would certainly have said, 'Well it was true, wasn't it?'

When I phoned the news of Mum's death to John Harvey, my former senior partner who had by that time retired to Dorset and who had been a really close family friend for the best part of seventy years, he commented 'She was always so determined and she got her own way. She never had to go into a home.'

Almost any reference to the *Sunday Post* brings to my mind a brilliant Rikki Fulton sketch: a man goes into a newsagents and in a brazenly loud voice asks for a copy of *Penthouse, Reader's Wives, Girls in Uniform* and a few other top shelf magazines before lowering his voice and, having checked that no-one is listening, whispers to the shop assistant, 'And a *Sunday Post*. It's not for me, it's for my mother-in-law.'

That was much the way I felt when I once bought a *Daily Telegraph* for a very nice English client before visiting him in hospital. When I handed it over, he commanded, 'Take the money out of my trouser pocket.'

'Not at all.'

'I insist.'

'Very well,' I replied, delving into his hung-up trousers, 'but if you insist on giving me the money, I insist on giving you the change.'

'Don't bother, keep it as a tip. I say,' client Ernest continued calling across the ward to a semi-comatose islander who was lying well below the sheets, 'do you tip your solicitor?'

'Aye,' came the muffled reply, 'I do. Right out.'

I was very amused, until I got back to the office and discovered that the islander was a client of my partner Mike Jarvie.

Ernest had three glamorous and attractive grand-daughters. A year or two after I had seen him at the hospital, he was dying peacefully at home. Once, on coming out of his unconscious state, he found the three grand-daughters round his bedside.

'Oh good!' said Ernest 'Is this me in heaven now?'

One of my many happy memories of family life was the orderly evening meals we always had, both alone with family or with a number of guests. The family meals certainly helped the communication links between us because, when we were alone, we always discussed what was happening the following day so that we could fit in with each others' plans as far as possible. At one dinner party, Sheriff John Christie, a long established friend of the family, told of a case he was taking in Dumfries Court when a witness who didn't seem very co-operative was ushered into the courtroom. He noted in his notebook 'reluctant witness' and prepared himself for having to issue a warning about the consequences of contempt of court. The Fiscal opened his questioning.

'You are Mrs Jean Brown, 24 The Rise, Dumfries?'

'No.'

The Fiscal shuffled through his papers before continuing.

'I am sorry, you are Mrs Mary McCulloch of 49 Newbattle, Dumfries.'

'No.'

The Sheriff decided to intervene.

'Who are you then?'

'Mrs Susan Green, 23 Baker Street, Dumfries.'

The Sheriff looked at the Fiscal, who frantically rustled through his papers before shaking his head and shrugging his shoulders.

'What are you doing here?'

'I don't know. I came into the building to pay my rates and before I knew it, they had frog-marched me up the stairs and put me in this box.'

Another illustration of the way in which the law and the people are not always on the same wavelength.

A classic example of that concerned a Glaswegian giving evidence in the High Court in Edinburgh who said, 'Then there came a chap at the door.'

That brought a question from learned QC: 'Can you describe this gentleman who came to visit you?'

At another family dinner party with about eight guests, the subject somehow went onto the modern trend towards marital infidelity. Mother had had just the right amount of wine and leapt into the conversation saying: 'Of course, I have no fears from Charles on that score. We have this arrangement, you see. If he ever feels like committing adultery, he has to phone me first and I shall tell him it is a bad idea.' The shock of saying that seemed to sober her up and she shot out of the dining-room adding as she departed, 'Does anyone want some more meat?'

The only real stricture about Mum's dinner parties was that you had to be on time. On one occasion I was late leaving Edinburgh and, in my MG on the motorway, overtook a police car when I was doing well over 100. I actually thought it was a taxi until I realized as I passed that the spelling of the sign on the top of the car was not quite the same. But it was better to incur the wrath of the law than be late for one of Mum's parties.

To me, the best of Dad's many good characteristics was his diplomacy. In Italy on holiday we had hired a car which turned out to be a bit ropey, to say the least. Dad did not have a word of Italian but when he returned the car to the Italian garage, he was able to renegotiate the terms of the hire and get some money back without any offence whatsoever. Indeed, Dad and the garage proprietor walked away from the garage together with their arms wrapped around each other in the best continental fashion. Another example of Dad's skill at reconciliation concerned an unpleasant argument that he and I had

had over something, the subject of which I have long forgotten. However, the fact that I was in my teens at the time would suggest that it was probably entirely my fault. I remember him coming to my bedroom and saying in a gentle voice, 'Graeme, we have to talk, let's go down to the dining-room.' I was extremely reluctant, but followed him. On entering the room, I saw that the log fire was still burning and Dad suggested that he put the lights out altogether.

'I don't particularly want to look at you at this moment and I am sure you don't want to see me either.'

So there, in front of the tranquil fire, we sorted things out.

At one time I also thought that Dad was a good judge of character until, many years on, Mum put me right: 'Nonsense, dear. He was a terrible judge of character. He allowed himself to be blinded by his own enthusiasms.' I obviously have Dad's failings. Once, with some justification, I thought the world of an attractive lady, who was also a very kind and caring person as well as being active about things which were wrong with the world. One day she felt it necessary to say, 'You are not being fair to me, Graeme. You put me on a pedestal where I definitely do not belong. I have as many faults and failings as anyone else. If, in your mind, you put me up there, there is only one way for me to go and that is down in your estimation.' That needed to be said to me and Pauline was not the only one about whom I made that mistake. But some need the adrenalin of enthusiasm to achieve anything.

Dad's legal practice in Cupar has been passed down from father to son for 200 years. Dad and I would not have had any serious problems had we gone into partnership together, but the lure of the Highlands was too much for me and it was typical of Dad that he never made the least complaint about my move or gave me any reason to feel guilty. Perhaps he was keeping in mind an incident from when he was only seven and his father had said to him, 'This afternoon, laddie, we are going to the Conservative Sale of Work.'

'But I don't want to go,' Dad protested, stamping his little feet.

'But you have got to. Your whole future depends on it.'

After all the money that Dad had paid for my education, both at private school and later on to get me fully qualified, he would have been entitled to feel aggrieved that I did not return to his firm, but he

Oban Solicitors centenary dinner at McTavishs' Restaurant, Oban
in 1988 and the launch of WILL AID

Office colleague Mairi MacRae atop Ben More, Mull not far
from the scene of the missing plane

Demanding Nelson Mandela's freedom. Taken at the Calton Hill, Edinburgh during a Scottish Parliament Rally in 1980

Leaving Concert Hall, Glasgow a free man thirteen years later – as close to my number one hero as I was allowed

A famous distillery producing one of Argyll's many
fantastic malt whiskies

A busy Oban Bay from home

General election 1992. Another victory speech for Ray Michie
at Lochgilphead Sports Hall. Husband Iain on her right

Preparing for the 18th of 30 Annual General Meetings of Oban Housing Association – Frances Black, Alan Buchanan, Heather Harris, Sheila Walton, self, Angus Simpson

Grahame Court, the Association's second development completed in 1977 thanks to Madam MacDougall of MacDougall and named after her late husband Leslie Grahame MacDougall

From my office window (top). The liner "Berlin" in Oban Bay,
spring 1995 and (bottom) the Colonsay ferry arrives back in Oban Bay
late on a November afternoon

Cycling on the Island of Gigha as the Islay Ferry leaves Kennacraig on the mainland

Heather doing her David Attenborough bit with puffins on the Island of Lunga off Mull

Celebrating with colleagues past and present from many different parts
of Scotland after my 30 years with Hosack & Sutherland

With some Oban jazz guys. "It's my party. I can pretend if I want!"

International jazz stars at Fort George during 2003 Nairn Jazz Festival

The ghastly Argyll road barriers. How could anyone in their right mind not understand that these things were "highly dangerous and lethal"

Peace, perfect peace. A sunset over Mull

shared from afar much of my joy in the Highlands and Oban in particular as well as my career here. Goodness knows what the school fees for my private education were at Bedford School. On one occasion, when the headmaster wrote to Dad complaining about my rebellious nature, he simply replied, 'I do not pay you X thousand pounds a year to have trouble with my number two son.'

My early days at Bedford were a revelation. Within the first week, I had to report to the administrative office, known as the bell room, which was run by a Mr Bull. He had been there in Dad's time and had the most incredible memory for names and faces. It was said that he could recall everybody who had ever been at the school during his time and still recognize them years later. When I reported to the bell room for my punishment drill form, Mr Bull commented, 'A sad day indeed for the Pagan family. Your father was five years at this school without ever once having punishment drill. You have not even been here five days and already you have one.'

Halfway through my education at Bedford it was decided that I was too thick to go into the right stream for university, but Dad persuaded the school to give me a chance. However, as the time approached for final exams at school, which would determine whether or not I could get into university, Dad withdrew me from school at the Christmas holidays of 1953 and paid for me to have intensive private tuition at home. Like most others, I would only get one chance to achieve the necessary level of passes. I then experienced the most important and just about the worst period of my life – pretty well solid studying for at least fourteen hours a day for six months, and I was no academic scholar. But it was all so worth it.

Dad was a good teacher and an extremely wise man. On one occasion when I very briefly considered moving to a different job altogether – farming would you believe! – Dad asked, 'Have you thought what it would mean not to be your own boss?'

'Come on, Dad, don't be so old-fashioned. That doesn't matter any more. Times have changed.'

'I think you are going to find that being your own boss will become more and more important.'

And my perceptive father was absolutely right. His words come back to me often when I hear ever more frequently about the highly unnecessary pressures put on employees by big businesses, everyone being answerable to someone higher up the tree. I have always had the view that, since we have to work for about half of our waking life, we might as well enjoy it and have a good laugh when it's appropriate. That, however, does not mean that, at the same time, you cannot be efficient and achieve good things. You can, because no-one can produce the goods when they are under stress and feel that they are being treated unfairly.

I remember many tributes to Dad after his death. One in particular stuck in my mind because it recalled an incident I knew nothing of. The letter read something like this:

> Dear Mrs Pagan,
> I was so sorry to read of your husband's death and wanted to send you my deepest sympathy. He was a great man. You will not know about this but many years ago, my husband and I decided to adopt a child and everything went through successfully. When I asked your husband to send me his account, he gave some excuse about being too busy at the time but that he would do it when he had a moment. He knew that we did not have much money and we never did get a bill from him.

The letter ended: 'With renewed sympathy from James and Moira S. and the child who cost nothing.'

Dad was not, of course, perfect and he enjoyed telling the story against himself about welcoming a client back into his office one day, because that is something that we solicitors are always pleased to experience. There is no better tribute or sense of satisfaction than to have a client return, especially when it is the next generation of the same family. However, on Dad's occasion, he greeted his client saying 'Good to see you again, what can I do for you this time?'

'You can hand over the money you won for me the last time.'

Proof, if it were needed, of Mum and Dad's great love for each other came from an unlikely source, namely a student friend. Peter Garwood, a rugby colleague who shared my digs, became over-stressed as his final medical exams approached. He was heavily into the Moral

Rearmament Movement and took life far too seriously without any real relaxation. He was heading for the inevitable breakdown when I suggested a weekend at Mum and Dad's wonderfully peaceful and hospitable home, Edengrove, which is between Cupar and St Andrews. The weekend restored Peter and his comments in the visitors book at home when he left read: 'Thank you for a wonderful weekend. It was lovely to see a couple who are obviously still so much in love with each other.'

During the weekend there was an incident which typified Peter's excessive conscience. A relation of Mum's from the south and a friend, both of whom were stationed at an Air Force base not far away, came to spend the Sunday with us. Peter and I and they took the dogs for a lengthy walk. We had some difficulty crossing the river to get home, being determined not to go all the way round the same way that we had already been. Peter was in charge of throwing the shoes from one side of the river to the other. Unfortunately, he missed once and one pair belonging to one of the RAF guys went straight down to the bottom of the river. Everybody agreed that there was nothing that could be done to recover them and that it did not really matter anyway. An hour and a half later, when we were finishing tea, someone asked, 'Where's Peter?' I knew instantly and jogged along the riverbank with my dog to where I saw Peter emerging from the bottom of the river, wearing only his Y-fronts and, of course, without having retrieved the shoes. Anyone who has experienced the joy of having an animal as a pet and friend, knows how deep their understanding can be. I have never seen such a real human expression on my dog's face as I did then. He was clearly saying as we watched Peter coming out of the water dripping wet, 'The man's off his head.'

Norman Mair cites another example of Peter's over-strict discipline. Norman had apparently been at rugby training every night for three and a half months, either active or coaching, and suggested to Peter that it would be reasonable for him to have the following night off. He sought Peter's approval but he should have known better because he got the answer, 'That, Norman, is a matter between you and your conscience.'

Nothing I have said about my father should give any impression that he was a soft touch. When it was required, Dad was more than capable of taking difficult decisions no matter what the consequences were or what effect they would have on his own popularity. He made it very clear early in my upbringing that one had to do what was right and that very often tough action had to be taken. I do not think he could have been a party political hack of today's kind. He would have had to be thoroughly convinced that the party line was correct before he could have given it support. He once confided in me about a particularly difficult business decision he had had to take, which was a useful guide to me several decades later when I was faced with a partner who was not pulling his weight. Despite the fact that I was older and more experienced than Dad had been when he had his problem, I found mine extremely difficult. I had agonized for a long time about what to do with the rather inactive partner because he was a nice guy with a young family and was a friend. Fortunately, a weekend to Solihull to visit my elder brother John was imminent. John, although having no qualifications, is an extremely astute, down-to-earth and sensible person. I had in mind that, some time during the weekend with him, after we had had a drink or two, I would discuss my problem at full length. It did not quite work out like that. I arrived in the middle of the night, pretty tired after a long drive and a dram was enough to have me blurting out my quandary immediately. He listened to me for about three minutes before saying, 'He's got to go, hasn't he? Have another dram.' That was the end of that. The decision was, in reality, a simple one and there was no point in wasting any more time on it.

Another example of Dad being no soft touch arose from the death of his brother George, one of millions killed in the First World War. He was G.H.P III, I am G.H.P IV and my son is G.H.P V. G.H.P I died when he was on his feet during a dispute at a church meeting. The local paper reported the first G.H.P's speech in full before adding, 'At this point Mr Pagan was seen to change colour, whereupon he fell to the floor'. When I told that story to friend Ronnie Frew, he asked, 'Was that not a rather drastic way to win an argument?'

G.H.P II was the daughter of the first; she was born after the ill-fated church meeting. She was an adorable great aunt, unfortunately stone deaf from the age of seven. For a time I had the smatterings of sign language, although she was an excellent lip reader. Great Aunt

Hilda was one of a large number of women I have come across in my life who never married, probably because of so many young men being killed in the First World War. The next time you are near a war memorial, count the names from the 1914–18 war and compare them to the numbers listed for the Second World War between 1939 and 1945. On holiday once in the Whithorn area, Heather and I came across a dramatic illustration of this in the tiny village of Glasserton. Its war memorial recorded the fact that seventeen from its small community had died in the First World War and one in the second. What percentage of its young men was that, I wondered. And in Ray Michie's father's book, John Bannerman mentions that of the 1913/14 Glasgow Accies Rugby XV, eight were dead and six wounded within the ensuing ten years.

My grandfather never got over his son George's death. Apart from normal grief, he had apparently mistakenly convinced himself that George was going to join him in the Cupar legal practice. Many an ex-soldier needing money for drink or for any good or bad purpose had only to call at my grandfather's office and say, 'I was in the war with George.' The pay-out rate was doubled if the soldier had actually been present when George was killed. Dad eventually had to put a stop to the pay-outs.

Dad enjoyed small, personal organizations where he could know and be at one with those he had to work with. He once lamented to me, 'I used to know all my staff by their full names. Now I do not even know the christian names of all my partners. However, there is one advantage: we can now field our own cricket eleven with me as twelfth man.' When anyone teased Dad about our surname, he told them that it should not be taken literally, pointing out that, in school, he had had to share a desk with and sit next to a boy called Christian.

Dad was very polite and courteous, especially to fellow solicitors, except when they were unworthy of it. On one occasion, in Cupar Sheriff Court, an unhelpful and uncooperative solicitor was on his feet – there always has to be one, doesn't there?

'I am requesting your Lordship to grant my application to lodge this document after the permitted time. I am sure my friend Mr Pagan will be as cooperative as he always is.'

Dad rose to his feet.

'I regret, my Lord, that on this occasion, I cannot agree to my friend's request,' and sat down.

'Unlike you, Charles,' whispered the awkward solicitor.

'I'll cooperate James, when you learn how to behave.'

There were quiet mutterings of approval from around the court table.

Dad and I were alone together one afternoon in Frankfurt.

'What are we going to do with ourselves while the women are away looking around all those boring shops?'

'That shouldn't be difficult, Dad. What do you and I most have in common, apart from sport, music and law? Foreign films. Where better to see one than in Frankfurt?'

'Don't be such an idiot. There won't be any subtitles.'

I suggested that we could choose a film that didn't require great academic skills and at that we passed a billboard showing a half undressed damsel and the words below: 'Angelique und der Sultan'. We agreed that it would be an experience to see a foreign film in a foreign city. Unfortunately, when we got in, we found that we were watching a Swedish sex film with German subtitles. Dad, claiming to be an expert, said, 'That doesn't look like Angelique.' I then remembered that there had been two words in German below the film title on the billboard and Dad and I were almost in hysterics when I surmised that presumably they translated as: 'Coming Shortly'. I then set off for the loo, for which I had been desperate for some time and, using one of my few words of German, said to the usherette, 'Toiletten?'

'Toiletten kaput,' came back the worrying reply.

I rejoined Dad.

'That didn't take you long, I thought you were desperate.'

'Toiletten kaput,' I replied. This was too much for us and our fits of laughter brought German shouts of, 'ShooSh!' We then decided to leave before we were arrested as we did not fancy a headline back home saying: 'PROMINENT SCOTTISH SOLICITORS ARRESTED FOR BREACH OF THE PEACE IN FRANKFURT CINEMA.' And so our only venture to a foreign cinema lasted less than quarter of an hour.

One thing Dad and I did not share was politics, although he was generous enough to admit his admiration for three leading Liberals: Jo Grimond, Russell Johnston and Menzies Campbell. When he told me this, I told him that I had a story to rival one he had told me years ago. Apparently when Dad was about eight, at the time when his father was the Provost of Cupar, there was a royal visit. He was with his father in the council chambers, when, to his father's horror, he suddenly realized he had left the chain of office at home about a mile up the street. The streets were deserted of traffic but lined by ardent royalists on all sides and Dad had the embarrassing but important experience of pedalling his bike through the empty streets, in front of all the masses, to reclaim the chain of office. When I recalled that story, I said that I had done better because, at only my second Liberal conference, at very much the last minute, I had had to rush to Russell Johnston's hotel to collect his speech.

'Not quite the same thing, Graeme.'

I was not sure whether he was indicating that, to him, Russell was not as important as royalty or whether he thought the chain of office was more important than a speech. It was somewhat unfortunate that on the last occasion I ever saw Dad, we had a dispute over CND. I knew that he did not approve of that organisation but we had long since had a silent agreement not to argue with each other about it. On that last occasion, Dad said to me as I was leaving after a visit with my then two children, 'Are you going straight home?' Not for the first time, I was too honest.

'More or less; we are actually heading in the Glasgow direction for a change.'

It was Easter Saturday.

'Would Easter demonstrations have anything to do with your strange route?'

That led to a disagreement, so much so that, on the journey away, my nine-year-old daughter said anxiously from the back of the car, 'Is everything alright Daddy? Grandpa seemed very angry.' I assured her that it was nothing important, just a divergence of view.

That occasion was only two months before the ill-fated Yugoslavian holiday and because Dad hated the phone, except on business and when it was absolutely necessary, there was a real chance I might never have spoken to him again. He nearly always left Mum to answer the phone but luckily, when I telephoned to wish them a happy holiday, Mum was out somewhere and Dad had to answer. I wished him a happy holiday and it was clear that there was absolutely no ill will from our unnecessary disagreement, which he had probably forgotten all about. I told him that if the Pools came up when they were still away, I would be out to join them in a flash.

'That would be fun.'

That was one of his favourite sayings and these were the last words I ever heard him speak. Mum was eleven years without Dad, which was exactly the same length of widowhood her own mother had. Mum was pretty blind for a few years before the end and much less mobile, which was fortunate for us because she had more time to share things with us. In her earlier years she had been constantly busy with her thrifty economic running of a lovely home and many charitable works. It seemed she could not sit still for a moment without doing something worthwhile. Like many elderly people, she did not like being away from her own home for too long despite her loneliness there without Dad. Nevertheless, she did make regular visits to the Highlands to stay with us and built up the kind of wonderfully special relationships which are often to be experienced between grandparents and grandchildren.

I am sure that Dad looked down with approval on those years of Mum's life. There was nothing that gave him more pleasure than looking forward to visits from family, both immediate and distant, and from close friends. Many people's picture of Dad would be of him standing, leaning on the grand piano, reading a newspaper or doing a crossword. He would often have more than half an eye on the window and an ear cocked for the sound of an approaching car at the exciting prospect of welcoming to his home someone whom he liked. His enthusiasm for those whose company he enjoyed was very infectious.

9

Never a Lost Cause

'Someone seems very pleased with life,' called out a customer at the building society where Heather worked. It was 12 June 1987, the day after another Westminster General Election.

'Yes,' replied Heather, 'Ray Michie has just won Argyll and Bute for the Liberals.'

'Great,' said one or two voices, but from the back of the customer queue, came the rather sour comment, 'They didn't win in many other places though, did they?' which was sadly true.

The news came to me at home, where I had decided to hide away, at least for the morning, pending the result, which was going to be a real watershed in my life. Being a natural pessimist, I had not really expected Ray to win, which was absolutely no disrespect to her. But if she had not won, at what was her third attempt, it was possible that she would not have stood again and that could have been the end of the Liberal challenge in this area and the end of years of hard but enjoyable work.

Before she first stood for Parliament, I had invited Ray up to my house for a private talk. I asked her whether she really wanted me to be part of her campaign because, as I pointed out, most of the things that I seemed to get involved with in life had failed. She simply laughed and said that Liberals were used to not winning but that the fight went on. I showed her, by way of an amusing example of my past history, a photograph of the Edinburgh University Cricket Team in 1955, which was headed 'Inter University Champions' and which showed me looking very proud of myself along with the rest of the team. But that did not disprove what I had said because all the university matches had been won before I had been promoted to the team!

As I sat at home on that post-election morning awaiting the result which would mean so much, my mind went back over the previous ten years and all that I had had the privilege of sharing with Ray and a reasonably small band of active supporters. It had all begun in the autumn of 1977, when I had suggested to my good friend Mary Faccenda, who was already involved with me in a number of housing and other campaigns, that we should go along together to the Argyll Liberal's AGM and see what the scene was. Mary's firm belief in justice and a fair society with individual freedoms made her a natural Liberal. The AGM was hardly encouraging – only a handful there and the excellent chairman, Oliver Whitley, threatening to disband the whole outfit unless members worked a bit harder to get more people to join. I had to leave early to attend a wedding and Mary joined the wedding dance later that evening.

'How did the rest of the meeting go?' I asked.

'Great,' laughed Mary, 'I am the Secretary and Treasurer and you are on the Committee.'

Shortly after that, I became the Press Officer and soon we all had to make the decision as to whether or not Ray should stand as the candidate in the 1979 election, which was not far away. At first, I was concerned because the local MP, the Nationalist Iain MacCormick, was a good representative of the area and I had voted for him successfully in the two 1974 elections when there had been no Liberal candidate. Also, I had just worked closely and happily with him in the 1979 referendum for a Scottish parliament. If Ray stood, it was highly likely that Iain would lose and that the Tories would win, which was the last thing that we all wanted.

It was a difficult political decision and there can often be conflict between voting for something slightly better and voting against it because it does not meet your full aspirations. It is not always the case, as the public might think, that politicians are more than happy to abandon their principles at the drop of a hat. The consequences have to be thought of but our decision was not really that difficult to make when Robin Clark put forward the unanswerable argument: 'What's the point in being a political party if we don't fight elections?'

'I'll need an agent,' said Ray.

'I'll do it,' said Robin, despite the fact that he already had an extremely busy life as the local surgeon and in many other ways. I have always regretted the fact that, by the time success came, Robin and his cheerfully energetic wife Marnie were away from the area and unable to attend any of the victory parties.

I was glad that Robin made the decision about Ray standing so easy. I had previously had good cause to be very grateful to him because, on a Sunday morning a year or so beforehand, he had abandoned practising on the church organ, just prior to the morning service, and had rushed away to the hospital to carry out a Caesarean operation to produce my first child. Just to show that the medical profession (like the legal profession) is not always right, a few years before that momentous occasion, I had been advised by the doctor I had before Ronnie Frew that, following on various tests, I was very unlikely ever to produce any children. He put it this way: 'You are in the worst of both worlds. You are unlikely to have children but I cannot guarantee you immunity if you want to sleep around.' Fortunately I didn't.

It was therefore more than a bit of a paradox that, ten years after the birth of my first daughter, I was in Robin's hospital for a vasectomy, lying starkers from the waist down. I had never been in such a position before and was highly tense, lying to attention with my arms at my side. When a nurse asked if I wanted to see what Robin was going to be doing, I declined the kind invitation, whereupon she put a net across my stomach so that I would be unaware of what was going on further down. This brought the comment from Robin, who was a keen tennis player, 'Graeme, would you mind folding your arms across your chest. You keep to your side of the net and I'll keep to mine.' A few weeks later, in the office, I was aware of a rather attractive client of one of my partners and eventually, not being able to place where I had met her, I approached her and asked. I was rather cut down to size by her reply when she whispered, 'I was present at your vasectomy.'

One client I had was not at all well looked after by the medical profession. She knew she was not well but her doctor refused to listen and dismissed all her ailments as depression, post natal blues, bad periods and all the rest. For long enough he declined to refer her to a specialist but, eventually, just to keep her quiet, or so he thought, he did set up an appointment for her. A massive internal tumour was found and she was rushed to hospital.

'I'll never forget when the consultant came to see me after he had examined all the results,' Nancy told me. 'He simply said that I had a tumour which was inoperable and that there was nothing that could be done. He then walked away with his retinue, leaving me alone in the side ward. You can imagine what I was thinking and how I felt.'

Fortunately for Nancy there was a young doctor on the ward, not long qualified, who had obviously not lost his idealism nor been taken over by power. 'He came to see me,' Nancy continued, 'and asked what the consultant had actually said. I told him.'

'What he means,' said the young doctor, 'is that he can't operate and that he can't do anything but that doesn't mean that nothing can be done. There are other kinds of treatment that we can try. I can't say that they will succeed but are you willing to give it a go? Will you help me fight this illness of yours?'

'Of course,' Nancy assured him.

'Right then. We fight it together.'

It was a long haul and eventually the battle was won.

All this was some time before I ever met Nancy and, when I first saw her, I had no idea that she had been so ill. Nancy has had a lot of misfortunes in life, some of which explained why she had to come and see me so often. One horrible incident was when her teenage son was knocked down by a car while he was crossing the street and was then run over by a second vehicle. Fortunately he survived and recovered. But despite all her difficulties and our many meetings, I do not think we ever had one without finding something to laugh at. She has great spirit. Come to think of it, I have not seen her for a while. Let's hope that means that her life is now running smoothy. I assure my many doctor friends that I do not tell Nancy's story to knock the medical profession. In most cases I am full of admiration for them. But people must learn from Nancy and not accept at face value everything they are told, no matter what situation they are in. If it's important enough it is always worth asking a few questions and not just taking the quick and easy way.

Ray Michie came from a strong political background. Her father, John Bannerman, had himself stood for Parliament on four or five occasions and on two of those had only narrowly been defeated. Ray told me how, in a general election for the Inverness Constituency, it seemed that her father had won and the declaration of a great victory was not far away when somebody suddenly remembered the postal votes. Unfortunately for Ray's father, there were a large number of them, because it was soon after the war and a lot of servicemen were still away. Once the postal votes were counted, John Bannerman lost. Almost fifty years later when Ray was on the point of having another victory declared, her agent suddenly shouted out, 'Have they remembered the postal votes?' I have never shut anyone up quite so quickly.

Ray got off to a good start in 1979, despite coming last, getting over 5,000 votes for the Liberals in their first attempt at the seat for fifteen years. At the next election in 1992, she set herself up for eventual victory when she got 9,500 votes and moved into second place. It was then pretty clear that, if people did not want to continue with the Tories, she was the one they had to turn to. Her own hard work and commitment to Scotland and the Highlands had already come across and, being very much part of the local community herself, the people, even if not natural Liberal supporters, knew that she was someone who could be trusted. There was still a lot of ongoing work to do and I remember canvassing in Taynuilt during the eventually successful 1987 campaign. I gave the man at the doorstep the usual spiel and got the reply which I think was the attitude of a lot of the voters at that time: 'I will vote for whichever party is going to get rid of the Tories. I shall be watching the campaign day by day and whichever party runs the best campaign will get my vote.'

Canvassing was never to me the most enjoyable of experiences. However, the camaraderie made it fun, especially when the ever present, indefatigable Helen Jackson was around. Canvassing also had some amusing incidents. Once, in the mid-Argyll area, the door was opened by a wee, timid man and, when he heard what I was about, he said, 'Hold on, hold on, I'll have to get my wife.' A large woman then filled the door frame and in a booming voice said, 'Tory, always have been, always will be, thank you for calling but goodnight to you.' As I went down the long pathway back to the road I thought to myself, 'What a bloody waste of time,' whereupon I was aware of a rustling in the bushes behind me and a voice whispering, 'Come here, come here.' I looked back and found the husband crouched in the overgrowth.

'I don't have to vote the same way – get it?'

As he scampered back up towards the house, he gave me a thumbs-up signal. When I recounted that story to the witty Ronnie Frew, he commented that he must be the only man in the country who really looked forward to a general election. 'He gets the chance to rebel every four years and no one can find him out.'

In 1987 Ray's hard work, dedication and personality, along with 'a little help from her friends', produced another 4,000 votes and she was elected MP with a majority of 1,394. She was the first female Liberal MP in Scotland. We celebrated in different ways. Dr Archie Hutcheson, who almost single-handedly had kept the Liberal flag waving in the area since before the war, until the recent more active days, told me that he was having his lunch when he heard the result and he 'wept into his potatoes'. Irvine Waugh, who was a very laid-back character with a fund of stories from election campaigns in the Borders in the '60s told me that when he came back from the count, he went into every room in his house until he found one empty. He then closed the door behind him and jumped up and down seven times.

I went out on my grass-cutting tractor, shouting and cheering at the top of my voice with no one able to hear me above the noise of the engine. If anyone had been watching, they must have thought that my machine had suddenly become electrified because I was waving my arms and legs in all directions like a demented dervish. I am not sure what Oliver and Elspeth Whitley did but they must have had a wonderful evening of quiet satisfaction. For Oliver, who was then seventy-five, it was the first time that he had ever voted successfully, which says something about our perverse voting system. He had made a very moving point, at the start of the 1979 campaign. In the early hours of a cold morning, while we were putting some posters up, he commented, 'Forty years ago today, Elspeth and I married. If you had told me then that I would celebrate my fortieth anniversary by walking along a cold roadside at 6 o'clock in the morning, putting up posters for a political campaign, I would have said you were mad. At the same time, however, if someone had said to me then that such activities were going to be possible forty years on, I would have been mightily relieved.' Understandably for those unlucky enough to be young adults in the 1930s and 1940s, the prospects and horrors of war dominated their lives.

The importance of Ray's victory, not just to the Liberals, but to the whole democratic process and the continuing fight for justice, came in a letter which appeared in the *Liberal News* not long afterwards. It was from a lady who was in her latter years and who had supported the Liberals all her life. She had hoped that the 1987 election was going to be the one that really justified her support for Liberalism over all the years and that it would at last be the big break-through. After another disappointing election, she was in some despair and felt that her whole life had been a waste of time and that it had all been a lost cause from the beginning. Then, the last result in the election came through the day afterwards and there, in some part of the country which she had never heard of, a woman whom she had never heard of either, had won a great victory for the Liberals against the Conservatives. She realized then that it is never a lost cause and that you never know when success will come. And even if you do not win, fighting for what is right can never be a lost cause. Even if you are alone, your time can still come.

I often look back to June 1980 and a rally at the Calton Hill in Edinburgh. It was organized by the Campaign for a Scottish Parliament and Ray Michie was to be one of the speakers. Marching with my children in the procession, I noticed a simple float in the parade which had nothing but two large posters: 'FREE MANDELA'. At that time I did not expect success in any of the three issues. I did not think then that we would actually get Ray elected as an MP, although I knew that we would do a lot that was worthwhile. The failed referendum on the Scottish Parliament was only a year behind us and most of us involved in the revived campaign did not expect to see a Scottish Parliament in our lifetimes, but we knew it had to come eventually. And I was convinced that Nelson Mandela would end his days by dying still a prisoner, which would have been such a waste.

And yet, and yet, despite my characteristic pessimism, only seven years later almost to the day, Ray was elected as Argyll's MP. Less than three years after that, on 11 February 1990, Nelson Mandela was released. Nine years later, there was an overwhelmingly successful referendum in favour of a Scottish Parliament. Elections to it were held in May 1999 and on the 12th of that month, the Scottish Parliament was reconvened, 292 years after it had been adjourned. We celebrated Nelson Mandela's release in the family with five of us sitting together in front of a roaring fire with a bottle of champagne at the ready. About an hour after he was due to be seen on worldwide television leaving the prison, my thirteen-year-old son, who was the first of us to have heard the news the day before, understandably got a little bit impatient.

'Come on, Dad, we all know he is going to get out. Why can't we open the fizzy stuff now?'

The great man managed to leave his glasses on his pillow. When, an hour or two late, he prepared to deliver the most carefully worded and most watched political speech in history, he had nothing to enable him to read it. Fortunately, someone came to the rescue, but if anyone watches a video of the speech, they can see how ill-fitting and wrong his glasses looked.

A year or two after Nelson Mandela's release I was, obviously, delighted to be invited to the Concert Hall, Glasgow in October 1993, where he was to give an address. As I rushed away from the Concert Hall to get back to Oban urgently for family reasons, I was suddenly aware of cars pulling up at a back entrance and thought that he might be on the point of leaving. I hurried back and was lucky to get close enough to him for a photograph, which now hangs proudly in my study at home. In fact, I was in danger of being arrested for pushing a burly policeman out of the way so that I could get near enough. Furthermore, it now seems obvious from the photograph that the man standing next to Mandela with a raincoat over his arm was a body-guard, with the coat possibly hiding a firearm of some kind. It is as well I did not try to get even closer.

Later I was talking to another great fan of his, the Rev. George MacArthur, whom I had met during my voluntary housing activities.

We discussed our emotions on hearing that Mandela was to be freed and confessed to each other our one reservation about his liberation: 'He'll never be able to live up to all the unreasonable expectations we have placed on him.' But we both agreed that he had 'and more than', which was truly remarkable.

George himself had an eerie experience of the apartheid regime because he had worked as a minister in South Africa during those awful times and no doubt had made his own views very clear. He had returned to Scotland for six months' leave and, passing a newsagent, noticed the billboard outside: 'SCOTTISH MINISTER BANNED'. Curiosity aroused, he went in, bought the paper, opened it and found his own cheerful face smiling back at himself. But the really frightening thing was that, when he got back to the house he had rented for his six-months' sabbatical, there were the banning papers waiting for him, served at an address which he himself had had no knowledge of when he had left South Africa. The tentacles of the South African secret police were obviously extremely and frighteningly long.

Ray Michie really had to push herself forward in many situations where most of us would have hidden away and not had the courage to stand up. I remember being with her at a European Parliament count in 1979, which was different because it was only a verification of votes and there would be no result declared in Lochgilphead that day. Normally the winning candidate, by tradition, thanks the Returning Officer, all the counters and so on, but what was the proper thing on this occasion? She turned to me.

'Don't ask me, Ray, I have never been at one of these before.'

At that, a powerful, large Tory gentleman came over.

'Ray, I've been thinking that someone really ought to do a vote of thanks.'

'It's alright Michael, it's taken care of. I'm doing it.'

After his defeat, the previous Tory MP wrote to the papers rather bitterly, but somewhat accurately, saying that he had only lost because the cards against him had simply been restacked in a different order. But he, as a supporter of the present unfair voting system, could hardly complain when the system at last worked to his disadvantage. The tone of the ex-MP's comments made it clear that he had never learned the simple lesson that his job was to listen to the people and represent their views properly at Westminster. It was not for him to impose his Tory views on his voters. Listening and representing were characteristics inherent in Ray's nature and something she never needed to learn.

I had originally joined a political party rather against my will but eventually I realized that not many people can achieve things working in isolation. The more I looked at what the Liberals stood for, the more I discovered that they represented my own views, especially on issues like the Scottish Parliament, international outlook, human rights, fair opportunities for all, the environment and changing the political system to make it more representative of the voters' wishes. Russell Johnston often quoted Ray Michie's father, John Bannerman, as saying, 'My trouble, Russell, is that I can't understand why everyone isn't a Liberal.' I have never been able to understand why, in times of war, forming coalition governments was deemed essential but that at other times we should spend all our time fighting one another. Surely we all want a united community working together for the common good. To me it is natural to want to work with others and there is a telling passage in Nelson Mandela's book *Long Walk to Freedom*. He recalled meeting up by chance on a plane with some political people he knew but with whom he did not often agree. During the flight, he found that they got on quite well together. 'High above the ground and far from home, we had much more that united us than separated us.' I was later to hear Russell Johnston's own words during one of his conference speeches: 'Unlike some of the more entrenched members of our party, I have never believed that Liberals were given a monopoly on wisdom.'

Not everyone knows the huge contribution that Ray's husband, Dr Iain Michie, made to her success. I had an early example of his irreverent humour, which was to keep many a campaign going forward with cheerful optimism. Very early on, Ray, Iain, Mary, Oliver and I had driven up to Ballachulish where we had arranged a public meeting. No one, but no one, not even the doorkeeper, turned up. We retreated back down the road but at Ray's insistence did some canvassing en route. As we stood at one door, someone called down from upstairs, 'Is that Dr Michie's voice I'm hearing?'

'Yes,' boomed Iain.

'You saved my life.'

'Too bloody true I did. If it wasn't for me you would have been up there strumming your harp long before now.'

Later his usual spiel at doorsteps was something along the lines of, 'Have you ever thought of voting for my wife, or does the whole idea fill you with horror as it does me?' Those kind of jocular comments disguised Iain's own caring nature and his sound common sense. His behind-the-scenes advice and guidance and his own personal popularity were important assets towards the Liberal successes here.

Ten years after Ray became the MP Iain was interviewed by *The Press and Journal* and made two particularly memorable comments. When asked for his most embarrassing experience, he gave the answer of playing Strip Poker with the wife of his Commanding Officer and losing.

'How would you best like to be remembered?' he was asked.

'As someone who cared about his patients – and that they were happy to have had him as their physician.'

Politics is often a hard and cruel business. One of the saddest sights I saw was after Iain MacCormick lost his seat in 1979 and he and his wife Micky were left to walk alone across the lawns of Kilmory back to their car. I contrasted that with five years earlier when Nationalist supporters swarmed round Iain and carried him away shoulder high. When Ray first fought to retain her seat in 1992, I remember saying to her daughter Deirdre and others in the car on the way to the count, 'I don't think your mother is going to lose, but if she does, we stand together and walk away from the hall united. We will have nothing to be ashamed of. Your mother has done a great job and if the voters no longer want her, that is up to them.' I hope Deirdre appreciated my words more than she did a year or two later when we were together in the loudspeaker car and I was doing the speaking. I had forgotten that the loudspeaker did not turn off at the microphone and we were driving towards Ganavan when, believe it or not, I saw a topless sunbather lying on the rocks. Unwisely and forgetting about the faulty loudspeaker, I said, 'You've got a nice pair,' whereupon the sunworshipper sat up and glared in our direction. Deirdre promptly banned me from speaking and insisted that I drove the car for the rest of the day.

After Ray's third victory, we had a memorable dinner to celebrate her ten years as an MP. Despite the speakers including Russell Johnston, Charles Kennedy, Ray herself (and of course me as Chairman!), for many people the highlight of the evening was the contribution that Deirdre Michie made. She spontaneously paid a tremendous tribute to Ray, not just for her political successes but, more importantly, for what she meant to and was able to do for all the family as a mother. I was relieved to hear that – not that I had ever doubted it – but because I had been very moved when reading Gillian Slovo's book *Every Secret Thing*. Gillian was a daughter of the great South African activist and courageous anti-apartheid campaigner, Joe Slovo – a real political hero if ever there was one. In the early hours of the morning soon after Joe had died from cancer following a long and difficult illness, Nelson Mandela, then President of South Africa, joined the mourning daughters. He told them that one day, when he had gone to hug his own grown-up daughter, she had flinched away from him and burst out, 'You are the father to all our people but you have never had the time to be a father to me.' Nelson Mandela went on to say to the grieving Slovo family that that was his greatest and perhaps his only regret: the fact that his children and the children of his comrades had been the ones to pay the price of their parents' commitment. In his own book, Mandela wrote: 'In life, every man has twin obligations – obligations to his family, to his parents, to his wife and children and he has an obligation to his people, his community, his country. In a civil and humane society, each man is able to fulfil those obligations according to his own inclinations and abilities. But in a country like South Africa, it was almost impossible for a man of my birth and colour to fulfil both those obligations.'

Charles Kennedy is a good Highland man with a very sharp wit. On one occasion I was at a Burns Supper in Oban when I noticed on the programme that one of the speakers was a Charles Kennedy, but not him. In fact, it made that clear by listing the man as 'Charles Kennedy (Fife)'. I sent a copy of the menu off to Charles with a note saying, 'It is a pretty poor show when anyone who has the misfortune to have the same name as you has to go around protesting "I am not that other guy".' At that time, Charles was President of the UK Liberals and I got a witty note back from him immediately which read

Thanks for the menu and your comments. Very amusing.
Regards
President Kennedy (UK)

At the Liberal conference in Ayr in 1984, being rather bored with what was going on in the debating hall, I set out in search of a pair of shoes and bumped into Jim Wallace who was Convener of the Agenda Committee.

'Have you any ideas for an important topical debate?' he asked.

'What about Road Equivalent Tariff – when did we last debate that?'

'Good idea, I'll put it to the Agenda Committee, but who'll do it?'

'Ray will lead the debate, don't worry about that.'

When I returned to the conference hall, Ray was unwise enough to accuse me of skiving, even if she was right.

'Not at all, I've been organizing the conference and you are leading the debate tomorrow on Road Equivalent Tariff.'

That night, Ray demanded that, seeing I had landed her with that, she needed from me an amusing anecdote to go with her speech. Luckily, I had one. My friend Norah Fairlie had once travelled on the Lismore Ferry from Oban and when she went to pay her fare she was asked for sixpence.

'Is that all?' she enquired. 'I thought it would be much more than that.'

'It is, but I just put you down as a parcel. You'll not be minding, will you?' came the typical Highland reply.

In 1986, the Road Equivalent Tariff reared its head again in a very unusual way. There was a huge storm that day, which happened to be my fiftieth birthday, and virtually all the delegates trying to reach Rothesay for the Liberal conference were storm-bound on the mainland. When I got to Colintraive for the ferry across to Bute, I found that it was also stranded by the storm. I came across Iain Michie ensconced quite happily in the hotel there and we thought that was a perfectly good place to spend the rest of the day celebrating my birthday. In the event however, the Council laid on a special ferry to go from Dunoon when the storm had abated slightly to get those stranded on the mainland across to the island. The conference then managed to get going properly. The problem was that the TV cameras had been rolling live from the conference hall much earlier in the day when there was virtually no one in the hall. One of the few delegates present was Carole MacIntyre from Islay. There was no alternative but to make her speak for about three hours on the subject of RET. She did well, and she must always be given the credit for being the first Liberal to have won an election in Argyll in recent times when she became a local Councillor. Later on, when I was Chairman, I commented at an AGM that it was my ambition for us to have both the Islay Councillors as Liberals so that I could say that I was Chairman of the whole of that great whisky island.

Of course, the best thing about conferences is meeting up with people who become good friends. It is especially important in small, semi-isolated communities like Oban that there are outside interests which allow you to come across people from other parts of the country, or better still, even further afield. I remember the Rev. Brian Wilkinson being on the National Committee of the Mission for Deep Sea Fishermen, which took him to quarterly meetings in Newcastle. Not necessarily the most exciting place to go, but he rightly thought it was very important that there was something that took him away from the area from time to time and allowed him to keep in touch with folk with different attitudes, different problems, different interests and so on.

In the case of the Liberals, when so often it seemed that the crusade for justice and a fair world was getting nowhere, for me it was good to encounter people who shared my own passionate beliefs in those ideals. At that time, one of the characteristics of a good Liberal was not to give oneself any airs or graces or make oneself out to be too important, but at the same time, to take the world and its problems seriously. I remember at my third conference, which was in Rothesay in 1980, having dinner with Fred McDermid, the Chairman of the Scottish Party. It was not just because I was such a new delegate but also because the dinner consisted of fish and chips from Zavaroni's shop and the venue was my car. I contrasted that to Margaret Thatcher having dinner in the grand dining room of the Hotel Majestic in Bournemouth, or wherever else.

One of the friends that I happily made was Des Murricane, who was very kind and very supportive. When he died, it was said of him that he was 'tolerant of the human condition', something which any friend of mine has to be! I first came across him when we were checking out of a hotel at the end of a three-day conference and I noticed him standing at the reception desk looking at his bill with a quizzical, enquiring expression.

'Night porter? £20? Never saw a night porter, but I'm sure it's right!'

It was only much later and by chance that I found out that he had been something of a war hero in the RAF. It was part of his life which he steadfastly refused to allow any mention of when he was standing in any campaigns. How I found out was when I went to the spring conference at St Andrews in 1987 and he commented, 'I missed you at the autumn conference, where were you?' At first I could not remember and then I recalled that Heather and I had been in a very nasty road accident at Loch Lomondside on the way to the conference after an encounter with a lorry owned, unfortunately, by one of my clients. Our car was totally written off and both of us could have been wiped out. In fact, the accident had occurred immediately after I had looked at the clock and had commented, 'Good. We are in excellent time and I shall be there for Russell's opening speech.' I was thankful for the love and tolerance of family, because the car in question was one I had had to borrow from my mother for my own family holiday a few months earlier. It had belonged to my father, who had died not long before.

I told Des that we were lucky not to have been hurt. However, we were both very shocked and when we went to Dumbarton station, with a view to going on into Glasgow for our separate missions, we quickly changed plans and decided to get back to Oban and the safety of home as quickly as possible. Fortunately, the timing for the middle of the day Oban train from Dumbarton worked well. Des enquired whether we had been able to walk afterwards and I repeated that we had not been hurt. He explained what had prompted his question and it was only then that one of his wartime experiences came out. He had apparently been flying in a bombing raid over Germany; all had gone well and he had set off confidently for home but suddenly he found himself surrounded by five or six enemy planes. Somehow he managed to manoeuvre his way between them all without coming to grief and arrived at the safety of the British airstrip full of assurance. However, when he got out of the plane, he said, 'I fell smack on my arse onto the tarmac. I was obviously far more frightened than I had realized.'

It is impossible to attend every funeral of every friend but there have been two in particular that I have regretted not making the time to go to despite the pressure of work. Des's funeral was one. It was less than a two-hour journey away and I should have been there. Des often reminded me, probably because of the RAF connection, of Oban garage proprietor, Jimmy Wilson, although I have no reason to think that either man knew the other. Jimmy had once flown his plane under Connel Bridge, much to the annoyance of his superiors. He was a man who was always welcoming and friendly. In fact, to this day, to many people, Airds Crescent in Oban will always be his street because you could hardly go into it without him emerging from his garage, putting his arm round your shoulder and making a very friendly but often derogatory comment about you. That was particularly so of me and my political affiliations, although he never quite let on which party he did support – if any.

Jimmy had a very difficult end with cancer but his discipline and courage – perhaps coming from his war experiences – were amazing. I had seen him in hospital by chance and he encouraged me to visit him whenever I could, which I was always pleased to do. Even through his illness, he was full of fun and amusing stories. On what was to be the last day of his life I arrived at his bedside, where his wife Alison was reading the *London Times*. Jimmy came out of his semi-unconscious state and declared immediately, 'Put that away dear; Graeme doesn't approve.' Jimmy's humorous bravery was all the more to be admired when I recall that after two of the most bizarre and freakish accidents – entirely different and separated by a number of years – that I had ever heard of, he lost, first, one of his best friends and, later, a son as a result of hugely unlucky falls.

Another Liberal friend was Bill Craig who, along with Ray Michie's father, John Bannerman, and a handful of other men, had set up the independent Scottish Liberal Party to keep the inevitable English dominance at bay. Typically modest, he had never said anything to brag about his connection with Ian Hamilton's exploit of removing the Stone of Destiny from Westminster Abbey. In fact, I knew nothing of Bill's involvement until I had known him for a number of years, when, quite by chance, on the day of a conference, the news of who the conspirators had actually been broke in the national press. I read then that Bill's part in the adventure had been to drive down to England a few days after the removal and recover the stone from the field where Ian had buried it. Again, quite by chance, I found myself standing beside Bill when I was in the queue to register for the conference. I remonstrated with him for not having shared his heroic experience with me. He smiled and said nothing other than, 'I thought you knew.'

When my son was eight, he misguidedly agreed to come with me to a one-day conference in Stirling and, not surprisingly, only managed to survive half the day before deciding, quite rightly, that there were better things to do in life. Fortunately, it did not put him, or his sisters, off continuing to help with various campaigns by leafleting, postering and all the rest. What was memorable about my son's only political conference was that it was the very day that Russell Johnston, arguably Scotland's greatest Liberal, received a knighthood. Not surprisingly, it did not change him and I enjoyed one encounter which I overheard:

'May I congratulate the noble knight?'

'Only if you tug the peasant forelock at the same time.'

My son was in fact the first to get Russell's autograph after he was knighted, but the only thing he could find for him to write on was the remains of a Jacob's Club plain chocolate biscuit wrapper which had been lying in his pocket for ages. I still have it showing the signature, 'Sir Russell Johnston 15th June 1985'.

By the time of Ray's last victory in 1997, she had made the seat her own, which enabled me to enjoy a count for the very first time. Normally they are far too nerve-racking for enjoyment, but in 1992 she had managed to increase her majority to 2,622 and in 1997 it went up further to a comfortable 6,081. She had served her constituents well and knew their needs. Certainly she was more in touch than an elderly Edinburgh MP who had been elected without serious challenge for a number of years. It was eventually suggested to him that he should hold surgeries so that his voters could come and discuss their problems with him.

'Surgeries? What do I need surgeries for? I'm in perfect health.'

The purpose of surgeries was explained to him again.

'What absolute nonsense. My people don't need things like that. They know perfectly well that if ever they do have a problem, they can come up my drive, ring the back door bell and leave a message with one of my maids.'

The fact that the seat was regarded as Ray's own was made clear in 2001 after she retired. After that election, the seat became a four-way marginal between the four main Parties, but the Liberals managed to hold on – just. After her retirement, Ray was elevated to the House of Lords and when she asked for my comments I told her I was pleased that her voice and her campaigning on behalf of the Highlands and Islands were not going to be lost. Her own comment was that she would be able to continue the fight for justice for the Chinook helicopter pilots, which indeed she did. Her induction into the House of Lords was memorable, with Heather, me, Mary and husband Guido and Helen all being present. During Ray's fourteen years as an MP, I had only twice managed to see her at the House of Commons. The most memorable part of the House of Lords occasion was when she took the oath in Gaelic as well as English. This brought a lot of comment, nearly all of it favourable. A leader from the *Press and Journal* went something along these lines, 'However, as it was after lunch and as it was the House of Lords, the question has to be asked as to whether any of the noble members were aware of the fact that she was speaking in Gaelic.'

The *Daily Telegraph* in its Diary, quoted Lord Carrington as having said, 'How pathetic, how pretentious', when he heard Ray and the Gaelic. I was enraged by this and wrote to him, sending a copy of an article from the *Stornoway Gazette* which had praised Ray to the heavens for her continuing fight for the Gaelic language. In my letter, I said rather sarcastically to the noble Lord, 'I do not suppose you normally read that paper.' I got the most charming, old worldly reply from the gentleman.

For me, being involved with Ray and the Liberal successes was one of the greatest honours of my life. Maybe there were other things I was lucky enough to have been part of which achieved more and which were as important. But, in the political battle, there were of course a large number of equally dedicated people who were fighting and campaigning to make sure we did *not* win. What Ray achieved with her supporters can truthfully be described as a proper victory. I was immensely proud to have been Chairman of the party for nine years, which, by happy coincidence, was most of the time that Ray was the MP. It was typical of her that when she generously gave me a letter opener to mark the successes, the inscription was neither triumphant nor bigheaded. It simply gave the date of our last victory – 1 May 1997.

10

'We know what's best for them'

'Not another one.'

The year must have been about 1968 and I was in the office of John Stevenson, whom I was later to succeed as Oban's part-time Fiscal.

'Not another what?'

'Another road-barrier death,'

'What's that all about?' I asked.

John then explained that it had at last come to people's realization that the wooden roadside barriers in Argyll were highly dangerous. They had originally been devised to control livestock, but were wholly inappropriate for modern transport by car. What was happening was that when vehicles went even slightly off the road and came in contact with them, the top barrier, which was an extremely heavy bit of timber, became detached from the rest of the barrier. It would then fly through the windscreen of the car before, usually, going out of a back or side window. They were like javelins but about ten times as thick. It was obvious that the driver and passengers were at serious risk of death or at least injury from parts of the barrier and in fact deaths were occurring at a high rate.

This type of barrier had already been banned in every other part of Scotland and an important witness at a later fatal accident enquiry was a Caithness councillor, who happened to be a brother of a local banker, John Carmichael. He explained to the enquiry why the barriers were so dangerous and why his local authority had got rid of them. Yet they still persisted in Argyll despite a local campaign to rid our area of that menace. The campaign was later spear-headed by people like my close friend and journalist, Stewart Fairlie and restaurateur, Jeremy Inglis – not to mention local police and doctors, who inevitably saw the aftermath of such accidents. They were vehement in their condemnation of the barriers. But could our authorities be persuaded to take the necessary action? Of course not. They knew best, despite the grotesque pictures of the accidents which frequently occurred in local and other newspapers.

In September 1972, about two and a half years after I became Oban's part-time Fiscal, there was a simple road accident at North Connel, which should not have had any serious consequences. Four elderly tourists were in a car negotiating a bend at a slow speed when, for some reason, the car left the road and went a few feet down into a ditch. Normally, one would expect nothing worse than a bit of shaking and perhaps bruising. Tragically, one of the back seat passengers was killed outright when part of the roadside barrier detached itself and went straight through the car. It was obvious that if there had been no barrier, there would have been no serious injury at all.

I immediately decided to get approval to hold a Fatal Accident Enquiry, which later took place at Oban Sheriff Court. I remember questioning Argyll's Road Engineer, who was principally responsible for the barriers and for the refusal to remove them. So far as I can recall, part of the cross-examination went something like this:

'Do you not agree that these barriers are highly lethal and dangerous?'

'Not if the car remains on the road,' was the uncaring and insensitive reply.

I was incensed and was on the verge of asking, 'Do you consider that decapitation is a suitable punishment for careless drivers?' but I checked myself. I had already been rapped over the knuckles by the Sheriff for some earlier questions I had put to the Road Engineer.

I hoped that the witnesses and evidence I produced at the enquiry were enough to convince the jury of the dangers of these barriers but any doubts that any of them might have had were removed at the start of the second and final day of the enquiry when another road barrier accident occurred on the Inveraray road near Dalmally. A commercial van went off the road and the barrier went straight through his windscreen as often happened, narrowly missing the driver who, miraculously, was not hurt – just seriously shocked. Eventually, after due deliberation, the jury returned with a finding that the barriers, in particular the top rail, were indeed dangerous and should be removed as soon as possible. One problem, as the enquiry accepted, was that the top rail was positioned at the same height as the average car bonnet, with the result that, on impact, the rail detached itself from the rest of the barrier and was guided by the bonnet straight through the windscreen at considerable velocity.

Four years after my Oban enquiry, a local lady who was known to me was killed when her car went off the road near Inveraray. Her two young children were in the back, and were totally unhurt apart from the trauma. As a result of that accident, Dunoon's Fiscal, Bill Stewart, having investigated the background to these terrible barriers, decided to have a second enquiry and asked me to be a witness to give evidence about what had happened at the earlier Oban enquiry. A doctor friend, Gordon Murchison, another campaigner against these barriers, offered to drive me to the enquiry as he was interested to see what happened. That enabled me to count the number of barriers which I was able to see on the journey.

After telling the second enquiry what had happened at the earlier one, I was also able to say that, during a 38-mile stretch of the journey between Oban and Dunoon, I had counted 126 barriers still in existence, despite the findings of the Oban jury. By that time juries were no longer part of Fatal Accident Enquiries, which were left to the determination of the Sheriff. However, he also had no hesitation in concluding that the barriers were dangerous and an obvious hazard. He added that money was no excuse for the failure to replace them. The campaign, it seemed, was at last about to be finally won. But not quite. In the same month as the second enquiry, there was yet another barrier death, this time involving a girl student from Colintraive. That led to a third enquiry, where again the Sheriff (a different one) reached the same conclusion as the Dunoon Sheriff. At long last, after fifteen years, the removal of these disgraceful barriers began and the campaigners against them were able to celebrate properly when a notice appeared in the *Oban Times* of 8 January 1981 which read:

DISPOSAL OF SECOND-HAND TIMBER

Large quantities of larch posts and dress rails from dismantled barriers are available in Lorn, Mull, Mid-Argyll and Cowal areas. Offers are invited for large or small lots.

The reference to Dunoon and Fiscals brings to mind David Thaw, who was Fiscal there for a number of years after being in, among other places, Hamilton. He was the Hamilton Fiscal at a time when Scotland's most notorious serial murderer, Peter Manuel, was on the loose and offered an interesting insight into the way in which the Scottish criminal justice system operates. Manuel was frighteningly different from most serial murderers in that there was no particular pattern. He simply killed at random whenever he felt like it and his victims were men, women and children, murdered in all different kinds of circumstances.

After what was generally considered to have been Manuel's first actual murder, (although he had already been convicted of various serious sexual assaults), the police wanted to arrest him and presented their evidence to David Thaw. He gave this deep consideration before reaching the agonizing decision that there was not sufficient evidence to justify an arrest and a charge. There then followed at least six murders committed by Manuel before, at last, in 1958, he appeared at the High Court in Edinburgh. After all the evidence was put before the jury, Lord Cameron directed them to return a verdict of not guilty on the first charge, because the evidence was simply not there to justify a conviction. David was mightily relieved to have had his decision of a few years earlier vindicated. However, he confessed to having endured many anxious moments. He would have been none too popular, obviously, if his decision had been wrong and if he had been responsible for allowing a murderer to carry on with his dreadful acts. David was later the man I would turn to for advice when I was unsure of what to do with my own Fiscal responsibilities.

Looking back to the Oban enquiry, I see that the young advocate the Council briefed to act for them and to defend the indefensible, was Michael Ancrum. Later on he became a leading light in the Conservative Party. Cynics might comment that that was appropriate and that he was well used to defending the indefensible, but I would never dream of saying such a thing! Thirteen years later I had a pleasant encounter with him when, as an Under Secretary of State for Scotland, he came to Oban to officially open the Oban Abbeyfield Home, which had a wonderful setting at Gallanach overlooking the bay.

I heard in my early days from my father of the obstinacy of authorities in all sorts of ways including matters of road safety. Dad instanced a set of crossroads near Cupar, where there were countless serious accidents and many fatalities. There were two fast major roads which crossed over each other – one between Edinburgh and Dundee and the other between Cupar and Perth. The authorities refused to put up signs or notices of any kind to warn motorists of the dangers. They claimed that the only signs they had were, 'Halt at major road ahead' and, 'Slow at major road ahead', and that as they had previously classified both roads as 'major', there was absolutely nothing they could do, and so the deaths continued.

Similarly, near Taynuilt in Argyll, at the West Manse on the hill coming out of the village towards Oban, there was a very dangerous bend: it was extremely misleading, being far bigger than motorists travelling in the opposite direction realized. They could see the road beyond what appeared to be a very slight bend and often assumed the road ahead to be clear when it wasn't. I remember once driving towards it and thinking it would be impossible for a car to be hidden by the bend but there were in fact three cars in it. Again there were a number of fatalities at that spot and for that reason. I remember when I prosecuted yet another driver because of an accident there, the Sheriff commented, 'How many more deaths are we going to have to experience before the authorities put up the appropriate signs?' Eventually, they put up warning posts along the sides of the roads, which emphasized the danger and extent of the bend and, so far as I know, that has cured the problem.

I am sure that wherever you go in Scotland you will be able to find some community which is campaigning for a road safety measure or something else important and sensible to them but not getting anywhere with the authorities. On one occasion while Heather and I were on holiday, cycling between Lochearnhead and the top of Glen Ogle on the old railway line there, we met a local resident who told us about a campaign they were having to improve safety for children on part of the road in their vicinity. Yet again it appeared to be a losing battle, with the authorities claiming that they knew best

Oban also appears to have suffered from centralized thinking when it comes to how our traffic systems are operated. At one time the authorities decided that the best way to ensure that traffic flowed smoothly through the town centre was to compel caravans destined for Ganavan, two miles from the town centre, to go the whole way through the town, round an extremely busy roundabout and then return back along a parallel road before reaching their destination.

I am no expert in town planning but it always seemed to me that a park and ride system in the vicinity of the cemetery just less than two miles from the town centre, incorporating a tourist welcoming office and something like a funicular railway would be worth thinking about. It would get people into the town on foot and encourage them to use our shops and eateries. Instead, the authorities in their infinite wisdom decided to place a sewage works at the cemetery, which is hardly the ideal welcome to our visitors. Certainly, something has to be done about our town centre traffic problem at the height of the tourist season. I remember a major traffic jam at the roundabout in the middle of the town, one of the victims being a bus party of elderly people, who were making their first visit to Oban. They were due to stay for lunch and a bit of shopping but by the time they got out of their bus, I doubt if there was much time for either. The bus driver's words were worrying: 'I have never been here before and I will never be back!'

Shopkeepers have complained about a traffic system which leads to people coming into the town, finding nowhere to leave their cars and then, before they know it, discovering themselves in a one-way system on the way back out of the town before having had a chance to experience its delights. What a waste!

High-rise flats, which were all the rage in the 1960s and in the decade or two to follow, were classic examples of giving people what the authorities decided they deserved, rather than what they wanted. They were also classic examples of trying to make everything the same instead of experimenting first with a new idea. It never seemed natural to me that people should live so far away from the ground, especially when access to it was so difficult. I once met an old lady struggling with her shopping at the bottom of a twenty-five storey block. There was only one lift working and naturally it was in constant demand. The other lift had broken down and both had been vandalized – another problem which, it is claimed, came from splitting up communities and concentrating together large numbers of people who did not know each other.

'It took me ten minutes in the bus to get here with my messages,' the old lady explained, 'but it will take me half an hour or more to get from here to my flat up there.'

But we are not all the same. Once, when canvassing, I tried to make political capital out of what I considered the unsuitability of putting elderly people out of reach at the top of huge multi-storey buildings only to be met with the reply: 'It's the most comfortable home I could have and I love sitting here looking out at all the views.'

I was once talking to a friend from Tyndrum, who mentioned that he was part of the voluntary fire brigade service there. I expressed some surprise by saying that I had not realized that he was involved with that. My friend then told me that the leader of the fire brigade was another guy who was actually known to me as a client.

'How did he become the leader of the fire brigade?' I asked in all my innocence.

'He was the only one who had a tow bar on his car,' was the perhaps inevitable Highland reply. I compared that with the qualifications no doubt needed by the leader of the fire service in, for example, New York.

In 1966, four years before I took over from John Stevenson, I stood in for him for a week to allow him to get away for a much earned holiday – he had been seven years without one. During that week there was a tragedy at the iron bridge pool at the River Orchy, which again was a known danger. There were what looked like innocent stepping-stones across the river but they were in fact extremely dangerous, slippery stones and below, out of immediate sight from the stones, was a severe fall to even more rocks further down river. Two or three other people had died in accidents before the lady's death I had to investigate on John's behalf. She and her husband were on holiday and were wandering casually near the river when she ventured on to the stepping stones and was quickly swept by the river's currents onto the rocks below. It took two days to recover her body because of the fierce waters. In fact, the police had to get help from Nuttals construction company, who were involved in the Loch Awe scheme at the time, about twelve miles away. It was necessary for them to sandbag and divert the river before the unfortunate lady could be found. To add to the tragedy, the post mortem revealed that she was expecting their first child. I asked the authorities why, despite all the deaths, there was no warning sign. They maintained that there had been one but it had rotted or been vandalized because it had been made of wood. Although no technical genius myself, I did suggest that they should put up a sign in metal, and I was glad to see one in place the next time I was there.

Fancy it needing me, with all my incompetence in practical skills, to find a solution for the so-called experts. After all, it was I who had a particularly embarrassing experience with my first car. Like most people's, my first car was a bit of an old banger. It was a Standard 8 and was not supposed to go very fast. One Saturday afternoon, after my morning's stint in the office, I was heading for Edinburgh. My wee car was in an especially good mood and we were bombing along on a fast, straight stretch of road near Stirling. We must have been doing at least 60mph when I decided to demand a bit more. All went well for a mile or two when there was a huge bang. Looking in my mirror I saw what, to me, was obviously part of the car lying in the middle of the road. Clearly the speed had caused the car to shake too much and something had fallen off. I, of course, had no idea what it was, so I put it in the boot and stopped at the nearest garage. In those days, garages not only served and sold petrol, they also repaired cars.

'Could I have a gallon of petrol please. Oh, and by the way, there is something in the boot which has just fallen off the car. Could you put it back onto the right place for me?'

The garage attendant opened the boot and took out a weird-looking object, at the same time giving me a strange look.

'What did you say this was?'

'I don't know. It's from the car. It fell off when I was driving near Stirling. I think I must have been going too fast.'

The attendant shook his head sadly.

'This,' he explained, 'is a piece of scrap metal. It hasn't been near a car for decades, until you ran over it. It must have been lying on the road.'

'Thank you. That's most helpful. You can keep it. Please make use of it in any way you like.'

I drove away as quickly as I dared but I wasn't going to risk too much acceleration in case something did fall off the car. I would have hated to prove the garage man wrong.

I have seen a number of examples of authorities trying to hoodwink the public. There was once a Sheriff Clerks' strike, which went on for a number of weeks, during which time there were no court sittings at all. It must have been obvious to the youngest primary school kid that that would lead to a delay in the administration of justice. Eventually a brilliant politician raised the question in the House of Commons as to whether Fiscals were dropping any cases because there were no courts. I would have thought the answer to that was perfectly obvious and during the strike I certainly had to disregard all sorts of minor crimes. I made that clear to the authority above me but I was shot down in flames. I was told in no uncertain terms that no other Fiscals were making that suggestion and that I would be phoned again and a different answer would be expected. They must think the public are totally moronic. No wonder that, almost 100 years ago, a cynic advised: 'Never believe a rumour until it is officially denied.'

A friend of mine, Michael Strathern, went to his own grave utterly convinced that a Nationalist political colleague of his had been murdered by the authorities because of his work on nuclear issues. The suggestion of suicide was ridiculous, partly because the gun which killed Willie MacRae was found some distance away from his body. There were many strange features surrounding the incident and parallels were understandably drawn with the mysterious death of an elderly anti-nuclear campaigner, Hilda Morell, in England. Anyone trying to find the spot where Willie MacRae died may be confused because there are two different cairns, a few miles apart, both apparently marking the spot. The suggestion has been made that the authorities changed the actual locus so as to have a more cooperative Fiscal to facilitate their enquiries and cover up what had actually happened. I know it is easy to read conspiracy into all sorts of perfectly innocent situations, but the authorities have only themselves to blame. Certainly Michael Strathern had no doubts about what had happened to his friend Willie MacRae. Asked on television if he thought the mystery of his death would ever be resolved, he strikingly replied, 'There is no mystery. Willie MacRae was murdered by the British Secret Service.'

Paradoxically, it is not only when you are attacking governments that you are liable to find yourself the victim of dirty dealings. I know of people whose phones were tapped during the 1979 referendum for a Scottish Parliament. They were campaigners actually fighting to secure the success of the government's own bill! Sometimes, of course, it is nothing sinister. But the Civil Service can be accused of deliberately trying to confuse the public with their extraordinary way of expressing themselves. In the old days when Death Grant was often payable, I received a letter which read as follows:

> Death Grant is not payable in respect of the death of Mrs X because the person on whose contributions the Grant is claimed has not in respect of any one year, ending before the relevant year, actually paid contributions of a relevant class from which the earnings factor is not less than 25 times the lower earnings limit for that year and this condition is not deemed to be satisfied (Social Security Act 1975, Section 32 (2) and Schedule 3 para.7).

It is as clear as crystal, isn't it?

Nicholas Fairbairn, in his own book, mentioned a statutory definition of a staggered weekend, which read as follows:

> Where a weekend which previously did not occur now falls in the middle of the week, it shall be deemed to occur on any two days, either

preceding or following the days on which it previously occurred provided they are not the same days upon which it previously did not occur.

As Nicky commented, 'It can happen whenever you want, on any day of the week, provided it is none of them.'

As has been pointed out elsewhere, it is better to have no laws at all than to have them written with such abundance and nonsense. The more that is written, the more there is room for argument, legal and otherwise, often leading to long-winded, expensive court cases. Often these cases are by one set of authorities against another set with us, the taxpayers, picking up the huge costs of both sides. It is easy to spend other people's money when you are given a free hand and when the result of such cases is of no real importance to those initiating them. Their jobs and lives continue as before. Often the only people to gain from increased regulations are the administrators.

Lawyers, of course, frequently get blamed for delays and sometimes it is justified, but often not. When I started in practice, there was a simple system in place for debt recovery. It was called the Small Debt Procedure. However, instead of reforming it simply by increasing the limits, which would have been easy and had happened before, the Civil Servants decided to change the thing totally and introduced complicated and over-regulated procedures which delayed things considerably. Similarly, in the criminal courts, the procedures have been changed, in many cases unnecessarily, and hugely complicated rules have been introduced. There is a new thing called the Intermediate Diet, which requires the Fiscal, the Accused and his solicitor all to make an extra appearance in court, between the time when they plead not guilty and the time of the actual trial, simply to confirm that they are still pleading not guilty. The expense of this must be colossal and it could very easily be streamlined to save such a dreadful waste of court time. I was once speaking to a temporary Sheriff who had to travel 100 miles to Dundee to hear seventy cases, all of which simply confirmed that the accused were still pleading not guilty.

My first example of the incompetence and delay caused by officials was perhaps something I deserved. At the time when I graduated, the two years of compulsory National Service were coming to an end. While at university, I was entitled to automatic deferment, although the Civil Service rules stated that if you were not at a recognized educational establishment, you would not get deferment but you could get postponement. One difference was that for postponement you had your medical in readiness for call-up but in deferment cases the medical was left until the time at university, or whatever it was, finished.

While sinking a few pints one evening with a student colleague, who later became a leading Scottish Sheriff (I won't name him!) he gave me a tip that if I enrolled in a thing called a Diploma in Administrative Law and Practice, I could do it over a two-year period, get automatic deferment and, with luck, National Service might be finally abolished before the diploma ended. He did point out that the course was a short one which could be done in a year, but suggested I tried for two. I therefore wrote to the National Service authorities in June to explain to them that in September I was intending to start a two-year course doing that diploma and I asked for automatic deferment. In December, three months after I had begun on the two-year basis, I was told that deferment would not be granted for two years but only for one. That was an understandable decision but it was, of course, too late, as it was impossible to reschedule the diploma. I could not understand why they could not have dealt with such a simple matter efficiently and told me before I began that they would only allow me one year. Eventually, after a lot of unnecessary correspondence, they conceded that they should have advised me properly from the very start and that therefore, grudgingly, they would allow the two-year deferment.

In due course, the time came for my second medical prior to call-up. I had passed the first a few years earlier, but this time, with the help of a doctor who was keen to keep people out of the army if they had something better to go to, I failed on the grounds of nervous dyspepsia and breathing difficulties. I explained that I suffered regularly from upset stomachs and, on occasions, from being rather out of breath – both of which were no doubt explained by normal student activities the previous night.

The other thing I looked at in my student days was Industrial

Relations. I was not at all surprised to read that it was not money but working conditions which were at the root of most industrial disputes. I have always had an inherent belief that if you treat people properly they will usually reward you – an obvious and simple lesson that far too few people in business have bothered to learn. How, for example, can you force a typist to type twice as quickly as she wants to?

I recall hearing of a bank manager in Hawick who was nearing retirement after many years there with the same bank. He was suddenly posted to Stirling against his will but reluctantly agreed to go, provided that he could keep his house in Hawick, where he intended to retire. He would commute to Stirling. This was refused on the grounds that the bank liked its members to be part of the local community. Eventually, the unfortunate elderly manager succumbed, sold his house in Hawick and paid a great deal more with a higher mortgage in order to buy a house in Stirling of a similar standard to the Hawick one. Within two months of his arrival there, he was made redundant because the bank decided to reorganise its systems.

In Oban we hear of people being brought here by large institutions and then being made redundant and left where it is not as easy to get the same kind of work. These feelings of resentment are accentuated when you read of the huge golden handshakes and big pay-outs to the so-called top guys in business. These seem to happen even when those big chiefs have not served the organization well. There was even the case of a local authority who paid a large sum in compensation to a man they sacked when they discovered that he had only obtained his job with them by giving false qualifications, to which he was not in any way entitled. Would it not have been more appropriate for him to have compensated the local authority in question? Is it any wonder that people employed by large institutions do not find it easy to accept that there is not more money available to cover a modest pay increase.

The pulling down of Oban's railway station offended many people – another unwelcome authoritarian decision. Fortunately, however, the train service has continued to operate so far and it is desperately needed. It is under threat from time to time. One thing that might make it more popular would be if the journey time to Glasgow were cut to two hours compared to the current three. That might encourage many to leave their cars behind. It should be possible to achieve that time because I am told that was all it took when the train was first introduced in the late nineteenth century. Obviously, the more people who use the train the better the chances that the service will remain with us. The worry is that the authorities sometimes make their services unattractive so that people do not use them. This then leaves them with an excuse to kill them off by saying, 'There was no demand for it.'

Targets, an unwelcome introduction from America, are the root cause of much bullying and unnecessary tension in business these days. Now it is not just in business but in organizations like health and education as well. I first met targets at a Shelter campaign meeting in Edinburgh in 1970 when I was a volunteer organizer for the North West Highlands and Islands. At the time, they had working for them a youngish lady from America who was appalled to hear that the Oban Shelter Group was arranging a coffee evening/folk night without setting a target.

'Well,' I countered 'we do have a sort of a target. We are hoping to raise about £200.'

'That's not good enough,' I was told. 'You have to set a target and it has to be well above what you can reasonably expect to make.'

I pointed out that our psychology must have been different from hers, because if our local committee members raised, at any function, much less than we thought was possible, we would be upset. We obviously did not need the sort of motivation that Americans seemed to require. I refrained from saying that it appeared to me that their way of doing things was to go around kicking each other's backsides as a way of encouraging people into action. We Scots, and especially Highlanders, do not respond to that kind of treatment. It usually has the opposite effect.

The next time I heard about targets was a few years later when I met up with a former university friend who was then working in England with a prominent English bank. He explained how his colleagues hated the system, which put them under a huge amount of stress, with threats of job loss if they did not produce the level of new money or new borrowings which their masters decreed. These levels were set, not by an understanding of what was sensible but by what the bank wanted so they would look good on the Stock Markets.

'It's all a charade anyway,' he confided in me. 'What we have to do if it looks as if we won't reach our set targets is to lend money to each other so the figures look good on the particular date and then have them repaid before any interest is due. It's all a stupid game.'

I was once taken to lunch by a local building society manager, who usually had a sensible, relaxed and laid-back attitude to life.

'I suppose you are only taking me to lunch to get some money out of me,' I said rather unkindly.

'Don't be ridiculous. I don't want any more money in the branch this month. I've already had too much. They will simply lift my targets for the same month next year and I will have terrible trouble and stress trying to meet them. Keep your money to yourself. I'll tell you when I need any.' So we had a very civilised lunch with no talk of the crude topic of money.

Now targets are being introduced into the criminal prosecution service with an aim to increase the number of convictions. That's worrying. Are they going to invent crimes and have people wrongly arrested just to keep the figures up or are they going to manufacture evidence (even more) just to ensure more convictions? You can't have justice if you have to decide in advance how many people will be found guilty. And what about the unfortunate refugees from other countries fleeing from horrific tortures and threats to life, many of whom have seen their own family members murdered in front of their own eyes? We hear that the number of such people who are to be refused sanctuary here is to be increased. How can you equate justice with that? Either they should be allowed in or they should not. You cannot dispense impartial justice while looking at figures.

Perhaps it is time that targets were exported back to America with a suggestion that they should be used in only one circumstance: that each day there should be an increase in the amount of goodwill they spread across the world. That way they might begin to 'unbreed' terrorists.

In January 1987, I attended a public meeting, which was called by sufferers of Multiple Sclerosis and their friends. Many people with that illness found that having treatment in de-compression chambers, of the kind used by divers when suffering from the bends, could help to alleviate some of the problems. A chap by the name of Phillip James, a PhD from Dundee, helped by Charles Butterworth, who lived in this area and whose own wife suffered from MS, made the discovery. The Oban meeting was addressed by one of his colleagues, Gordon Gillies, who had travelled well over 100 miles to address our meeting in order to explain the benefits of the chamber. He pointed out that he could not possibly have driven himself and attended our meeting without the benefits of the chamber treatment he was getting, which was keeping some of the effects of MS at bay. In particular, his balance, vision and incontinence, all of which he had suffered with MS, had been kept under control. Many of the sufferers in this area were, at that time, having to travel to Maryhill to get the benefit of the chamber there, but sometimes these benefits could be nullified by the travelling involved.

It was a few years before the Oban chamber was able to get going and it has been very well used, not just by MS sufferers but by those with leg ulcers, cerebral palsy and other problems. In fact, recent research showed that 95 per cent of a selection of people questioned after suffering from strokes showed that they or their family members believed that there had been quite significant improvement in their condition because of treatment in the chamber. My wife Heather is one of the many volunteers at the Oban centre and I find it difficult to understand why the medical people cannot give support to it, at least in some shape or form. They consider that the benefits are pure imagination but if people feel the better for having chamber treatment, what can be wrong with that? I once asked my friend Dr Ronnie Frew what he thought about the chamber and got this answer: 'It doesn't do any bloody good. But I will tell you something. If I had MS, I would trample everyone else to death in the rush to get in first.'

I once asked a friend from university days who had retired after forty years in general practice, what he thought of hyperbaric chambers and their help to MS and other sufferers. He confessed to have had very little experience of them and felt he could not comment. But he did add, 'The more I worked in general practice, the more I felt the need for alternative medicine.' It must be said, of course, that treatment in the chamber may not be of help to everyone with MS. Some have had adverse effects and some have found it of no help at all. But that surely is not a reason for denying the benefits to those who are helped by it, whether for real or by imagination. There are enough chambers in operation throughout Scotland to prove how beneficial they are to many people. They have to be run, however, by voluntary efforts because the authorities refuse financial support for them.

There is a brilliant designer and inventor by the name of Professor Stephen Salter at Edinburgh University, who has already come up with a number of great devices. For some years he has been working on an apparatus called the Dervish Landmine Clearance System. It is claimed that, when fully developed, it will be the quickest, cheapest and safest way of ridding the world of landmines. There are millions and millions of them lying around all over the world and it is estimated that it will take several lifetimes before they can be got rid of. Meantime, they are a source of constant danger to anyone having the misfortune to live anywhere near any one of them. People, often children, are being blown to pieces as they go about their normal daily routines or games. If they are lucky, they may only have a leg blown off. Lucky to have a leg blown off? What have we allowed this world to become?

Despite all this, Stephen Salter has not been able to get the financial support he needs from the authorities, even although his device is already at a very advanced stage and has been shown to operate successfully. Those who believe that there are vested money interests in trading in arms of all horrific kinds will not be surprised by the resistance which has been experienced by people like Henry Disney, a Cambridge academic, who has worked voluntarily as a fund raiser for the Dervish for some years.

There cannot be many people who have not experienced or heard of the problems that teachers and health workers are now experiencing because of increased management and red tape. I was talking once to a very committed primary school teacher in Oban who eventually retired because he could get nowhere near the children whom he loved to teach. His whole time was taken up in form filling and regulatory red tape. In fact, it went further than that when, following a visit by the school inspectors, he was rapped on the knuckles because he 'showed too much care and concern for the children'. How many more times am I going to hear someone say, 'I wish they would leave me alone to get on with my proper job.'

Years ago all letters from Civil Servants, however offensive, demanding or dictatorial they were, ended, instead of the now usual 'Yours faithfully', with these words: 'I remain, dear Sir, your most obedient servant.' A slightly eccentric client I once had in Glencoe was in receipt of many such letters and always ended his replies by saying, 'I would remind you, dear sir, that you have the honour to remain my most obedient servant.' Those elected by the people and the officials they take on to help with their functions should remember who pays them and who they should be answerable to. Some such people find it far too easy to ignore us and to spend our money too readily. Thomas Jefferson once said, 'When a man assumes a public trust, he should consider himself a public property.' They should also remember the title to this chapter and the simple fact that they will never know what's best for us unless they ask and listen.

II

'We had a dream'

It wasn't that long ago. Several of us, all supporters of the Shelter Campaign group in Oban, were making visits to the slums of Glasgow to see for ourselves how bad the situation actually was. Angus Simpson was certainly there when Mrs Devine kindly volunteered to let us see the dreadful conditions in which she was being forced to live. It was a one-roomed home in a tenement which should have been demolished decades earlier. It should certainly not have been possible to find it towards the end of the 1960s. There was no inside toilet, no bath and no heating and there were more broken than intact windows. All that was bad enough, but there was one thing we had never envisaged. Mrs Devine saw one of us noticing the fact that her bedroom slippers were on the table, 'Are you wondering why my slippers are not on the floor?' she asked and went on to explain that the room was so damp that if she left her slippers on the floor, they were filled with snails by the morning. That left a permanent impression on Angus, who often recalled Mrs Devine living in 'the most undivine circumstances you could possibly imagine'.

Fortunately, nowadays it is not easy to find such extreme examples of bad housing but no one should be complacent. The concentration on improving the condition of homes has not reduced the number of homeless people. Quite the opposite, in fact. It is now commonplace to see people sleeping rough on our streets with no protection from the weather and liable to all kinds of abuse and attacks – sexual and otherwise. I once joined others in a sleep-out to draw attention to the problem and to raise funds. Despite it being mid-summer, it was not in any way a pleasant experience, even although I knew that when

6.30a.m. arrived, I would be able to go home and have a hot bath. Also, I have to admit that I popped into the office in the middle of the night to use the loo. How can the homeless ever make themselves presentable at a job interview, I wondered. Do not ever allow yourself to imagine that it is only drinkers and drug takers who end up on the streets. Though, after even my own very brief experience, I could well understand how people would turn to any kind of solace and oblivion to enable them to cope with such horrors day after day, night after night. Remember also that now, with so many more marital break-ups, children can often be forced out of what was their secure home with no provision being made for them. Step-parents are not always willing to live with adult or near-adult strangers who are not their own. There are numerous examples of the parent's new partner saying in reference to the child of a previous relationship, 'Either he/she goes or I go.' When the child is only two, few mothers would have difficulty in deciding between partner and child, but when the child is twenty-two and the parent is also two decades older, it can be a very difficult decision. Some of us do not want to be alone and that feeling can get stronger as the years roll on.

Our Shelter group visit to Glasgow also showed the importance of seeing things for ourselves. Reading about things is often not enough. There were at least two things which we were ignorant about at the time. One was that it was not just Glasgow that had a problem with slums; later I saw far worse conditions in a part of Dundee only eleven miles from where I had been brought up in privileged isolation. The other thing was that Oban itself had a major problem, which we did not then realise. It was not a new problem for Oban. I later heard of a manager of a woollen shop being posted to Oban in the 1920s from the Borders. He asked the permission of his bosses to stand for the local Council but was refused: 'If you get on to the Council, you will be plagued all the time with people looking for homes and you won't have any time left to work for us.'

Another thing I discovered from the visits to Glasgow's bad housing areas was that it was wrong to regard the problem as one just for the people of Glasgow. One of the first people I met in Glasgow's slums came from the island of Lewis. Scotland's communities (and the world's) are too small for anyone to say: 'That's their problem, it's nothing to do with us.'

Later on I was made to realise that one of the reasons why we as housing volunteers sometimes encountered hostility from the authorities was that we were drawing attention to their failures to produce the homes which they were duty bound to provide. One example came when a member of our local Housing Association, Bill Gregory, sensibly suggested that the Council help us in a joint venture to establish a caravan park as temporary accommodation for the homeless. The site was available and all that the Council was asked to do was provide the access, water and drains, which could serve the caravan park for as long as it was needed and which could then be the basis for a proper housing development when the money was available. This was rejected, which hardly surprised us, because by then we had become used to the unwillingness of authorities to support new initiatives. Presumably our caravan idea would simply have drawn attention to the number of people without proper homes.

The first director of the Shelter campaign nationally, Des Wilson, a New Zealander, brought his own style of leadership, which involved an understanding of the press and how to get the best out of them. On one occasion, after seeing some appalling housing conditions in Northern Ireland, he managed to negotiate with Liverpool Council that the prefab houses which they were in the course of replacing, but which still had a reasonable lifespan remaining as acceptable housing, could be made available to the local authority in that particular part of Northern Ireland. Anticipating officialdom's likely reaction to being offered cast-offs from Liverpool, he crossed the Irish Channel having alerted the press, who used his story under the headline: 'SAVIOUR DES ARRIVES WITH HOMES FOR THE HOMELESS'. After that, the authorities could hardly refuse.

I once met Des at a Liberal conference in Inverness. In a couple of minutes I tried to explain what an effect he and the Shelter campaign had had on my life. He smiled before replying, 'It is a charge to which I am happy to plead guilty.' Much later on, I was honoured to have as a friend The Rev. Bruce Kenrick, who moved to Argyll in his later years and who had been one of the main people responsible for setting up the Shelter Campaign in 1968. He had been working with a housing group in the Notting Hill area of London providing relief to many. In those days, the Notting Hill area was notorious for its bad housing. Less than forty years later it became *the* place to live. Along with others, Bruce worked to launch a national campaign to expose the scandal of the bad housing which was still being experienced in the country nearly a quarter of a century after the Second World War had ended. Bruce's own quiet faith was inspiring and I could have done with his guidance about life much earlier.

One of the things which had motivated me to get involved with housing problems (regarded at the time as Britain's biggest social injustice) was that many came into my legal office looking for long-term tenancies. We never had anything available and, because of pressures on my time, I paid little attention to their needs. In fact, one day I had been particularly impatient with an enquirer and the following night on television there was an excellent Panorama programme about the fact that professionals involved in housing were often wholly uninterested in the needs of those who had to rent. I did not feel very proud of myself.

As Angus Simpson commented when he retired after twenty-seven years of voluntary efforts for the homeless, it had not initially dawned on us that more homes were needed here as well. But our work with the Shelter campaign made it clear that Oban's needs were as great as and often far greater than many other parts of Scotland. We found that a lot of young people were leaving our Highland area, not because they could not find work but because they could not find a place to live. House prices, particularly at the lower end of the scale, were often twice as high as in many other parts of Scotland. All communities need their young people and there was a danger of Oban becoming a place dominated by the idle rich and wealthy retired incomers.

The iniquities of our society were brought home to me at that time by a very wealthy client who lived in Sutherland and who already owned vast areas of land and properties there. He phoned me one day with instructions to buy a largish house, for what in today's market would be worth something approaching £400,000. Obviously, as his solicitor, I needed to know for what particular purpose he was wanting to buy this expensive property.

'No particular reason. I just thought it would be nice to own something on the other side of the loch for a change.'

I had this dream that, instead of him spending that money on what seemed to be a totally unnecessary purchase, he would donate it to our Shelter Group in Oban so that we could build some flats for the homeless. After all, when the Oban Housing Association did get started in 1971 its first block of twelve flats costs less than £50,000!

With such a divergence of mind between me and my wealthy client in Sutherland, it was perhaps not surprising that he soon removed his business to somebody more on his wavelength. Also, I have to admit that I had been involved with Edinburgh solicitors in a Court of Session action on his behalf over a disputed boundary involving an equally wealthy neighbour. It seemed a trivial matter to me but a QC whose advice we sought recommended that my client should pursue a court action with all vigour to establish his rights. A few days before the court hearing was to start, the counsel who had given the favourable opinion received another case, presumably of more benefit to him, and we were therefore left with a new counsel, who was probably superior anyway. Unfortunately his immediate comment was, 'You do realize don't you that you do not have a snowball's chance in hell of winning this case?' The client, nevertheless, decided to continue and duly lost, having to meet heavy expenses, which in today's terms would be something approaching £20,000. I sort of apologised to him, not that anything was my fault, and got the reassuring reply, 'The money doesn't matter. I now know that I cannot walk on that piece of ground any more.'

Interestingly enough, at the same time that my landowner's case was proceeding, a criminal trial involving forensic detection began in the High Court just along the corridor. I sneaked off more often than I should have done – not that my services were needed in the land dispute case – to hear a case which involved, for the first time, the conviction of a murderer on the basis of the teeth marks which he had left on his unfortunate victim.

After my inevitable replacement, my former wealthy client had the gall to phone me one day.

'I want you to do me a favour. I have lost the telephone number of my new solicitor in Edinburgh. Kindly look up your records and advise me of it. Phone me back as soon as you can.'

I was enraged, but I complied and gave him the information. What should I do, I wondered. Sending him a bill would have looked both petty and pointless because, with his wealth, it would have been like asking a baker for a crumb of bread. I therefore decided to try and forget about it, but it continued to niggle. At last I got a welcome phone call from a very close friend, David Macpherson.

'It's time we paid you another visit. Can we come up some time next month? I am still determined to catch my first ever salmon.'

'That would be great. Furthermore, I think I know where I can get you some free salmon fishings.'

I put the idea to my wealthy former client and was given a brush-off along the lines of, 'I'll have to think about it.' I knew that he would not seek any further unpaid favours from me.

A very nice ex-army man who was involved with me in a local charity was also not immune from the desire to look for unpaid favours. When his wife died, he phoned me asking for my advice as to how to go about getting a valuation of her furniture so that he could provide his Edinburgh solicitors with the necessary information to administer her estate. I do not think he liked my reply: 'You get advice from the solicitors you are paying to do the job.'

That may have seemed unnecessarily rude and unhelpful but if I had once allowed him to think that he could disturb me whenever he wasn't clear about something his Edinburgh solicitors were saying, I might as well have moved into his home to be permanently at hand to help. Another local character used to pride himself on getting free advice from whichever solicitor he happened to bump into in the street. Eventually he stopped asking me after an encounter which went like this:

'You don't mind me stopping you and asking for free advice, do you?'

'Not at all, Edward. As long as you appreciate that whenever I give free advice, it is always wrong.'

At last the local Shelter supporters managed to do something practical for those who were so desperately in need of homes in the town.

Mainly these were newly-married couples who could not afford to buy a home and did not qualify for Council housing because they had no children. Advice being given at the time by Council officials was simple: 'If you want a home, go and have a baby.' Of course they were only applying the directions of central government but it was an utterly crazy system and all it did was to force couples into having children when they were not ready for them, simply so that they could put a roof over their heads. We came across numerous examples of couples living in caravans or other appallingly inadequate housing with no heating, no running water and no inside toilets or baths. Many others were having to stay with one set of in-laws, which no one wanted. Some were sleeping on their friends' floors. Others were in winter lets, waiting to be kicked out once the tourists arrived.

Local surveyor Malcolm Michie, who was another member of the Oban Shelter Group, came to see me one day.

'We have got to do something for local young people here with nowhere to live. Why don't we form a Housing Association and get some government grants?'

'OK,' I said. 'You build the houses and I'll do the admin.'

After Malcolm's untimely death, I was both interested and surprised to learn that he had been instrumental in initiating a number of other local organizations. He appeared to have the ability to recognize the things that needed to be done and at the same time ensure that they happened.

The first director of the Scottish Federation of Housing Associations was an inspiring, charismatic leader by the name of John Davidson – yet another to die before his time and who was much needed on earth. John had a way of manipulating people with great charm – not for his own ends but simply to ensure that some vital aspect of housing work was achieved. Once I read a minute of a meeting I had been at which John had prepared and which, to my surprise, read as follows: 'It was agreed that detailed figures would have to be produced to enable further consideration of the proposal. Graeme Pagan offered to provide these a week in advance of the next meeting.' I phoned John to complain, saying that I had no recollection of making any such offer.

'I know. But there was no use leaving the minutes open; otherwise we would never have got anywhere and I thought you were the man to do that.'

On another occasion, I had a phone call from him asking me to chair a meeting in Glasgow on some aspect of housing in which I was not in any way involved and which I knew nothing of.

'You've got the wrong man, John; I have no experience of this.'

'That's exactly why I am asking you to chair this meeting because you will have no axe to grind and you will be able to do it impartially. I have spoken to Bill Law [who, incidentally, had been instrumental in helping to get the Oban Housing Association formed] and we both think you are the ideal man for the job.'

Reluctantly I agreed, but as the meeting date got nearer, I began to worry. I then noticed that there was to be another meeting about the same problem in Edinburgh the night before mine. I decided it was time I had a day off and also time that the two older children visited their grandparents. I thought that if I attended the Edinburgh meeting I would at least know something of what I would be facing the following night. After the Edinburgh meeting, I was talking to John Davidson when Bill Law came up.

'Who is chairing the Glasgow meeting tomorrow?' he asked.

'Graeme's doing it.'

'Could Peter not manage?'

I cannot describe the look that John gave me. It was a sort of apology but at the same time saying 'I'm sure you know why I conned you into doing it.' In any event, he was as totally disarming as ever and I took no offence. I don't think anyone could with John.

I once attended a dinner at Stirling University during the annual conference of the Scottish Federation of Housing Associations. The guest speaker was George Thomas (later Lord Tonypandy), a former Welsh Labour MP, who became a well known Speaker of the House of Commons partly because of his distinctive voice. He told of an occasion in the 1920s when he had been visiting a part of his constituency on a dark, snowy December afternoon. Outside an old folks' home he had found an elderly couple sitting on a bench holding hands. He remonstrated with them, saying that if they did not go inside they would both die of pneumonia. He was humbled by their reply.

'Once we go inside, we are separated with the men in one part of the home and women in another. We would just like to be together for a wee while longer.'

During the course of his speech, George Thomas kindly praised the work of the Oban Housing Association. Afterwards, I asked the chairman for the evening, Bill Law, how on earth George Thomas had heard about us.

'What happened was that, halfway through the meal, George asked me to tell him something about one of the more rural Housing Associations. I could not think of any and then I saw you going out for a pee and that reminded me about Oban.'

I was glad that my weak bladder had some beneficial results.

George Thomas's story from the Welsh eventide home would no doubt have been dismissed by some delegates on the basis that that sort of thing did not happen anymore. But now we are finding that with many elderly care homes being centralized, older couples are often being split up and separated by a distance of many, many miles when one of them has to go into a home. Therapeutically, it would be of huge benefit to both if they were to continue to see each other on a daily basis and not just once a month or whenever they can manage the journey. How cruel it is to separate couples at that late stage of their lives.

Fortunately for the creation and future success of the Housing Association, not all landowners were like the former client I fell out with. Madam MacDougall of MacDougall was the principal benefactor of the association and on being asked, immediately agreed to donate enough ground to us for our first twelve-flat development. Without her we might never have got started at all. How wonderful it was in those early days, when we were trying to persuade the authorities to release the public grants, to be able to say when they and other sceptics asked, 'Where on earth will you be able to find ground in Oban to build on?' 'We've already got a site.'

The demand for housing was proved yet again by the more than a hundred applications which we received for our first twelve flats. The Rev. Hamish MacColl, always a vital part of our housing activities, and I went to see Madam MacDougall and explained about the demand for flats, which was still colossal. Without hesitation, she agreed to donate further ground for another development. We also got her permission to call the first development MacDougall Court and the second development Grahame Court, after her late husband, Leslie Grahame MacDougall, who had himself been an architect.

Madam MacDougall's generous cooperation was so vital. One year after our first twelve flats were allocated, one of them became vacant and we advertised for new tenants. We received eighty-seven applications, one of them being from a couple with a three-year-old child who had applied to us the previous year. They had been married for four years but had been unable to find a proper home. They were still living in a derelict tenement, fifteen miles out of Oban, which should have been demolished years before. They were just about the only people still living in what had been two blocks, with a total of twenty-four flats. It was not only the horrible conditions which caused concern, but the fact that they were more than a little isolated, which caused great difficulties to the husband in getting to work. He had a good job and he was determined to hold on to it. Fortunately, the committee was unanimous in deciding that the vacant flat we had should be allocated to them. It was quite late in the evening before our meeting ended, but I decided to give the couple the good news as quickly as possible. I had to struggle through an unlit tenement, negotiate several pools of water and avoid one or two rats or mice before finding them. The next morning they were at my office almost before it opened to get the keys to their new home.

'Where's the kid?' I asked.

'After you left us last night, we started packing immediately and stayed up all night. Tracy stayed up to help as well. We're not going back. She has now crashed out and is at my mother's.'

If you are wondering why they did not qualify for a council house when they had a child, it was because they were regarded by the authorities as already being housed. Some home!

A few years later, I called on another couple living with their child in a wholly inadequate caravan to offer them the tenancy of one of our flats. Their child was also about three years old and when I arrived she was playing with an older girl. It was Tracy. She said she remembered me and, as I left, she was adopting that delightful characteristic of assumed adulthood, explaining to her younger friend what would be involved in the removal and what her new home would be like.

Many years later I met Tracy's mother, Cathy, in the street and we recalled her early home, if it could be called that. She reminded me that one of the rooms in that awful flat was totally unusable because the ceiling had fallen in. It was also the case that they couldn't get water in their own flat and that they had to collect water from one of the few remaining flats which was still occupied. Cathy was very glad to hear that her terrible experiences were not being forgotten.

But it was not always happy endings. Angus and I have never forgotten another man, living with his family in another sub-standard caravan, who committed suicide the week after he missed out on an allocation. He had been experiencing other difficulties as well but maybe getting a decent home would have been the encouragement he needed to turn his life round. There was little danger of the Housing Association Committee becoming smug and complacent. When, twenty years later, the authorities took it upon themselves to dictate and further regulate our activities, they forced us to adopt a points system for allocations despite our own system having been shown to have worked fairly and impartially. From then on, all decisions about allocations would be made by computers and robots, thereby removing all flexibility and human compassion. Perhaps that was the idea.

I was told by a number of sources over the years that Madam MacDougall was proud to be associated with the Housing Association, which was just as well for me personally. When one of our later developments next door to MacDougall Court was nearing completion, I was very satisfied one lunch break to visit the project and to see the roofers finishing off their side of things. Returning to my desk, there was a letter from our lenders' solicitors suggesting that we owned only half of the site on which the new development was being built. 'Absolute balderdash,' I said to myself aloud before going back to look at the original title granted a few years earlier. To my horror, I found that a small area of ground which I thought we had always owned had not for some reason been included in the earlier deed plan. Nervously, I approached Madam MacDougall's local solicitor, Lake Falconer, and then had a few sleepless nights before receiving the very welcome letter: 'Madam MacDougall will be only too happy to cooperate by granting the extra title you require.'

After my initial meeting with Malcolm Michie about setting up a Housing Association, I immediately spoke to my banking friend, Cameron Sommerville, because I panicked about the sums of money that might be involved. He was always a calming influence. Later on, when we were looking for a treasurer for the association, the name of Angus Simpson inevitably cropped up because of all the stalwart work he had done for the Shelter campaign locally. But I was reluctant.

'Angus is so busy with all sorts of good causes that he can't take anything else on and I am fed up wasting time on pointless phone calls.'

Fortunately, I was told that I would have to ask him so as not to cause any offence and, as soon as he was approached, he jumped at the chance of further involvement, thereby, yet again, proving me wrong. Thereafter, he personally wrote and countersigned every single one of the thousands and thousands of cheques that the Housing Association had to issue over the next quarter of a century, as well as keeping impeccable records and handling all the money. We worked well together over all those years, with no time being wasted unnecessarily. It was all streamlined so as not to interrupt our main jobs any more than was absolutely necessary.

Like me, of course, Angus would say that the advantage of having a bank structure behind him made the job a bit easier but that did not stop him dealing with everything himself. In my case, my legal firm provided a ready-made office with telephonists, receptionists, typists and all the rest to help me with the massive administrative work that would be involved. Obviously I could not have undertaken that work if I had been a travelling salesman. Also, of course, Angus and I were lucky to be our own bosses to a large degree and did not have people breathing down our necks demanding that we spend less time on voluntary work and more on producing some money for our businesses.

Over the years a large number of people, including tenants themselves, served on the Association's committee and we had fun. One amusing occasion I recall was when we decided to mark the occasion of granting our 300th tenancy by arranging a photo call for the hand-over of the keys, with the kind and helpful cooperation of the tenants involved. Everything was set up and cameras were about to fire off when someone realized that no one had the keys. Fortunately I had my car keys, which were used as a substitute. It brought to mind a story from a friend of mine who gate-crashed a party in Glasgow. As the guests gathered, the car keys were thrown into the middle of the room and my friend thought he was going to be in for an interesting and certainly different experience. However, it turned out that it was a party of environmentalists, who were taking a common pledge to save petrol by walking home.

The constant battles with officialdom, whose people often behaved as if they were trying to put us off, was a constant irritant. Angus recalls the first meeting the association had with the Oban Town Council when the Provost welcomed us with an attitude which was not exactly friendly and which certainly displayed ignorance.

'I understand that you are here to tell us how to solve Oban's housing problem. We have been trying for years and years. What is your magic formula?'

I explained that he had got it wrong. We had no secret remedy; we simply wanted to try to help by providing a handful of the many, many extra homes that were needed and that we were asking for cooperation. I told him that we knew we had much to learn from the Council and their experiences.

Perhaps I should admit that my own fury at the injustices of the housing situation and my reaction to the unfeeling bureaucracy which we encountered may have antagonized various authorities over the years. Eventually, when our voluntary efforts were finally brought to an end by officialdom, I asked Oban accountant David Mudie, who had given a great deal of good guidance to the association over the years and who was always very straight, 'Do you think it is my fault that the authorities seem so determined to kill us off?'

'Not necessarily,' he replied, 'but it has to be said that sometimes you do not use your diplomatic skills to the best advantage.'

We laughed at his understatement as to how I sometimes reacted. I have often thought that if ever Oban had a competition to choose the best guy in the town, David would probably win.

Mary Faccenda was secretary of the association for twelve years and, as with Angus, her common sense and calmer reaction to various things that worried or enraged me were characteristics I needed alongside. Sheila Walton took over from Mary for five years before being succeeded by Frances Black. Frances also did a tremendous job like Mary before her. Frances will always be remembered for the vital work she did in establishing the Hameart holiday flat, which we set up to provide free holidays in Oban for cancer sufferers and carers. I worked with Mary on a number of things and we had the same attitude to nearly everything, which made it such an excellent relationship. There was just one thing that we did not agree on and that was publicity. Some love publicity, others hate it. I was in the former category and no doubt open to some criticism of being a self-publicist. On the other hand, Mary was so wary of publicity that at conferences, if a television camera was brought into the same room, her inclination was to dive under the nearest chair.

I had known Sheila Walton since she left school at age fifteen, when she worked briefly with me at my legal office. She was a lovely person but life was not always kind to her. However she had four fine kids and, after a difficult marriage, married again very happily. Tragically, only very soon afterwards she contracted multiple sclerosis. As if that was not enough, she was then struck by a particularly virulent cancer and died before she was fifty. I remember once going with Sheila and her wheelchair to a housing opening ceremony in Dunoon. It really was an eye-opener for me as to what it meant to be dependent on a wheelchair. I know that things have improved since then, but I am sure it would not be too difficult, even today, to drive around for an hour or more trying to find a place which would provide coffee and a loo for a wheelchair. My dominant memory of Sheila was her cheerful optimism and helpfulness to others. At least one member of my own family has a lot to thank her for.

The compassion and passion shown by volunteers with the housing campaigns was in marked contrast to the attitude of government and officials. I remember, at a housing conference in Stirling, hearing an address from the then Secretary of State for Scotland. I had hoped for something inspiring and encouraging. Instead I had to listen to a boring delivery of pages and pages of carefully drafted words, which took at least half an hour to read out. Sitting immediately in front of me were two faceless officials from the Scottish Office, each of whom had a copy of the complete speech and each of whom followed it through with their fingers under each word as the boring epistle was delivered. The only glimmer of hope I had was that I might witness a repetition of what had apparently happened to another politician who had all his speeches written for him and who never gave any credit to those who did the work behind the scenes. One such speech writer was on the point of retirement and had written his last ever speech for his master. He handed it over for delivery at an important gathering that night. All went well until the second last page of the speech was reached and the self-important politician carried on, 'Finally, ladies and gentlemen, there is one desperately important matter which I have to commend to you.' He then turned over to the last page and, to his complete chagrin, found that all that was written on it in large handwriting were the words, 'FROM NOW ON, YOU BUGGER, YOU ARE ON YOUR OWN.'

As will no doubt have become clear already, I am a huge admirer of Nelson Mandela. In his book, he explained how, during the treason trial in South Africa, a large number of people of different colours had been herded together in the same dock but when the day's hearings were over, they were taken to prison and segregated with different standards of treatment. He commented in his book: 'When the proverbial inflexibility of red tape is combined with the petty small-mindedness of racism, the result can be mind-boggling.' That brought to mind a number of examples of mind-boggling red tape I came across during my housing experiences. On one occasion, an urgent housing development was held back for two months while the question of the value of the ground was referred to the District Valuer for a determination as to whether it was a reasonable price. The fact that we were being given the ground and were paying nothing was not apparently sufficient to stop the referral.

Nelson Mandela's quote about bureaucracy reminded me of an incident told to me by a friend who was working with the Shelter Advisory Aid Centre. She was representing a client whose application to have a benefit backdated had been refused. It went to a hearing on appeal against the apparent injustice. The official from the DSS or whatever it was called in the '70s gave evidence to the effect that there was no excuse for the applicant not knowing about the benefit to which she was entitled and making proper application at the proper time. The cross-examination at the hearing went something like this:

'I agree that the benefit was a fairly new one but it was well publicized and thousands of leaflets were produced to draw attention to it. Your client has no excuse for not putting her application in when she should have done and cannot now get back-payments.'

'But,' countered the Shelter worker, 'I was in your office yesterday and I could find no leaflets at all relating to this particular benefit.'

'That is perfectly correct. You see, people kept taking the leaflets away so we had to put them round the back.'

I could write several books on examples of petty officialdom holding back the desperately needed homes. There was one particular official in the Scottish Office whom I will call Mr Colclough. One day, when I had been inundated with people coming into my office urgently looking for homes to rent, I decided to phone him to ask why approval for our next development had still not been granted months and months after the application had been lodged.

'The matter is still being considered. I am at a loss to understand the urgency of the situation,' was the wholly unhelpful and uninterested response.

That led to a fairly angry encounter because I felt that if he was in control of housing projects in Scotland, he jolly well ought to understand why it was urgent for people to have a decent place to sleep in at night. Nevertheless, despite our encounter, we decided that when, at long last, the houses which he had delayed were ready we should invite him to our opening party. He did not turn up, which did not surprise me but there was an explanation. The next day my phone rang.

'Mr Colclough here. I am terribly sorry I could not make your party yesterday. I did set out from Edinburgh but my car broke down at Lochearnhead. I expected to get a bus from there but I had not realized that the bus service between Lochearnhead and Oban was so poor.'

Of course, there wasn't one. Surely the officials that we pay to run our country properly have the duty to know what the reality of life is. A few months later, it was necessary for me to phone him again.

'I'm sorry, Mr Colclough is no longer in housing. He's now in drains.'

I won't repeat what I thought.

I also recall with fury an encounter with the one-time Director of Housing for Argyll. He phoned to complain that we were breaking the law by housing, in a newly-built, modern, warm, one-bedroom flat, a single mother with a five-year-old girl.

'That is illegal overcrowding,' he complained.

I pointed out that if we were illegal, the Council must have been even more illegal because, previously, that mother and her child had been living in a caravan without proper heating and where water had to be carried in cans. He did not seem to think that made any difference. Nor was he impressed by the argument that it was the mother's choice to rent a decent modern home from us. He was displaying the frequent behaviour of officialdom: 'We know what's best for them.'

When, in the mid-1990s, Scottish Homes decided that it was time to get rid of the Oban Housing Association, they gave as one of their reasons a suggestion that we did not give a good service to tenants. I produced a recent tenant survey, which we had instructed an independent organization to carry out and which gave a satisfaction level of over 90 per cent. The Scottish Homes official I was dealing with at the time refused even to look at it. Obviously, she also thought she knew what was best for other people and was not in the least interested in knowing what our tenants wanted. Eventually, despite the fact that on any decent assessment the Association had met all the criteria laid down and had a high reputation in the town, we were compelled to give up because we would not be allowed to continue unless we spent £64,000 per year on administration. At that time we were spending barely £10,000 and the extra money was not available except through huge rent increases, which were simply not possible. It was a bitter end for many of us, with 80 per cent of the committee resigning in the last year of our operations. I was told that we were entitled to appeal against the bureaucrats' findings, so I did. One day I enquired when the appeal would be heard.

'It's already been dismissed,' I was informed. 'I spoke to my superior and she said I was right.'

Hardly justice, but it seemed pointless doing anything more. We had other things to do with our lives and we didn't have to put up with authorities who were clearly determined to finish us off.

My main concern was, and remains, not for us or for the past but for all the thousands and thousands of volunteers throughout Scotland on whom millions of sick, poor and disadvantaged people have to depend. All volunteers, it seems, are now subjected to all kinds of pressures and regulatory controls. It doesn't matter whether you are trying to help a lifeboat, or an Abbeyfield home or refugee children, you will be up against unimaginable and unnecessary restrictions. Government-speak says, 'We are keen to support and encourage the voluntary sector.' What they really mean is, 'We will be happy to allow you to work for us without any pay or other rewards provided that you will accept our instructions and our regulations and our full control over everything. The ratio of paperwork to actual productive activity will be 90 per cent to 10 per cent.' This is not an attitude which will produce the volunteers the country requires and who are needed for the good of its soul as much as for the practical benefits they bring. What is particularly worrying is that some charities themselves are no longer exempt from some of these criticisms.

Between 1974, when the Oban Housing Association provided its first homes, until 2000 when it was finally abolished, we managed to house a total of about 1,000 people – people who were completely unable to find any other homes. We also provided employment for local builders and others, and produced ninety-two homes in all, which were valued at £5,000,000. Our tenants, of course, also contributed to the local Council's finances and I calculated that, in the final year alone the total Council Tax paid by them was £65,000. The fact that we did not spend very much on unnecessary administration led to a separate Charity Trust, which was able to make fairly substantial donations. Fortunately, it is still able to donate about £10,000 a year to various local and other charities in Britain and overseas. It also provided the Hameart holiday flat for cancer sufferers and carers.

Times change and the Oban Housing Association had probably run its course but there was still a lot we could have done to help some local and other people. In one way it was perhaps surprising that it lasted as long as it did. The fact that it did manage to carry on its good works for so long was down to a whole succession of caring and enthusiastic committee members over a period of years. They came from all walks of Oban life and included tenants and former tenants wanting to 'give something back'. Somehow we managed to encourage each other along, believing that what we were doing was really necessary and worthwhile. Eventually, however, we had to accept defeat. Despite the sadness of the ending, Angus Simpson summed it all up for us when he commented at his retirement party, 'I am very pleased to have been involved in such a great adventure in life.' His own burning zeal and Highland wisdom had contributed greatly.

12

Mysteries of the Air

It was Christmas Eve 1975 and a few of us were heading for the late night service. I was not to know then that, only a few miles away, an extraordinary sequence of events was beginning to unfold, which would eventually lead to my being quoted in Richard Wilson's book *Scotland's Unsolved Mysteries of the 20th Century.*

As in many small communities, Oban's ministers played an important part and we had a number of good men to choose from on that night. The Rev. George Higgins was an unusual character for a minister, but that only helped to open up religion and Christianity to many who would normally have eschewed it. So it was his church that we attended. As we left George's service we were vaguely aware of a plane flying overhead, which was quite surprising in view of the bad weather at the time, but no one thought very much about it.

The following day there was a lot of activity in the air and clearly something was happening. As Oban's part-time Procurator Fiscal, I soon got a phone call from the police to say that a plane and its pilot had gone missing on Christmas Eve after taking off from the small airfield at Glenforsa on the island of Mull. Its pilot was a man by the name of Peter Gibbs, fifty-four years of age, but looking younger than that. He was a former spitfire pilot and had at one time been leader of the BBC Scottish Symphony Orchestra. He was obviously something of an adventurer, then based in London dealing in property transactions of one kind or another. He and a lady friend had decided to spend the Christmas holiday at the Glenforsa Hotel on the island, in the course of which Gibbs was intending to suss out the local airfield and flying conditions with a view to possibly establishing a business in the area. Gibbs had hired the plane, a few days before its mysterious disappearance, from one of Scotland's great legal characters, Ian Hamilton, who lived near Oban. He was at one time a Sheriff and was then practising successfully as a QC.

Massive searches were carried out on the island and elsewhere by the police and by many volunteers, but they found absolutely nothing. As the weeks went by without anything being found to give any indication at all as to what had happened to the plane or its pilot, a number of rumours started to go round. There were suggestions of jewellery smuggling, drugs and all the rest, of which there was absolutely no evidence that the police could find. I remember receiving one call from a freelance reporter by the name of Ron MacKay, whom I had known as a very fiery campaigner on behalf of the Shelter charity. He put a number of questions to me but there was nothing that I could tell him, nor would I have done so unless it had been something that could have been given to all the press and public.

I remember Ron causing me great embarrassment once when I was sitting beside him at a conference. It involved a rather upper-class lady who did some voluntary work for the homeless but in a way which Ron certainly regarded as being patronising, paternalistic and Victorian. She mentioned in a speech that there had been a problem because of a personality clash between her and Mr MacKay – whose name she deliberately or automatically mispronounced. Ron was on his feet in a flash.

'There was nothing of the f… sort, a personality clash between you and me. It's just that you didnae get on with me and I didnae got on with you.'

One of the extraordinary things about the missing Mull plane was that whenever something turned up as if to throw some light on the mystery, it simply raised more questions than it answered. And so it was to be when Peter Gibbs' body was found four months after he disappeared. I was on a short holiday in Edinburgh at the time but had to keep in constant touch with my then secretary at the Fiscal's Office, Brenda Morrison, as well as the police, in case any emergencies arose. The phone rang and I heard Brenda's voice: 'They have found a body.'

I immediately assumed that because it was now the spring, some unfortunate mountaineer who had got lost in Glencoe in late autumn, had been found with the melting of the snows. But I was wrong. Mull shepherd Donald MacKinnon, while out on his normal rounds of the hills, had come across the body of a man lying backwards over a fallen larch. 'It was almost as if he was resting peacefully.' David Howitt, one of the last people to have seen Peter Gibbs before he took off on his ill-fated flight, recognised the clothing, including the flying boots – and Gibbs' identity was later confirmed by the dental charts. According to an *Oban Times* report at the time, even before the finding of the body the police regarded the disappearance as, 'one of the most intriguing cases they had ever had to deal with'. The finding of the body simply added to the mystery, because it was in a position only a few yards from where the shepherd, Donald MacKinnon, had regularly passed with his dog throughout the winter. Also, it was very close to where a search for Gibbs had been made at the time when the plane first went missing. Some were therefore suggesting that the body had been planted there at some time after the death, but the excellent Dr W.D.S. McLay, Strathclyde Police Chief Medical Officer, who gave a lot of forensic help in various cases in which I was involved, was adamant. He told the eventual fatal accident enquiry that 'the condition of the body was entirely consistent with his having lain there for a period of four months'.

The real mystery, in the continued absence of the plane, was what Gibbs was doing so far up the hill. The most likely theory as to the whereabouts of the plane was that it had ditched in the Sound of Mull. But why had Gibbs, after, presumably, getting out of the plane and struggling ashore, crossed the main road and started climbing up the hill before eventually dying from exposure? Dr McLay's findings were that there were no injuries on the body, apart from a small cut on the front of Gibbs' left leg. Nor, to add further to the mystery, was there any trace of salt water on his body or clothing – not even in his watch.

Dr McLay did tell me that, when people die from exposure, they often appear to have acted in a very bizarre way beforehand, as if in some kind of hysteria. He mentioned a case where someone lost in the snowy mountains had removed all his clothing before finally succumbing. He added: 'Unfortunately, we have not been able to question anybody who has died from exposure as to exactly what they were going through.'

The fatal accident enquiry at Oban Sheriff Court covered all the facts in some detail and heard evidence from Ian Hamilton and Dr McLay, among others, as well as from William Cairns, the Board of Trade Accidents Inspector and a former civilian test pilot. The enquiry unearthed nothing new and I am quoted as having said to the jury: 'Some mystery will always remain unless the plane can be found. There is nothing sinister about this incident. It was just a series of surprising happenings.'

Events proved me wrong. In November 1976, only four months after the public enquiry, the finding of a tyre and tube from a Cessna plane on the shore at the Sound of Mull, only four miles from Glenforsa Airstrip, did not bring the mystery any nearer to a solution. When proper tests were carried out, they established that the tyre and tube had been in the sea for some time until the wheel broke up. The *Oban Times* report at the time said, 'Police investigations are still continuing – bedevilled by the fact that each piece of evidence that comes to light tends to add to the mystery rather than solve it.' We were no further forward and it was to be another ten years before there were any significant developments.

Meantime, in September 1981 I made my television debut when Ludovic Kennedy headed a series of programmes about unsolved mysteries. Fortunately, my contribution was pre-recorded because my nervousness at appearing in front of the camera for the first time necessitated a number of takes. I remember being interviewed for half an hour or more and, like many others, being surprised and somewhat peeved that my contribution had been cut back to fifteen seconds, which simply related to what medical man Bill McLay's findings had been.

However, it led to a memorable family occasion, my two older children being then six and four and, being well indoctrinated, obviously wanted to see their father's brilliant television performance. We had no videos in those days but it was agreed that they would be wakened at 10 o'clock, well after they had gone to bed, in order that they could see the great moment. My six-year-old seemed to enjoy things, being especially proud of the fact that Oban itself was shown on television. The four-year-old, however, could not keep awake, except to swear vengeance on those who had disturbed his peaceful night's sleep. My daughter did not, of course, know then that in a few all too short years' time, she would herself make a career in television.

At last, in September 1986, a professional diver by the name of George Foster, while searching for scallops in the Sound of Mull discovered 'a dark shape, 100 feet down, 500 yards from the shore'. He was surprised to find the remains of a plane, the wings from it having parted company, but one was lying flat in the mud about 100 yards away. All this was only a mile and a half from the Glenforsa airstrip. When the diver had a chance to examine the plane further, he peered inside the cockpit but found no body or remains – just a large lobster. The windscreen was described as being 'completely out'.

Inevitably, some things were missing but that did not necessarily mean that someone else had found the plane first. With this extraordinary mystery however, nothing could be ruled out. George Foster's most significant finding was that the doors of the plane had been firmly shut on impact and on sinking and presumably Peter Gibbs had escaped through the smashed windscreen of the cockpit. Some had held the theory that Gibbs had managed to get out of the plane before it ditched in the Sound of Mull. This was completely discounted by most of the experts but it would have got over the problem of there being no salt-water traces on or around Gibbs' body.

Perhaps the biggest mystery was the first one. Why did he take off at all? It was a bad night; it was, of course, dark and there was no lighting on the airstrip. He had had dinner with his attractive companion with no more drink than some wine. So why on earth did he set out on a flight in the first place? Simply to test the night flying conditions, was the only explanation offered by the various witnesses. And there the mystery ends, at least for the time being, unless anything else comes to light. Having been wrong at least twice, I should probably not go as far as to say that that will be the end of an extraordinary tale, but it probably will.

And I was right to be wary of being proved wrong again because early in 2004 just as I was finishing this book, I casually flicked through ceefax one Saturday morning and was alerted by a headline: 'MYSTERY PLANE FOUND IN SEA'. Since the Cessna 150 flown by Peter Gibbs had been identified as the one found in 1986 I thought to myself 'It will be nothing to do with our mystery but I wonder where it was'. The Ceefax story however really staggered me because the location was described as being 'near Oban' and there was speculation that this was Gibbs' plane. The discovery was made by Royal Navy mine sweepers only a few miles from the site of the earlier finding. Over the next few days further enquires were made but the search was eventually called off, the Royal Navy spokesman concluding, 'we are not ruling out any possibilities but any identification of the plane at the moment is just speculation'. They were satisfied there were no bodies. But the latest finding did suggest that the plane was very similar to Gibbs' one. So yet again a new development has simply added to the mystery. Surely there weren't two missing planes! Or were there?

Before finally finishing with the amazing case of the Mull plane, it is worth recalling another of those peculiar coincidences of time. Ian Hamilton, from whom the plane was hired and who is regarded as one of the great personalities of what can often be the rather boring legal profession, is particularly renowned for his brilliant escapade, when, as a student, he was involved in the removal of Scotland's Stone of Destiny from Westminster Abbey. As Richard Wilson points out in his book, the removal of the stone was twenty years to the day before Ian Hamilton's plane went missing on Mull. A few months after its removal by Ian Hamilton and his friends, the stone was found and taken back to England. A further two decades after the Mull plane saga, the Stone of Destiny was officially returned to Scotland. Argyll and Bute's MP, Ray Michie, was asked by an English press reporter for a comment. I doubt if he understood her reply: 'I never thought Westminster Abbey was a suitable place for keeping stolen property.'

In my nearly ten-year reign as Oban's part-time Procurator Fiscal, there was only one other plane crash which, strangely, was just over a year before the Mull mystery. In that other case, two men in their thirties had travelled to Oban for a business meeting, one of them arriving by plane at Connel airfield. For some strange reason, when the two men set off together by the plane to return south, it failed to take off properly and ended up in the water at Dunstaffnage. Only one body was found, but the fatal accident enquiry which had to be held was useful in that the jury was convinced by all the evidence that both men had been killed in the accident, even if one of the bodies was not found. This meant that the missing man's death could be registered as well and his widow and family would not have to wait seven years for a Court Petition to establish his death. That is what otherwise would have been required. It can easily be imagined what terrible extra stress can be caused to families if they have to wait all that time before they can begin to sort out the financial and practical matters involved after a death – not to mention the terrible emotional turmoil. There can be many agonies in life. The disappearance of a loved one must be among the worst.

Although the purpose of fatal accident enquiries was usually just to bring things into the open and not necessarily to prove anything positively, nevertheless, it was always a responsible task on the Fiscal. However, the presence of official and experienced accident investigators in plane crashes certainly made things easier – especially for someone like me with very little technical understanding. The Dunstaffnage enquiry had one particular memorable moment and a classic example of a Highlander standing no nonsense from the sometimes out of touch members of the Scottish legal establishment. A local crofter, who also had the job of being the airstrip's Safety Officer, was questioned about various safety aspects of the airfield which may or may not have been present, presumably in an attempt to establish liability of some kind. The Edinburgh advocate abruptly abandoned his line of questioning when the Safety Officer replied – 'It is time you were advised of the extent of my duties as Safety Officer. My sole responsibility is to remove my sheep from the runway if a plane is likely to be landing.'

I remember another occasion of learned counsel being flattened in Oban Sheriff Court by a local witness. It was a slightly complicated case in that a good number of the witnesses seemed to have the same name and were related. When another similarly-named person entered the witness box, counsel decided it was time for him to enter into the spirit of things by asking, 'I presume you are the brother of the previous witness.' The current witness replied, 'No' and looked at counsel in an apparent sense of bewilderment at such a question, before adding, with a sense of timing which would have done justice to the late Tony Hancock, 'He's my cousin.'

Another much more serious air mystery also occurred in Argyll in recent times, but it was not in the Oban area and was not anything with which I was involved. It concerned the tragedy of the Chinook helicopter crash in the Mull of Kintyre near Campbeltown when, in June 1994, a large number of important Irish and other officials were on the way to a top level secret meeting. In bad weather and flying low, the helicopter crashed into the hillside. All twenty-nine on board were killed, including the two pilots. The establishment, and in particular the Air Force enquiry, decided to throw all the blame on to the two unfortunate pilots, despite the fact that there was no evidence at all to indicate their being at fault. On the contrary, the pilots had been very concerned about the safety of the machine in question and had raised those doubts with a number of people before the accident. Interestingly enough, it was the Conservative government in office at the time which refused to hold a public independent enquiry despite demands from the Labour Party. Now their roles have reversed with the Labour government refusing an enquiry. Public cynicism about politicians can be understood unless you believe, like me and others, that it is the Civil Servants who are in control of the whole show.

Meantime, the campaign to clear the pilots, in which Ray Michie has been closely involved, continues. It is categorically stated in the Air Force Regulations that no pilot should be blamed for an accident unless there is proper and clear evidence to legally establish such blame. In this case there is no such evidence. Indeed, such evidence as there is exonerates the pilots. How their poor families are coping with the disgraceful stigma that has been heaped on them by the authorities, I do not know. But I hope they can take some comfort from the fact that an independent Scottish fatal accident enquiry before a Scottish Sheriff made it absolutely clear that there was no satisfactory evidence on which blame could be brought to the two pilots. I hope that one day the authorities will learn that the more they try to pull the wool over the eyes of the public, the worse it gets. What is the reason for a cover-up in the Chinook case? One of my main political heroes, Russell Johnston, once quoted in a major speech an American president who said, 'Tell the truth and you will not have so much to remember.'

It is time the truth came out for the two pilots.

A small additional anecdote on mysteries of the air. In August 1977, from my own home, during a convivial evening with close friends, near 10 o'clock on a Saturday evening, a strange flying object was seen coming from the west, from the Morvern direction. We went outside to investigate and were struck by the unusual lights, the fact that there was little or no sound from the craft and that it was flying very low and at no great speed. I remember being amazed when it changed direction, not in a gentle curve like a normal plane but in a sudden sharp manoeuvre, like a car turning right at traffic lights.

This further mystery cannot be explained by Bowmore or Macallan. Other people in Oban saw it as well, as it flew over the Bay, and were puzzled enough to check with air traffic control at Prestwick, only to be told that they had no record of anything and that there should have been no planes in the area. Guido Faccenda, Chairman of Oban Round Table at the time, was interviewed by the local press. You may wonder why being a Round Table Chairman gave him authority to pronounce on the authenticity of UFOs. The fact is that he was the only completely sober person present at my convivial gathering, whose number included *Oban Times* editor, Stewart Fairlie.

13

'Death is not extinguishing the light . . .'

'Read that, Pagan, and tell me what the answer is'.

My apprentice master tossed a letter on to my desk, giving me the usual severe look as he left the room for the privacy of his own office. He did not like to emerge from there too often, obviously frightened of the dangers of mixing with the common herd. On one occasion I heard him say to a colleague, Brian Jones, 'Tomorrow, Jones, we leave on the 10 o'clock for Aberdeen. Kindly book two seats. A first class for me and a third class for you.' The second class had been recently abandoned, which was just as well for my apprentice master, otherwise he could have found himself on the train far too near to his staff member. Maybe it is the same attitude that causes some managers nowadays to send emails to their staff even when they work in the room next door! However, the office got its own back when the master was on a trip north to visit one of his many wealthy landed estate clients. The switchboard operator was a nice enough, doddery old man, but quite the most useless telephonist I ever came across. However, he did have the guile to refuse to accept a reverse charge call from the boss on that far away visit, explaining to the operator, 'A man in his position should pay for his own bloody calls.'

I looked at the letter. It was from a lady client living in West Byfleet in England and she was clearly very distressed. Apparently, her son had died after falling off a railway platform just as a train approached. Being England, there had to be a public hearing into the circumstances and the coroner returned the verdict that the young man had committed suicide. This was something that his mother could not accept at all. I was horrified at this early encounter with English law, setting out with enthusiasm to investigate a possible miscarriage of justice and change the coroner's verdict. However, no matter where I turned, it seemed that there was no right of appeal or review, and after weeks of enquiry and advice from the south I had to abandon my efforts on behalf of the grieving mother. There was nothing that could be done to console her.

It was not so much the fact that the coroner might have been wrong which disturbed me, but the fact that something private, like suicide, was made public. What did it have to do with anybody else, I wondered? It contrasted badly with the Scottish system of private, discreet enquiries and especially our Procurator Fiscals, who would not normally make public those things which were nobody else's business. Large insurance companies trying to escape making payments from policies in such circumstances were well able to make their own enquiries. I did not see any reason why the poor mother should not have been allowed to go to her own grave, when the time came, without carrying the stigma of her son's suicide. Surely she had the right, if she wanted, to believe that it had been a gust of wind and not a deliberate act which had caused her son to fall under the train. Faced with such agonies, why should people not be allowed to think what they like? It was said that when my jazz hero Bix Beiderbecke died so tragically young, one of his musician friends, on getting the news, simply said: 'I don't have to believe it if I don't want to.'

The unfortunate mother in West Byfleet had a logical reason for thinking that her son would not have committed suicide. At the time of the tragedy, he was on his way back from London, having gone there particularly that day to hire a morning suit for a friend's wedding. She maintained that he would never have gone to the trouble to hire the outfit if he was intending to kill himself. I later discovered that there was often no rhyme or reason for people ending their own lives – at least not one which allegedly normal people could understand.

Graeme Obree was, I imagine, Scotland's greatest ever cycling champion. He achieved a number of major international successes and was BBC Sportscene Personality of the Year in 1993. I was both sad and surprised when I read a *Herald* article about him and learned that he had suffered from mental illness from quite early on in his life, being bullied at school because his father was a policeman. He made a number of suicide attempts and on two occasions was only prevented by chance interruptions when other people arrived in places where they were not expected. He has described that sometimes he feels so depressed that absolutely nothing matters, 'but that's how this dreadful illness affects me. Sometimes I will hear other folk remark "I am a bit depressed today". But what they really mean is that they are cheesed off, they are a wee bit exasperated and wished they had stayed in bed for the day. For me though, the depression is an all pervading sense that I am entirely worthless and those nearest and dearest to me would be far better off if I was dead.' He could see no possible ending to those feelings despite there being no doubt about his undying love for his wife and children.

In the article he also explained how the pressures of success weighed on him: 'I kept worrying that if I stopped winning, I would be regarded as a failure and a flop. Although that offered me motivation at the beginning, it soon became an incredible millstone.' That made me think that those of us who are not geniuses and who are not famous have a huge amount to be thankful for. As if Obree's illness were not enough, he was also faced with another battle when the International Cycling Union took exception to and tried to outlaw his unique riding position. But eventually he won that fight. And yet, despite all these difficulties and personal problems, when a young friend of mine, Lee McKillop, who was mad keen on cycling, had a very nasty biking accident, Graeme Obree came to Oban from Irvine just to visit her in hospital and to encourage her on the road to recovery. Lee was back on the saddle far sooner than she should have been!

One of the most sadly fascinating lectures I ever attended was on the subject of suicide. It was delivered, when I was a student, by Professor Douglas Kerr, who was an expert in forensic medicine and who had also lectured to my father's class three decades earlier. He told us of one case where a father had spent the whole evening discussing the summer holidays with his wife and children. He had then filled up the booking forms and had gone out to the pillar box with the necessary cheque, only to return home and gas himself as soon as the family was in bed. What was particularly strange was that he had brought home in his briefcase that day a length of rubber piping, which he was going to have to use in his sad act.

Professor Kerr had also encountered a strange case where a man had gone looking for a friend and, on reaching the top of a tenement, had failed to find him but had instead struck up an instant friendship with a total stranger, who he had never heard of or encountered before. They spoke for some time at the top of the stairs before the enquiring man left to continue his search for his friend. At each landing, he looked up and called out something along the lines of, 'Cheerio again, so nice to meet you, we must meet up again soon.' When he was just one floor from the ground level, he called up again, saying the same thing. 'I'll be down before you,' came the disconcerting reply as the newly found friend threw himself over the banisters from the top of the tenement. No logical explanation could be found.

The first time I encountered death by suicide involved a distant cousin, who was a young schoolteacher. He was a man of great charm and charisma, who appeared to be worshipped by everybody. Young people used to flock round him and his motorbike and my father thought very highly of him. I often heard him say, 'Guess who is coming to visit – Peter.' When Peter killed himself, his brother Adrian consulted my father, both as a family friend and adviser. He was looking for guidance as to what enquiries he could carry out to discover what on earth had caused his seemingly confident brother, with a huge future ahead of him, to take his own life. Dad advised him against any enquiry, unless it would help the surviving brother in his grief. He pointed out that almost certainly he would not find any logical explanation or reason that he would be able to understand to explain the tragedy. Often it is like that.

The agony for those left behind can only be imagined, but they should never blame themselves. It is impossible to be with people twenty-four hours in the day and, if they are really determined to end it all, they will usually succeed. I had one case where a man was attempting to gas himself in his car while parked in a lay-by alongside a loch. He was disturbed at least once, but was able to escape from one good Samaritan and drive to another remote spot over thirty miles away before successfully bringing his life to an end.

Sometimes, of course, suicide can perhaps be understood. When that great comedian Tony Hancock finally ended his tragic life, he left a note which, among other things, said. 'There was nothing left to do. Things seemed to go wrong too many times.'

Like all of us, I have my downs but only once remember feeling that I was in danger of ending things. It came at a time when the lack of children had become an issue. My own attitude was very much one of, 'If children come, they come,' and I was quite relaxed about the situation, except that I knew it can be very different for some others – especially women. At the same time, I have never thought that anyone has some sort of divine right to have children, demanding scientific human intervention if necessary. Furthermore, there can be a lot of advantages in not having children and sometimes much more can be achieved in doing worthwhile things in life without them. In my case, like most or many other parents, once mine arrived, I could not envisage life without them – nor did I want to.

The chance moment which triggered me off into suicidal feelings came when I was walking in Dunoon one day on a charitable mission of some kind, in perfect sunshine, when everyone else seemed so content and adequate. I passed an empty parked estate car with children's seats fitted at the back and that was almost sufficient to propel me into a catastrophe. Another chance incident along the same lines, on the same day, could perhaps have led to that. Who knows? What is known is that more people take their own lives not at depressing times like dark winters, but at more optimistic times when everyone else appears so cheerful and happy and content and when for no good reason they feel so inadequate.

I am sure that suicide can often happen very much on the spur of the moment. That fits in with perhaps the most common reaction afterwards from those people who knew them. 'James was not the sort of person to kill himself, no way.' How often have we all heard that? Professor Douglas Kerr did explain to us that there is such a thing as accidental suicide, when attention-seekers threaten action which they do not really intend to go through with. He gave as an example the neglected wife who comes into the room when her man is watching football on the box and threatens to swallow all the pills unless he gets up to pay her some attention. As the learned professor added, 'Unfortunately, some men are very slow to get out of their chairs.'

When I first started coming across people facing bereavement, however that may have come about, I often used to deliberately avoid mentioning the subject at all in case it brought memories back to the mourner and caused tears. What stupid thinking. I have since learned, of course, that there is never any length of time when the deceased is not in the mind of their loved ones. Talking to a large number of clients who have had to consult me about administrative matters after death, I have learned quite a lot but not nearly enough.

At one of the best attended funerals I was ever at, the husband of a young teacher who had died of cancer shook hands with one particular friend outside the church where there was a large gathering of those who had not managed to get inside for the service. He then found everybody queuing up to shake his hand. I said later, 'You were a brave man standing there, shaking hands with everybody.'

'I did not mean to do that, but at least it will stop them crossing to the other side of the street in future when they see me coming.'

Naturally, funeral services are among the worst of life's experiences but when they can be celebratory of a long, worthwhile life they can ease some pain. And if some humour can be introduced, that can help as well. I remember reading in the *Scotsman* a few years ago of how, at the cemetery, a daughter had, before her father was finally put to rest, handed out an envelope to all the male mourners. They were told to open them there and then. Inside each was a £5 note with a handwritten note from the deceased attached which read, 'Thank you for attending my burial this afternoon. Buy yourself a drink with the enclosed but remember when next we meet it will be your round.' The daughter said that the smiles on the faces of her father's friends as they each read the note helped her to cope.

We are all different and we all cope differently when faced with horrors of any kind but, if there is any generalisation which could be made, it surely is that we should offer to be there if any person we know wants to talk. They can always immediately change the subject, if that is what they want. We must never decide how other people should cope. One friend, in a different part of Scotland altogether, told me that when her husband died, one member of the family, with the best intentions, decided that it would be less painful for her if all her husband's clothing was taken out of the house, which she proceeded to do. 'But,' said my friend, 'it made things worse, for whenever I open the wardrobe there is this empty half where my husband's clothes used to be. He is still part of me, so why should his clothes not be here?'

Another mistake we must not make, as I did once, is to assume that because someone has spent years and years looking after an ill and dying partner, it will necessarily be a relief when the end finally comes. I tried to suggest that once and was, quite properly, corrected. 'Actually, while it may be a relief in some ways, for me it is going to be even worse than it would have been normally. After all those years looking after my husband full time, I am going to be even more lost. I just don't know what I am going to do with my time. I've forgotten how to lead a normal life.'

On one occasion, I was totally surprised when a client, again a husband whose young wife had died far too soon, came to see me about the business matters. I was really the solicitor for the family into which he had married and I did not know him at all well. Nor did I expect him to want to talk to me about his private feelings. But when I casually enquired how he was getting on he was obviously more than ready to talk, because an hour later we were still together and I learned a lot from him. What upset him particularly was when neighbours or friends were visiting and Liz's name cropped up, many would react by saying, 'It's time we were going,' and either leave or make a clumsy attempt to change the conversation totally. It made Keith feel that Liz had been some kind of criminal or someone to be ashamed of. 'To me, she was wonderful. She is still wonderful. I loved her. I still love her. She was with me. She is still with me.'

Liz had had an Aberdeen connection at one time and Keith had set himself a mission of arranging a memorial stone in special Aberdeen granite which, strangely enough, he had great difficulty in tracking down. After failing in the Aberdeen area, he tried various places in

Europe before ending up with somewhere in Fife which was able to supply exactly what he was looking for. The fact that it took so much trouble actually helped him because, as he explained, 'I felt as though I was doing something for Liz. It was like buying her a present and the more effort it took, the more worthwhile it became.'

The trouble is we cannot normally tell how other people are feeling at the time. On one occasion I remember Heather and I seeing a friend who had lost her husband walking alongside Oban Bay apparently in good form. We had a normal kind of conversation with her but, when I said something, she became tearful and went on her way. The next day I phoned to apologise for upsetting her.

'What are you apologising for? It is I who should be apologizing. I was just having a bad day.'

I told her that Heather and I thought that she was looking great, which was true, and that cheered her up.

Recently I went to a meeting of the Lorne Counselling Service to hear a bereavement counsellor explaining what his role was. The most interesting part of the evening was a very brave contribution from a man who described himself as a private person and whose only close friend, with whom he could share everything, had been his late wife. He spoke brilliantly and bravely, sharing all sorts of things with his audience, despite the fact that he had never spoken in public before. He said that his friends had been wonderful in rallying round and offering support at any time – day or night. Nevertheless, he explained, when he needed to talk, he did not want to talk to friends but wanted a properly trained counsellor. I asked him, having in mind the unexpectedly open conversation I had had with Keith, whether if he had met a friendly stranger in a pub, he could have spoken to him, rather than a close friend. 'No,' he replied, 'I needed a properly trained counsellor who I knew would listen to whatever I had to say with patience and without judgment.'

I respect that entirely, but I think it would be unfortunate if we ever got to the stage where people who wanted to talk could only do so through a proper counsellor.

Sometimes counselling is offered in ways which can make the situation worse. Children, as many have discovered, can be extraordinarily resilient and often cope without professional help – so do others. I recall the tragic death of an architect with whom I had just become reasonably friendly and who was killed by one of Argyll's ghastly barriers in a road accident. He had a very young family but the children seemed to cope well, with the young boy often saying to visitors with great pride, 'I have a dead Dad.'

Sometimes even making light of a situation can be of help. On one occasion I had two funerals more or less at the same time and I had worked out an elaborate plan whereby I would manage both, in some shape or form. That involved rushing from part of one service to my car, strategically parked alongside the Bay, so that I could join the other procession when it went by. But it never arrived. I could not understand why I had to wait so long and what the hold-up had been. A while later, when I went to investigate, I found that I had missed the procession altogether. Perhaps a large lorry pulled in to the side to let the procession pass, thereby obstructing my view. I don't know, but when I phoned the daughter at night to apologise for my absence from her mother's services, I explained what had happened.

'I am so glad you phoned. That was kind of you. Also, it is the first thing I have been able to laugh at all day. The thought of you sitting in your car and missing the procession . . .'

A friend told me of a funeral where the minister made clear his view that those who were grieving were actually displaying self-pity. In a sense they were being selfish because the person who had died had simply embarked on a happy journey to a better place. And is that not the answer when someone asks, after an especially tragic death – particularly if it involved a young child, 'How can there be a God? No decent God would allow such a thing to happen.' But that assumes that there is nothing else but the world we know. There is something else far bigger than us and far too complex for us to understand. Which is why we are told to believe as a child believes and to believe without seeing. In his excellent book *Why Y2K?* John Blanchard emphasizes very strongly that the basic meaning of 'death' is not termination but separation.

I have always felt specially sorry for a friend, Christine, whose father was killed in a road accident when he was on his way to collect her from a wedding dance out of town. It was, I suppose, natural that for a time she sought to blame herself and wished that she had made other arrangements for her journey home. But we all know that life cannot be like that. These things are going to happen from time to time if life is to be lived – and it must be. Even if we were to stay wrapped up in bed all day, we could not be guaranteed safety.

As I have said, we all cope very differently and it is not for us to judge what people want to do when faced with bereavement. I have no idea how I would cope if faced with a tragedy. My wife Heather's father died of cancer when she was just twenty. Timing – which is something over which none of us can have any control – is all-important in life and that was far too soon for Heather. When, twelve years after her father's death, I first came into her life, his death was not something she could normally talk about at all. Even now she is still affected by her loss.

One of those uncanny circumstances of life occurred in 1990 and ended up being used in a minister's Sunday sermon. In that year the two Paisley MPs died within a few weeks of each other. Given that there are 659 MPs, the death of two 'adjoining' ones at virtually the same time was coincidence enough. At the same time some friends in Oban and I were trying to set up a holiday home here for use, free of charge, by cancer sufferers and their carers. I do not know the Paisley area at all well but set out one day to help the Liberal cause in one or other of the two by-elections – it did not matter to me whether it was Paisley North or Paisley South. Reporting for duty, I was dispatched on my own to leaflet in a part of Paisley I had never been in or even heard of before. As my leafleting stint came to a welcome end, my eyes were diverted across an open field to a largish building with a minibus outside, whose driver was about to get into it. I could just make out the words on the vehicle: 'ACCORD HOSPICE'.

I stood transfixed and stared in amazement at what I had, by sheer chance, caught sight of, thinking to myself, 'That's exactly the kind of place we want to make contact with for our holiday flat.' I stared so long that the driver stopped and stared back, obviously thinking, 'What the hell are you gawping at?' Three hours later I was where I most like to be – in my Highland home, in a comfortable chair, with a glass filled with a good malt – always particularly welcome after a visit to the 'cities'. Heather, who originated from Crosslee and who lived or worked in the Paisley and Renfrew areas before moving up here, asked where exactly I had been that day.

'Paisley. Apart from that I haven't a clue.'

I described it and particularly the astonishing incident across a field to the Accord Hospice.

'I know exactly where you were. You were virtually alongside the Hawkhead Hospital. That's where Dad died.'

There had been no hospice in those days. Of all the places where I could have been sent to campaign, the chances of going to the Hawkhead area must have been several thousand against.

The coincidences continued the next day. At lunchtime I passed my office switchboard on my way out somewhere. The phone was ringing, which I would not have noticed if I had stayed at my own desk, that being my normal practice. Also, in those days, the office was closed during the lunch break. Something, however, made me answer the ringing phone.

'Hello,' said the caller, 'I'm not sure if I have the right number. I am looking for someone called Graeme Pagan. Can you help at all?'

'Yes, I am Graeme Pagan.'

'That's a lucky chance. You won't have heard of us but I work for an organisation called the Accord Hospice. We're in Paisley.'

I told him where I had been precisely twenty-four hours earlier and he was absolutely dumbfounded. He had heard something of our holiday flat proposals and was phoning to ask about it. A lot of holiday-makers have since come from the Accord Hospice to make use of our Hameart holiday flat.

During the leafleting exercise the day before, there had been an amusing incident which showed again how easy it is to get the wrong end of the stick. As I made my lonely way up and down various streets in the Hawkhead area, I was aware of two people in green, slightly ahead of me, also shoving leaflets through the doors.

'Ah,' I thought to myself, 'SNP. Why are there always two of them to one of us?' Eventually I got nearer to them.

'Be careful in that next house,' one of them called out. 'There's a wild dog in there. He'll take your fingers off.'

'Thanks,' I called back, thinking at the same time, 'Balls. It takes more than that to stop a good Liberal from campaigning properly.'

Fearlessly I approached the next letter-box and nearly lost my hand as a ferociously barking dog moved in for the kill. I just got it out in time. 'Serve me right for misjudging the Nationalists. That was good of them after all,' I thought to myself. A few streets later I wondered what their leaflet was actually saying about the campaign. Luckily a leaflet fell out of the next letter-box by sheer accident, right into my welcoming hand. I looked at it. It was nothing to do with the SNP. It was a flyer for the Co-op Bank!

Evelyn Nicoll, an enthusiastic area organiser for the MacMillan Cancer Fund, also helped with the setting-up of the Hameart holiday flat. Naturally, when I met her at a coffee morning a few weeks later, I told her about the coincidences of my extraordinary visit to Paisley. Her minister husband listened with equal astonishment. Two or three years later the phone rang on a Saturday morning.

'I'm stuck for my sermon tomorrow. What was that incredible experience you had in Paisley a few years ago?'

I used to have a particularly close friend who worked with me into her eighties. Amusingly, when Dorothy reached eighty, she got – not the first person to do so – a wholly inappropriate letter from a government department. The DSS wrote: 'According to our records, you have now reached the normal age for retirement.' Dorothy took great delight in writing back to them, pointing out that that event had actually occurred twenty years earlier. Dorothy finished her days as one of the best advertisements for Abbeyfield there could have been, because she still lived life to the full. In fact, in the first month after she moved in, she set off on her first ever visit to Leningrad!

Also, she was fearless in travelling all round Oban in her electric buggy and persuaded a close companion at Oban's Abbeyfield home to get one as well, so they were often seen together. When he died, she was inevitably very distressed. Talking with her one day I happened to remind her about a BBC religious programme which had been filmed in Oban and which had contained a shot of herself and her late companion alongside Oban Bay. It had been a very moving scene into the sunset, where Dorothy was alone in her buggy and suddenly her companion and his buggy came into view. I thought it might be harrowing for her to see that again, but on the contrary, she said she might find it consoling. We were able to persuade the BBC to send her a special tape of the programme and after that she watched it frequently, often conversing with it before and after she went out on her lonely excursions. Earlier, I had asked Dorothy whether, when her own husband had died, she had found bereavement cards rather than letters somewhat impersonal and uncomforting.

'On the contrary. It does not matter what people send. If you know they are thinking about you, it is a great help.'

I got the impression that if someone had sent her a tin of prunes, she would have been happy!

When dealing with the Executry business on behalf of clients, I often like to leave it to them as to how the administration should be carried out. Sometimes clients find it helpful to have administrative work of some kind to do after bereavements. Others find it unnecessarily harrowing to have to go into banks and building societies with the death certificates. I usually try to arrange the operation in ways which help with the bereavement process, when that is possible.

There was a brilliant article in the *Scotsman* in October 1986 by a lady called Marlena Frick under the title 'A TIME TO LIVE, A TIME TO DIE'. She wrote that article after she had read about Jacqueline Picasso, who after thirteen years of grieving for Pablo, had shot herself in the head, in the very bedroom where he had died. Marlena Frick recalled having herself been in the same position seventeen years earlier and, like Jacqueline, had brooded about the pointlessness of going on without the one you love. Eventually, she was made to realize by valuable friends that life should go on. 'Let it be his life not his death that you carry around with you,' she was told. Having shown the full article to one or two clients who apparently found it helpful, I made contact via the *Scotsman* and told Marlena Frick how I was using her article, which she was happy about. I suggested that she should consider having it published in leaflet form for use in doctors' waiting rooms and so on. I hope that what she wrote will get as wide an airing as possible.

I have a very close friend, Kay Hamilton, now living in the

Aberdeen area. She has had more than her share of sadness, including the death of a daughter, but remains very upbeat and cheerful despite having to face ill health. She described bereavement to me as, 'a burden to be carried for a little while and then quietly put down by the roadside before walking on'. Frances Shand Kydd who, of course, also lost a daughter in tragic circumstances, was interviewed on television and was asked how she coped. 'We just have to remember the Lord's words. "Let Thy will and not ours be done."' Frances is someone else who has had more than her share of knocks, despite the many things she has done to help others and what she has done for our community. I once asked her how life was then treating her. 'Not bad,' came the reply, 'but sometimes it's like riding in the Grand National and reaching Becher's Brook, only to find that you are on a Shetland pony. But you just have to get up and get on.' That in a way summarises what many feel in bereavement – very much up and down. The fact that Frances's daughter happened to be one of the most famous people the world has known does not, of course, in any way lessen a mother's grief. In fact, the public interest often brought back memories in the wrong way and some things published were, as they often are, unkind and untrue. That cannot lessen the grief.

My own sister, Judy, had to face the loss of her husband at a time when she was having a frightening problem with her own health. Fortunately, she won over the latter and has been very brave in her bereavement. One day I phoned her cheerfully before adding, 'You don't sound too good. Is something the matter?'

'I am having a bad day and I have been doing so well in coping without George.'

'Why today?'

'It just happens sometimes and today it was triggered off by the fact that I had a bad round of golf and no one to come home to moan to.'

Unsympathetically, I suggested she gave up golf, which brought back the fighting spirit in her. Fortunately she has a good sense of humour and herself laughs at a family tease at her expense. After Mother died, various items in the home had to be valued, including a painting of Judy herself (aged 8) and one of the family dog. The one of her had a nil value put on it whereas the one of the dog was valued at £5!

Another friend has found it difficult to cope whenever a regular client comes into her office because he always wears the same kind of shoes that her late husband used.

When I was at university, I was friendly with a guy called Harry Rutherfurd who went on to join his father's medical practice in Kirkcudbright. Many years later, I read of the death of his father and phoned to commiserate. 'I can't complain, Graeme. Dad had a good innings and was reaching a time when things were starting to go wrong. I'll tell you something though. What has really struck me during forty years of medical practice in a small community is the way in which ill fortune often keeps hitting the same family. It doesn't seem to be handed out equally among all of us.'

In one letter of sympathy shown to me, the writer had said to a client after a particularly tragic death: 'These are things beyond human power and understanding. Our faith in something far, far greater than the world we know must somehow be increased and not diminished by ghastly events like this tragedy. We must all look at the positive side of things and take life forward in the pursuit of what is good.'

From the day we are born, we are dying. We know from the moment we can think that we are going to have to cope with death on many occasions – that is if we live long enough ourselves. We have got to learn to accept it and to cope and not to give up our lives whenever we are faced with the death of a loved one. Of course, life will never be the same, but as Marlena Frick said in her brilliant article: 'Life is worth living, even without the one you love to share it. There are always new places to see, new songs to hear, new paintings to enjoy, new friends to make and even new lovers.'

Someone once said that they were comforted by the fact that everyone else has been there before. I am no expert but having had, mainly because of the nature of my job, many experiences with other people's bereavements, I hope it is helpful to pass some of these experiences on. Some people have gained comfort from what was once written by Rabindranath Tagore, the first Asian to get the Nobel Prize for literature: 'Death is not extinguishing the light but putting out the lamp because the dawn has come.'

14

After 300 Years – One Minute Late

We were on our way to the Island of Gigha. The 'we' were Ray Michie, Margaret and Hilary King and myself. It was not exactly a holiday, catching the ferry at Tayinloan at about 4 o'clock on a winter afternoon, by which time it was already dark. The purpose of our mission was to start off the 1979 referendum for a Scottish parliament. The meeting took place in the local primary school and it brought to mind a story of Ray's about one of her father's campaigns, when a similar public meeting had taken place in a wee school on the island of Coll. Ray's father had made it clear to the islanders how much more could be done for them by an in-touch and concerned government. The local laird responded by arguing that he was sure the islanders would not want to change anything as the Conservative MP, Sir John Bloggs, was doing such an excellent job. Ray's father was on his feet in an instant and using the Gaelic, which the laird did not understand, reminded the islanders that the ballot box was secret and that they could vote for whoever they liked. This brought a somewhat amusing response from the adult and elderly islanders seated at the tiny school desks, who banged the desk tops up and down in a demonstration of approval.

My next visit to Gigha was with Heather, almost a quarter of a century later, when we made the short crossing to the island for the day with our bikes. By that time the Scottish parliament was at last in operation. The timing was appropriate, bearing in mind my earlier visit, because the parliament had introduced legislation about community buy-outs and the islanders had recently managed to get together to achieve the purchase of their own island. Used properly the new legislation could achieve a huge amount towards the regeneration of the Highlands and Islands. But there is, of course, still much for the people of Gigha to do. While there, I generously purchased a community polo shirt for £20 (well above my normal budget!) as a contribution to the one million pounds they have got to find within a very short period of time.

What had caused me to start the Argyll group of campaigners for a 'Yes' vote in the 1979 referendum was the danger of complacency. The government, with customary wisdom, had already spent millions of pounds in getting the parliament building near the Calton Hill in Edinburgh ready, which left many with the impression that there was nothing more they needed to do to bring the Parliament into being. Maybe that was the idea. It was, therefore, vital that those who wanted the parliament realised that they still had work to do if it was at last to be won. I have been involved in quite a number of campaigns over the years. Normally they were not so much to change public opinion but to persuade people to speak out and fight for what they already believed in. Some say, 'What's the point? There is nothing we can do about it anyway.' But that is not the case. If one person speaks out, it's amazing how many more will speak out with them. We should all remember, if starting new campaigns, the experience of great people like Ghandi and Martin Luther King. They said of those who opposed them, 'First they ignored us; then they laughed at us; then they fought us; and then we won.'

I genuinely believe that, properly led, Scotland could become the greatest community in the world. That is partly because we are a small nation and already have a great sense of society. That, in turn, may be because we all seem to know each other, which usually means that we are not allowed to adopt high and mighty attitudes. If you go abroad, you will almost certainly come across someone from back home who knows someone you know. I was once visiting a brandy factory with Dad and some other members of the family while on a brief holiday in Germany. After the tour, Dad went up to the German guide to thank him and to congratulate him on his excellent command of the English language. It brought this whispered reply: 'It's not surprising, I'm from the Teacher's whisky family in Scotland and I'm just doing a student holiday job.' My friend, Stewart Fairlie, tells of a visit to Massachusetts, when at a dinner it transpired that the chef was the son of a friend he had once known in Oban. It elicited this response from one of the American hosts: 'Yea. We know all about Scotland. There are only ten of the buggers and they all know each other.'

In my experience the vast majority of Scots do have an inherent belief in what is kind and decent. I don't think we normally find it easy to be aggressive and rude to someone we know – or might know of. We were very lucky in Argyll in having as our chairman of the 'Yes' campaign Lord Kilbrandon, who had already produced a much-praised report on the whole subject of devolution and home rule for Scotland. He had also, incidentally, written a visionary report on the way to deal with children who had gone off the rails and which had led to the setting up of Children's Panels. The weekly meetings of the 'Yes' campaigners used to take place in the jury room in the Oban Sheriff Courthouse because with me being the part-time Fiscal, I held some keys. I might have got into serious trouble over that but with Lord Kilbrandon at the helm, I reckoned I was in very good company.

The campaigners were a mixed group of people from different walks of life and from different political parties, or from none. As some-times happens, we initially viewed each other with some suspicion. Eventually, by the end of the four-month campaign, we had gelled well together. Indeed, during the final meeting Lord Kilbrandon felt able to tell the humorous story about an old, pompous lord who used to sit in his London club every day in his leather seat, looking out of the window and staring blankly. Eventually, somebody asked him why he found it so interesting to sit there day after day, just glaring out of the window, to which came the reply, 'I like to see the poor getting wet.'

That brought back to me one of my favourite club stories about an equally bizarre lord, who used to go into an exclusive private club every day on his way to the House of Lords in order to use their facilities. Eventually the club committee met and decided that someone had to tell his Lordship that if he wanted to go on using their loo, he would have to apply in the normal way to be admitted as a member. The committee drew lots as to who should have the unwelcome job of advising the eccentric peer. The unfortunate member went up to the lord on his next visit to explain the situation, which he did with great deference and nervousness only to get the disarming reply, 'Good heavens. Is this a club as well?'

On my only visit to the House of Lords' own loo, I came across another strange lord – a man younger than me. He explained to me, a total stranger, that he was in a bit of a predicament. He was going to a function of some kind that evening and had ordered his 'carriage' for 9 o'clock, only to be told by his wife that she wanted to go on somewhere else and would not be going home as early as that.

'I can't accept that load of nonsense, can I?' he asked.

I gave the impression that I entirely agreed with him before rushing away to rejoin more normal company, including my own wife. I hoped she had not overheard the conversation I had just had.

The 1979 'Yes for Scotland' campaign argued that it was a once-in-a-lifetime opportunity to finally get our own parliament and that we would never have the chance again. We believed that to be true and for Lord Kilbrandon himself and many others like Michael Strathern, Wendy Wood, John Smith and John Macintosh, that was sadly the case. But some of us were lucky enough to live and fight again much later. At Lord Kilbrandon's funeral in September 1989, Bishop Holloway's tribute summed him up well when he said 'He took life seriously. But he never took himself too seriously.' There is an important message there for all of us. Interestingly, Lord Kilbrandon's many skills included playing the organ and singing. This no doubt explains in part why a grandson, Donald Shaw, later married one of Scotland's loveliest singers, Karen Matheson. Together they created the popular and successful musical group Capercaillie.

The 1979 referendum was my first real foray into political activity, if you discount an alcohol-induced student experience. In the university union one night, rather the worse for wear, I became enraged when it was announced that our alcohol supplies for the rest of the evening were about to end because it was closing time. I leapt onto the bar immediately, preaching Home Rule for Scotland and a government which would have only one policy. That would be no licensing hours at all, so that drink could be available throughout the day and night.

Suddenly I found one of the union officials at my feet demanding that I came down from the top of the bar. The next I could remember was him wiping his glasses with his handkerchief and it was alleged that I had poured my pint over him. My impression was that I had simply fallen on the slippery top. However, I was rightly suspended from the union and had to appear before the Committee of Management, which led to a letter in these terms:

> As you know, a case of disorderly behaviour in the Smoke Room Bar has been considered against you.
>
> The Committee decided that, while it deprecates your action on that evening, in view of your apology to the Committee member involved, no further action should be taken on this occasion.

Forty years later, my own son, with the same initials, was in the middle of his university career when I came across the letter by chance. I photocopied it and sent it to him with words emblazoned on it saying:

THIS KIND OF CONDUCT WILL NOT BE TOLERATED.
DAD

My son got quite a fright until he read the thing properly and spotted the date. One reason why I had kept the letter at all was to remind me of my misdemeanour whenever I was involved in court with people who had done much the same thing, no matter whether I was prosecuting them, defending them or sentencing them. In my student days, pubs closed at 10 o'clock, but instead of being turfed out into the street with nowhere to go, we had the privilege of staying in the union for another two hours or more. If I had been on the street at the time of my misconduct, I would almost certainly have spent the night in police custody with a charge of breach of the peace hanging over me.

When I did start my legal career in Oban, I had as a client a man who seemed to get arrested every weekend for making a nuisance of himself after the pubs closed. It was said that he kept his own library of books in Oban's police cells because that is where he spent virtually every Sunday, awaiting the Monday morning court.

The 'Yes' campaign actually won the 1979 referendum but because it was not by a sufficient margin to meet the terms of the Parliamentary Bill, it was counted as failure. The parliament therefore did not come into being at that time and many of us wondered what to do next. Most thought it was lost for all time. Fortunately, a Glasgow University academic by the name of Jack Brand managed to get people together to keep the campaign going and I phoned him one day, asking if there was anything I could do to help.

'Yes,' he replied, 'you can join the National Committee.'

The thought now of someone getting onto a national committee about anything in such an informal way is odd, but such was the paucity of activity at the time that that was the reality of the situation. For a year or two, I travelled up and down to Glasgow for the monthly evening meetings, returning in the early hours of the morning. I was glad to have done something to keep the campaign going and to meet a number of people, the most revered of whom was probably the late Jim Boyack.

At long last, eighteen years after that, the weight of public opinion, helped of course by the continuing campaign, led to another referendum. Thirty-three Home Rule bills, one of them put forward by Russell Johnston, had all failed during the 292 years that the Scottish parliament had been in abeyance. The further referendum was held on 11 September 1997 and was overwhelmingly successful. It was a happier date for Scotland than it later became for America and for most, if not all, of the world.

And then, on 1 July 1999, I skived the day off work, donned my kilt, drove to Dunblane and got the train to Edinburgh to join the many happy plebs in the street, celebrating the official re-opening of our parliament after 300 years. From the train there is an excellent view of the Wallace Memorial at Stirling and I do not think I ever felt more humble or more proud at one and the same time. Ray Michie has described to me her proud and humble emotions on many occasions when on leaving late sittings of the House of Commons she walked alone in the early hours of the morning through the great Hall of Westminster, where Wallace was condemned.

We were fortunate in Argyll and Bute to find as our Liberal

Democrat candidate George Lyon from Rothesay, who is a man of standing and who had been an impressive leader of the Scottish Farmers' Union. He was just the sort of person I considered parliament should have in it – someone with direct knowledge of the problems of Scottish life, as well as an understanding of the particular difficulties facing Highland and Island communities. I was glad to campaign for him and it was fun, although nerve-racking, as one never knows how these things are going to go. However, he eventually won convincingly, if not exactly comfortably.

Sadly, there were not nearly enough people of such calibre in the parliament. I would like to have seen many more who had been directly involved in the Health Service, housing, education and all these other things that are so important to the well-being of the Scottish people. One person I particularly regretted not seeing there was Bishop Richard Holloway, an outstanding man in all kinds of ways. In particular he had been involved in the setting-up of the first Voluntary Housing Associations in Scotland, first in Glasgow and then in Edinburgh, drawing attention to the very serious housing problem in Scotland, which many knew nothing of. Canon Kenyon Wright should also have been there. He had been a leading light in the Scottish parliament campaign over many years but even more important, was a head figure in the ecumenical movement. For some reason, I often have great difficulty in pronouncing that word and find it easier to call them 'joined up Christians'. It probably explains it better anyway. After all her years of championing Scotland and the desperate need for our own parliament, Ray Michie herself should have been in it. Unfortunately, the timing was wrong and as I have said before, that is something in life over which we have no control.

The first Transport Minister in the new Scottish government was Sarah Boyack, a daughter of Jim Boyack, who had done much to bring the parliament into fruition and whom I knew from earlier campaigns. By happy coincidence, so far as I was concerned, Sarah Boyack's first public duty was to open the new road bridge at Creagan over Loch Creran, fifteen miles north of Oban. I was not present at the opening ceremony but George Lyon, the local MSP, and Ray Michie as the Westminster MP were present and that was good enough for me.

Quite apart from the public benefit, the value of the bridge for me is that the six-mile stretch of road round the head of the loch is hardly now used by vehicles and makes an ideal bike ride at one of Argyll's many glorious spots.

The Scottish parliament is succeeding in a number of ways but there are many justifiable causes for complaint. For example, it has been taken over by the party political machines, which has kept out of the parliament many who should be there. Further, it has failed to avoid the criticism that it is sometimes just the old style of secretive government influenced by behind-the-scenes anonymous creatures, rather than being a government of the people. However, there is still plenty of time to get it right, if enough people will stand up as individuals and if we elect such people as MSPs.

One of the needs for a Scottish parliament of course is to enable essential reforms to be brought into effect when they are required. Most people in Scotland are protective and very proud of our own separate and distinctive legal system. How on earth it managed to survive all the years without our own parliament, I do not know. My own father brought me up with many complaints about the rules of intestate succession in Scotland, which even in my father's early days were sadly out of date. The result was that widowers and widows received very little money from their spouses if they were to die without leaving a will in favour of the other. Scottish lawyers spent over forty years campaigning for an automatic right for widows and widowers. It is something which should have been introduced far, far more quickly than it was. The only excuse ever given for the failure to bring in such essential reform, was that Westminster simply did not have time to attend to our separate laws.

However, do not ever imagine, as many do, that with the new laws, husbands and wives are now perfectly alright, even without a will. That is not the case and I still come across situations where widows are in danger of losing their homes because of claims made on their husband's money by brothers and sisters-in-law for example. I also read of a case, following on the dreadful Piper Alpha tragedy in the North Sea, where one of the men killed had been separated from his wife for many years without there ever having been a divorce. For a long time he had had another partner with whom he had lived happily in a house, which unfortunately was in his name alone. After the tragedy, the legal wife re-emerged and successfully got the house which was her legal entitlement.

For years, Scottish lawyers have tried to persuade clients that they simply must make wills and the Law Society has promoted a wills week, which unfortunately never seemed to attract a lot of activity from clients. Eventually, following on Bob Geldof's example with Band Aid and Live Aid, a charitable scheme originated in Oban in 1988 whereby Scottish solicitors offered for one month to do clients' wills for them without a fee, provided they made a donation to a group of charities specializing in famine relief and development work overseas. Will Aid has taken off. Despite my arguments to solicitors when I was phoning them persuading them to participate, that it would only be once in a lifetime, the scheme now runs every two years over the whole of the UK, being organized by the charities themselves. But no one should forget that it was an initiative of Scottish solicitors, which is maybe why it succeeded! So far it has raised approximately four million pounds for overseas relief and educational work and goodness knows how many extra wills and legacies have resulted from it. We were lucky with the initial Will Aid event in 1988 to get the support of that very popular Scottish actor, the late Gordon Jackson. He was such a modest man and very kind. Sadly, he died just over a year later.

One of many examples of why people should not make their own wills concerned a professor of Mathematics, no less, who, having inevitably made it rather more complicated than it should have been, came to the final part of the will where he directed his executors to divide what was left into four equal shares. 'One share I bequeath to my niece Annie Brown, one share to my nephew Peter Brown and the final share to my friend Thomas Lever.'

I recall getting a phone call from an Edinburgh solicitor saying in a rather friendly way, 'I don't like this Will Aid idea of yours.'

'Why on earth not?' I answered defensively. 'I can't see anything wrong with it.'

'I'll tell you what's wrong with it. The other day a client came in asking me to make a will. I pointed out he had only made one two months ago and enquired why was he now wanting to make another.'

To that he had received the reply, 'I just like the idea of getting you to do something for me for nothing for a change and this is too good an opportunity to miss.'

I remember, with embarrassment, my first ever radio interview, explaining how the Will Aid scheme worked. It was going out live on the Jimmy Mack programme and I had to go to a wee room in an office in Oban, which served as the BBC's linked-in studio. I was highly nervous and that condition was not helped when I went to collect the key to the room and found that no one knew where it was. I was told, 'The last person who had it was a pregnant woman with red hair, whose name I do not know. She was meant to return it yesterday but she has obviously forgotten.' After more panic, I managed to find a way into the room somehow, only to be confronted with all sorts of technical explanations about how I had to link myself in to the controller in Glasgow. Things continued to go wrong and I was sitting there with headphones on and holding a phone to half an ear, when I heard a voice from Glasgow saying, 'And Graeme Pagan is waiting by in Oban to speak to us. Hello, Graeme.' I wasn't sure which thing I was meant to be talking into but decided to play it cool. Unfortunately I opened by saying, 'Hello, Jimmy. Can I hear you?'

'Yes, Graeme, and I can hear you too.'

It was not the best of beginnings. However, it gave the family much to laugh at. Heather had taped the programme but was not decent enough to at least cut out the 'bad bit'. Later on, I became a bit more relaxed about such interviews, or so I thought. In fact, I once did seventeen in two hours, being linked in by brilliant technology to live local radio stations, one at a time, throughout Britain. However, a year after that achievement, I was doing a live interview from the BBC studio in Glasgow. I had been asked in advance if I objected to the fact that they were also bringing on to the programme a tax expert who worked in Devon.

'Not at all,' I replied, 'In fact I would welcome it as it is not a subject I am an expert on.' I fielded my first question without much difficulty and then the interviewer turned to the Devon solicitor, putting to him a highly complicated question and I remember thinking, 'I don't even understand the question, let alone the answer. Thank goodness that's not for me.' I was startled into reality.

'Hello, Mr Blackstock. Are you there? Mr Blackstock are you there? We seem to have lost Mr Blackstock but fortunately Graeme Pagan is still on the line from Glasgow. Graeme, how would you answer that question?'

I cannot remember how I got away with it, but I had had a few years of experience of listening to politicians.

No one should be surprised at my problems with things like live interviews. After all, I was the guy who, before my second only speech at a Liberal Conference, got so nervous and flustered that I ended up in the wrong toilet. I only realized that when I began wondering why they had suddenly introduced tampax machines into the gents!

One essential reform did manage to get through the Westminster parliament, but only by chance. Very soon after David Steel was elected to that parliament he became one of only a handful of MPs who, by lottery, had the opportunity to introduce a private members bill. He was inevitably approached by a number of lobbyists before deciding that abortion law reform was a real must. As with divorce, people obviously have very strong views on that, but if abortion is going to happen at all it is essential that it does happen under civilized conditions. I remember being told by Douglas Kerr, the forensic medicine professor in Edinburgh, about the large number of women who died as a result of illegal abortions. They knew the dangers but simply could not cope with their lives without an abortion and decided to take the risks involved. If they did not die, they sometimes suffered severe wounding from these back-street abortionists. That practice had to be stopped. David Steel has never been forgiven by some people for successfully introducing such an essential social reform but he has been the saviour of many women, even if they do not always realize it. Now abortion can be carried out legally in a proper medical establishment by suitably qualified medical people.

There was an interesting but sad story which emerged not long after we entered the new century. It concerned an extraordinary case in Orkney, where the remains of three newborn babies were found, having been buried there by their mother, or by someone on her behalf, between seventy and eighty years previously. Not only, of course, was abortion illegal at the time, but there was nobody in the area even to carry out an illegal abortion. It now seems to have been the case that the murder of illegitimate babies was relatively common at that time and no doubt in many other parts of the country as well.

Our new parliament will have the opportunity to ensure that all the reforms we need are put into effect and are carried out quite quickly after proper advice. We just have to hope that the parliament will not make work for itself and introduce all sorts of unnecessary new rules and regulations. Already, over the last few decades, there has been a danger of that happening from all sorts of governments.

There has been a lot of criticism of the new Scottish parliament building and its massive costs. Certainly, there seems to have been a terrible lack of control but it got off to a bad start before our parliamentarians were ever elected. However, I believe what some have predicted, that in due time it will become the most visited place in Scotland, taking over from Edinburgh Castle as the major tourist attraction. Certainly, I think and hope that our grandchildren will be proud of the building and will be surprised about all the fuss. After all, it is costing less than an addition to the Westminster parliament and we hear next to nothing about that. The Millennium Dome in London alone cost nearly twice as much and was a real white elephant if ever there was one.

My first visit to the Scottish parliament was with my youngest daughter and it was memorable for a number of reasons. A tribunal I was attending in Edinburgh ended early and after a quick visit to the High Court to see a murder trial in progress, I persuaded my daughter to accompany me to the parliament on the understanding that I would not be there too long. By chance, I bumped into one of the most impressive of the MSPs, George Reid, whom I knew of and whom I had met briefly many years before. I was having difficulty in finding the right way in and he was kind enough to show us where to go. As we walked down The Mound together after leaving the parliament, I suddenly stopped and said to my daughter, who is adopted, 'Good heavens, I've just realised what a coincidence that was – what they were debating at the time. It was adoption and children's rights.'

'I had noticed,' she replied, 'but I didn't think anything of it.'

It was actually a debate which showed the Scottish parliament at its best, with contributions from those who really knew what they were talking about, including one MSP who was himself adopted. It was also good to see MSPs applauding speeches by members of other political parties. As far as I am concerned, there is only one thing wrong with adoption. My youngest daughter insists on having two birthdays a year.

The next time I tried to visit the parliament was not so successful. Heather had never been into it and, although it was on holiday, we agreed it would be nice to have a look around. Unfortunately, the visiting time ended at three o'clock and we were seconds too late. I pleaded with an official: 'Are you really going to keep me out? I've waited three hundred years for this. Surely I am not going to be penalized just because I am a minute late.' He smiled, but rightly stuck to his guns. After all, I might have been some mad Englishman trying to secrete himself into the building with a view to removing a stone later on.

15

Through Life's Changes

Television. Photocopiers. Contact lenses. Videos. Penicillin. Frozen foods. The Pill. Credit cards. Radar. Biros. Air conditioners. Dishwashers. Electric blankets. Tumble dryers. Drip-dry clothes. Disposable nappies. Computers. Artificial hearts. None of these existed when I was born. People of my age have had to learn how to cope with change. But we are not alone because that is the way it is continuing. One very close friend of mine who died at the age of ninety-four said that it was the changes which kept her going. 'Every day something new happens or is discovered. I look forward to each new day. It's exciting.' From a business point of view, arguably, the most useful new invention was the photocopier. Imagine having to do as we did when I first started, and have everything we wanted copied typed out separately and checked over. Now everyone copies everything to everybody. But despite public perceptions and the claims of manufacturers, some new devices have actually had the effect of slowing up business.

Of course it is not just new inventions that have altered the world in the last sixty years and more; expressions have been changed from what they used to mean. For example, my own nickname, which stuck with me for a long time, almost from the time I was born, was Gay. Now it has a different meaning. At one time, it meant something cheerful and celebratory with balloons, ribbons and all that and a gay person was the life and soul of a party. Goodness knows why it was applied to me. Perhaps I could not pronounce my own name properly.

Possibly the biggest change, sad to say, is that people are less honest and are ready to tell mistruths far more often even over unimportant matters. That's a very worrying trend in business and in the court scene. Justice is impossible without truth. And it cannot be a good thing when, apparently, a fifth of all employees consider that their senior managers and directors are to be 'positively mistrusted'. Hardly any employees seem to believe in their own company's magazines and corporate videos. How can any business succeed properly when the people working for it cannot trust each other? And if they cannot trust their own colleagues, how far can they trust other people with whom they have to deal? A friend of mine worked mornings only in the Oban office of a huge organization. I phoned her once, the call being re-routed – presumably to cause confusion – to a call centre, no doubt in another country. 'I'm sorry, Sandra isn't available just now but you will be able to speak to her this afternoon.' My response, asking how on earth I could do that when I knew she didn't work afternoons, did not seem to upset the operator one little bit.

On another occasion, I was having, not for the first time, an argument with an insurance company which was trying to avoid meeting a perfectly legitimate claim. The man I was speaking to gave his name as Robert and his telephone number. Two days later I phoned the number Robert had given to enquire why he had not got back to me as he had promised.

'I'm sorry, we don't have anyone called Robert here'.

Someone must have been lying.

No-one likes to be done for parking misdemeanours but when we are at fault we usually have to accept it. Once, however, I was the victim of a faulty parking meter on a public holiday. It took a whole year of unnecessary correspondence with Glasgow Council before they were forced to admit they had been wrong. They had even fabricated various facts before they accepted that they should not have pretended that the meter had been checked on the morning of a public holiday. An imaginary meter inspector, carrying out his duties on Easter Monday, could not be found. The argument was all over £40 and no doubt cost Glasgow's Council taxpayers dear. And that did not include the cost of a free parking voucher, which I was given by way of apology. Incidentally, I never used it because I kept forgetting to take it with me and eventually gave it away!

All my three children, while students, had huge problems with their

Council Tax payments, from which, of course, they were exempt anyway. But that did not stop correspondence going on for years with Sheriff Officer's letters, potential black listing and all the rest, despite countless letters and visits to the Council Tax office from the family. Apart from the waste of Council taxpayers' money caused by such inefficiency, the concern about all this is not so much for those who should be able to look after themselves, but those who cannot. And when an old, disabled lady client nearly had her power cut off because the electricity board decided it was easier to do that than to deal with correspondence questioning the account, it was necessary for me to take severe action against them. They then claimed to have improved their systems but maybe that was just another lie.

Another, to me, unwelcome change is many people's obsession with money. Many are now unwilling to do voluntary work because they don't get paid and are often suspicious of those who do such work. 'No-one does anything for nothing any more. They must be getting something', is a very common thought. And legal and other businesses in small country areas like ours can have difficulty enticing people here from the rich pickings to be had in the cities.

I have been careful to call this final chapter 'Through Life's Changes' and not 'Through Life's Stages'. Life, of course, is not a natural progression with all of us going through stages in an organized, programmed procession. Tragically, some never get beyond what might be called stage one and some don't even get to that stage at all. What stage was my grandmother at when at over ninety, she got smashed on champagne at a family christening? As I escorted her into the taxi – she never normally needed to be escorted anywere – she turned to me and said, 'Darling, please reassure me that I am not getting old. I would so hate to be old.'

On another occasion, the family drove to Waverley station in Edinburgh to bring her to our home in Fife for a holiday. After the long journey from London she was asked if she wanted a cup of tea, which she declined.

'Are you not tired?'

'Why should I be tired? I was only sitting on the train, not driving it.'

If forced into thinking in terms of stages, I suppose I would have to admit that my grandmother was then in the later stages of her life. Sadly, it is a time when some old people can begin to lose their minds. I was lucky with my grandparents and with my parents but I remember feeling very sorry for a close friend at the time of my own mother's death. Her father, at the time, had totally lost the place and, having been a dignified, professional man, was reduced to living in a home, needing everything done for him and behaving in his mind very much as a child. I suspected at the time that my friend envied me for the fact that Mother had died in a dignified and relatively peaceful way and I certainly could not blame her for that.

I have met a number of people over the years who have been very upset by the change in behaviour of elderly relatives, who can behave in a very bizarre as well as a very offensive way. Some unfortunately took it personally, without realizing that the person was no longer responsible for the way he or she was behaving. Sometimes I have found that if you can laugh at some of the more strange behaviour without showing any disrespect to the person, that has helped people to cope.

I remember being told about an Edinburgh lawyer who, every two weeks, at the weekend, travelled to visit his elderly mother in a home in Dunoon. One night, after a particularly difficult journey, he sank into his leather chair in the New Town of Edinburgh, poured himself a large dram and was just beginning to enjoy it when he remembered that he had forgotten to tell his mother that he was safely home. She tended to worry about these things. He struggled out of his chair and went to the phone to tell her.

'That's nice dear. Where have you been?'

But my favourite of such stories concerned an elderly spinster lady in her upper eighties who was in a home in the very north of Scotland and whose affairs were looked after by an accountant. When his retirement came, he asked whether I would be willing to take over and I said that I would, provided that she was mentally capable of granting a power of attorney in my favour. The accountant said that he would be visiting her within the next couple of months and would let me know after that how he got on. I then received a telephone call from him when he read out his notes which began as follows: 'The old lady seems fine. There is no reason why Graeme should not prepare a power of attorney for her to sign.' The accountant then explained to me that shortly after he had written that, the dear old soul had looked round her room to make sure no one was listening and had then leant across to him before whispering, 'You do know, don't you, that it is going to have to be a Caesarean.'

Fortunately, we all know very elderly people who do not show their age and who carry on like someone a few decades younger. One slightly eccentric lady client I had was a very formidable woman. I remember her losing an eye when, at aged ninety, she decided to chop up some firewood. She was a woman to keep well away from if she was in her car. It was said that it had no brakes and that, when she wanted to stop, she just drove as gently as she could into the nearest tree or fence. Once there was a private funeral service in the magnificent Castle Stalker in Loch Linnhe at Appin.

'Are we all here?' enquired the minister.

'I think Mrs MacCarten has still to come,' replied one of the mourners.

At that moment there was the sound of a motorboat coming across the loch at some speed in the direction of the castle.

'That will probably be her now,' said another of the mourners.

Seconds later there was a loud bang as the motorboat crashed into the rocks below.

'That's definitely Mrs MacCarten,' said a number of voices in unison.

Of course you do not have to be old to experience mental diffi-culties. Very early on in my career, I was more than somewhat taken aback when I opened a letter from a newly acquired client and read as follows:

How dreadful a mistake I made in lowering my dignity to stoop and take you into my business affairs, Mr Pagan, let alone confide anything to you for your manners are uncouth to say the least! Furthermore I have a good mind to put you into the circulation of my new book [1963] as a fella who has a devil of a lot to learn. Your so called help is and was of very little value and for your benefit and to ponder over when I come into your mind (which will be often) [she was right!] I shall fight my legal battles myself and I shall win hands down. You remember what I told you at the head of your stairs? There will come a day soon now Mr Pagan when you will be glad to know me. Shall I know you then Mr P. I think not.

God knows what is eating you but you seem to be a cover up man to me. All smiles in front of others but when you get me alone you are a brute! When I contact London this week I shall get my son to get cracking and to tag your ancestors and descendants etc. like I did with two other persons recently. Maybe I shall get an unpleasant shock when I receive all information required as to how and where you sprang up and from. I will not tolerate anymore of your insolence or rotten trampish matters and manners. Tell me what your half hour time cost me and I shall see as you get the money (if it is worth it to me). If not I shall cut your fee by half. I only hope that when your illness overtakes you before the end of March 1962, you can be as brave as I was and as I still am. Your peculiar talk this afternoon Sir made me really wonder if your brains were a wee bittie addled.

I am

Yours most sincerely

Maybe it is not really fair to laugh but if we took such incidents too seriously, life would be impossible.

Certainly I laughed when I got a phone call from a solicitor who had acted for the buyers when I sold the house of a close friend in Perth. Apparently, my friend seemed to have forgotten that he had sold the house because he kept going back to do the garden. Not that the purchasers minded too much because, like so many young people, they were far too busy for things like gardens. But there would come a time when they would want to dispense with John's help. John's case was actually a particularly sad one. He was never a strong man and his wife controlled him to a degree with loving devotion. She later on suffered from dementia and the roles had to be reversed, with John caring for her twenty-four hours a day. When she eventually died, John had a reaction which led to him becoming more than a little bit confused and he was an easy target for unscrupulous rogue builders who kept repairing his roof. On top of all that he lost his sight completely.

Before his end he had become aggressive and used to shout offensive things at me. Fortunately, thanks to other people's experiences which they shared with me, I knew that that was not the real John and I could still remember him as a cheerful, gentle and uncomplaining person and a very loyal friend.

Life is, of course, all about changes; sometimes the very thing we want most not to happen will occur. But some have discovered that an unwanted event changed their lives dramatically and for the better, in ways which they could not have foreseen. Somebody once said that if you ask for God's help, it will come in many disguises.

People are different in the way they react and cope and it depends on whether they are the kind of people who view a bottle as being half empty or half full. Then there is the classic story of three stonecutters, all employed on the building of a cathedral hundreds of years ago. Their attitudes were different. The first of the three, when asked what he was doing, replied that he was cutting stones. The second replied that he was earning a living for his family. The third had a larger vision: 'I am building a great cathedral.'

Sometimes, of course, we do have to recognise that we have moved on to a different stage in life and that we are going to have to change our lifestyles. In my case it had to do with alcohol. I have never had a very large capacity, but like most Highlanders, including the adopted ones, I enjoy my dram. Two incidents within the space of a few months when I was still under fifty warned me that I might have to be a bit more careful in future.

The first was at a dinner of Argyll solicitors, which takes place on a two-yearly basis. I have never been allowed to forget my performance at the dinner in Campbeltown in 1982 after a visit to the Glen Scotia Distillery. I made it through the soup course but did not manage to survive the rest of the meal, or the speeches, although I remained seated at my place sound asleep. All I can remember is my partner, Mike Jarvie – a bigger man than me – interrupting my deep slumber from time to time, picking me up and saying, 'On your feet sunshine, it's another toast', then putting me down again. When, a week or two later, I presented the bill for the function to my cashier, Mairi

MacRae, she wittily commented: 'That must be the most expensive bowl of soup in history.'

Four months after that disaster, I paid my first ever visit to a live jazz bash, which was at the Edinburgh Jazz Festival. I was very excited, meeting up with people who shared my interest and tastes. I could probably have got intoxicated on a glass of water but it was certainly not that I was drinking on this second disastrous night. I got in tow with a Canadian band who shared my worship of the legendary Bix Beiderbecke and they mentioned that they had a leading jazz singer, Jodie Drake, joining them for part of their session, which was soon to happen.

Unfortunately, after being introduced to Jodie, I remember nothing more until someone was shaking me awake and telling me that it was time to leave the club. To my horror, it was 5a.m. and I had lost six or seven hours.

Two days later, I checked the jazz programme and went in search of Jodie when she was singing at a lunchtime bash. When she came to the bar she treated me like a long lost friend: 'Oh Graeme, I hope you are alright, I was worried about you.' I apologised profusely for what had happened a couple of nights before but she simply laughed. Then I told her about the Campbeltown experience.

'Do you make a habit of not eating your food?' she enquired.

'What do you mean?' I asked.

She went on to explain that I had apparently asked for chicken and chips when the band and she were ordering their food. I denied that, saying that it was not what I liked, but she insisted that that was what I must have ordered.

'It was absolutely hilarious. The waiter arrived with all the food. He asked who wanted chicken and chips and got really quite angry when everyone denied having ordered that. Then as one, seven thumbs pointed towards you where you were crashed out in the corner.'

'Oh dear, who paid for it?' I asked.

'I did.'

'How much do I owe you?'

'Absolutely nothing, I have never had such a laugh in ages.'

It seemed to me unusual that someone in the jazz world had to meet up with a boring country solicitor to have such a good laugh.

My social graces are not always of the best. At one legal dinner in the WS library in Edinburgh, I somehow managed to set fire to my menu by leaving it too close to the candles. It was actually at a dinner being hosted by my partner, David Preston, who was then President of the Law Society, and there was a large number of distinguished guests and dignitaries present. One of them wrote to him later, thanking him for a marvellous dinner in tremendous surroundings with great company and then added: 'And as if that wasn't enough, the attempted arson added a frisson of excitement to the occasion.' She must have noticed a waiter carrying the burning menu on a silver tray the whole length of the long dining room.

Looking back, I recall that I once had occasion to be very grateful for alcohol. What happened was that I got into the Bedford School Cricket Eleven for a very important match simply because two of my friends, who were better than me and who had been in the team all season, were banned for two matches. They had been away at a two-day match at another posh public school and had broken out from the confines of the dormitory to hit the nightspots in the local town. They were apparently discovered crawling back through the dormitory window in the early hours of the morning, having enjoyed a good night of alcohol and women – both of which were regarded by the school authorities as the most heinous crimes of all time.

I could never understand why such efforts were made to isolate us from female company, not that I was unduly interested in those days. That was perhaps as well, because speaking to a girl in the streets of Bedford was a beatable offence. At the same time, however, the authorities were equally against homosexual behaviour. In fact, at the start of one term, they decided to have a purge against anyone with homosexual tendencies. So determined were they that they invited all of us to report to our housemaster in strict confidence anyone whom we suspected. The result was inevitable. We all queued up to shop our enemies and by the end of the week all seventy-five boys in the house had been branded as homosexual.

It is not surprising that, decades later, I was vehemently against the government's dreadful idea to invite neighbours to report anyone they suspected of getting state benefit falsely. It was noticeable that the government did not even dream of introducing a similar scheme to deal with business and company frauds. They were apparently to be allowed to continue.

Another wicked crime at Bedford School, only marginally behind homosexuality and speaking to women, was smoking. Fortunately there were two safe places to indulge in such anti-social behaviour. One was the large bell tower in the town, to which a friend and fellow smoker had access for legitimate reasons. Actually it was not as safe as I imagined because, within seconds of my first visit there, three o'clock struck and I nearly fell to the street below. The other safe haven was the school photographic darkroom, which was the only room where we were allowed to lock ourselves in. Many keen camera boys were not keen at all. They were smokers. Fortunately the school authorities never seemed to realize that gloves, toothpaste, peppermints, heavily scented soap, air fresheners and various other such items had nothing to do with developing photos. Many years later I met Paddy Ashdown, who was a year or two (or more) behind me at Bedford School and who had by then become leader of the Liberal Democrat Party. He also had made full use of the photographic society for the wrong purposes and I was glad to hear that he had helped to keep the school traditions going. Later he did a marvellous job in advancing the traditions of liberalism.

Another school tradition hit the front page headlines of one of the less intellectual Sunday papers the term after I left. This had to do with pub crawls following Sunday morning chapel. I never understood why that was considered newsworthy, but the headline might have misled readers into thinking that it was worth a read: SHAME OF TOP PUBLIC SCHOOL EXPOSED. A schoolfriend of mine, not realizing who he was talking to, and no doubt exaggerating a bit, was quoted by the reporter as saying that boys of all ages went straight from chapel to the nearest pub to see how many pints they could get down before lunch and then added: 'It's all part of a long-standing school tradition.' On my first return to the school after leaving, I came across one of the masters with whom I had had a few earlier encounters. 'It is an amazing coincidence,' he said to me, 'that the pub story should have broken the term after you left. Some of my colleagues wondered whether that was because you had used your good influence to keep the others in check while you were there or whether you were a main participant. I am afraid I had to make my own views on that abundantly clear!'

My mother and father were very pleased about the fate of my two friends who were banned from the school cricket team, because that allowed me into the team for the important match. The match was against an old England Eleven on the occasion of the school's 400th anniversary, and it was to be attended by royalty in the person of Princess Margaret. Later I was able to show my proud parents a photograph of me, which also included the princess and a former England cricket captain. I hoped that, after all my reprimands, Dad at last felt that my presence at Bedford had been worthwhile.

What I most remember about the match was playing against the West Indian, Learie Constantine, who, at the time, was regarded as the greatest all-round cricketer that the world had ever seen. I remember him, then aged fifty, coming in to bat and being warned by the elderly man at the other crease that he could no longer manage a quick single. Learie reassured him but then to his first ball he played it only a yard or two in front of himself and called for a run. The old England cricketer almost had a heart attack trying to reach the other end and, when he recovered his breath, reprimanded Learie for going back on his word.

'I know, man,' came the disarming reply, 'but the last time I played on this ground I was out for nothing and I am not going to do that again.'

I was very proud to have been in the same company as the great Learie Constantine, not just because of his sporting prowess, but because of his fight against racial discrimination. On one occasion he had booked into a London hotel, only to have it claimed when he arrived that there had been a double booking and he would have to go elsewhere. It was clear that it was simply his colour that had suddenly made him unwelcome at the hotel and he raised an action against the hotel proprietors for defamation and damages, which I am glad to say he won. Later he settled in Britain and worked tirelessly to break down such discriminatory behaviour. Nine years after my lucky cricketing encounter with him, he became the first black man in the House of Lords under the title of Baron Learie Nicholas Constantine of Maraval and Nelson. He died in 1971.

When I was at Bedford School, we had some kind of association with an organisation called the Holborn Boys' Club, which was set up for some deprived children in what was, at the time, a very poor area of London. Once a year the school authorities invited them to come to the school, which they presumably thought was a magnificent gesture of kindness. I seem to remember we played one game of cricket against them, gave them some juice and a bun or two and then sent them back on the train to where they had come from. I suppose that the authorities thought that such generosity would instil a very grateful attitude into the boys from the Holborn Club and that they would then devote the rest of their lives fighting to make sure that the sort of privileges we enjoyed at Bedford would continue. Instead, I would imagine that the visit simply resulted in feelings of resentment and a determination from the boys of the club to change the country's dreadful social divisions at the earliest opportunity.

I have, of course, had many other sporting heroes apart from Learie Constantine, although I never had the honour to meet or even see, except on screen, Scotland's world champion racing driver, Jim Clark. However, there was a sort of connection between us, of which he would have been totally unaware. This was that he was born sixteen days before me, sixteen miles away from Cupar where I was born. Later, he moved to the Borders and twenty years after his death I at last managed a visit to his memorial museum in Duns with my own family. We also paid our respects at his grave at Chirnside, where his headstone rightfully and proudly records that he won twenty-five Grand Prix races.

Many people remember where they were and what they were doing when American president, John Kennedy, was assassinated. I am sure that many Scots of my generation will recall what they were doing when they got the awful news of Jim Clark's tragic death in 1968. He was only thirty-two. It was a Sunday and I had spent the day with Willie Melville and my Dalmatian dog in the hills above Helensburgh. On the way home, Willie decided to phone his wife Margaret to warn her that we were running late. He stopped at a phone box at the top of the Rest and be Thankful, there being, of course, no mobile phones at that time, before returning to the car ashen-faced.

'Jim Clark's been killed at Hockenheim.'

We said nothing for the next few miles and I then reacted, as many do, clinging to false hope.

'Does Margaret know much about sport?'

'Not a great deal.'

'Maybe she's got the wrong man.'

But of course she hadn't.

I am sure Willie and I would have wanted larger than normal drams that night.

Many years later there was an amusing encounter between Willie and his optician when, despite his being a bank manager, he managed to get wrong a cheque for an account which was due. The exchange of correspondence went something like this:

'I thought a bank manager would know how to write a cheque.'

'Oops, sorry. It must be those new glasses.'

'Put more water in them next time,' came the bright reply.

One of life's changes for me – I refuse to recognize it as a stage – was when I became entitled to my old age rail discount card, which from time to time is extremely useful – a fact I commented on at Dunblane Station one day when I was getting a ticket for Edinburgh.

'Handy things these, aren't they?' I said cheerfully.

'Indeed they are sir.' Pause. 'When you remember to renew them.'

Mine was already six months out of date.

On another occasion I was buying my concessionary ticket at Queen Street Station in Glasgow one morning in front of a large queue, prior to getting the 8 o'clock train to Edinburgh.

'That will be 9.15 sir.'

'Bloody ageist nonsense,' I said to myself. 'How dare they keep old people off the 8 o'clock till later on in the day.' I made my protest.

'£9.15 is the price of the ticket , sir.'

No hole opened up in front of me, unfortunately, and I had to walk past those in the queue who were all sniggering at my stupidity.

Naturally, Oban itself has seen great changes in the last forty years and more. We now have one hospital instead of five but, although beds no longer have to be moved into the middle of wards to avoid leaking roofs, staff morale is not what it was. When I first arrived in the area, there was of course no Ballachulish Bridge. Early on I made a journey north with fellow solicitor Robin Banks and was impressed by his instant sizing-up of the situation. He was driving and as we approached the pier, he did not even reduce speed before carrying on towards Kinlochleven and round the loch without making use of the ferry.

'Why did you not join the queue for the ferry?' I asked in ignorance.

'As soon as I came round the corner, I saw that the queue was already beyond the rowan tree. If it is, then it is quicker to drive all the way round the loch.'

That was a distance of about fourteen miles. Many years later, my son entered a bicycle marathon of some kind which involved cycling twice round Loch Leven. He was the youngest competitor by a large number of years and by the time he finished the course a lot of the older participants had left for home. But he finished.

One of many regrets is that I never travelled on the Oban to Ballachulish railway line, which was closed down in the late 1960s. The route it took is still visible at many spots and serves as a frequent reminder that I kept saying, 'I must go on the train before it is too late.' One of my colleagues travelled on it every day for a few years from Ballachulish, crossing the impressive bridges over Loch Creran and Loch Etive at Connel. The Connel Bridge also celebrated its centenary in 2003. When I first came, one of the few perks I got from my job was a season ticket to drive over the Connel Bridge. It was a particularly worthwhile one because the cost of the crossing each time was five shillings. That would be the equivalent now of at least £5, which was a lot of money for a short crossing. When the train still ran, it was not possible for cars to drive over the bridge at the same time and there was a memorable scene, once the train had passed, of the man in charge of the bridge getting on his bike and cycling back across the bridge, the cars following behind him. He then opened the gates and allowed the traffic to flow one way, as it still does.

City dwellers might ridicule the thought of cars having to follow an old man pedalling his bike, but does city traffic often move faster than that? Contrasting lifestyles were well illustrated by a telephone conversation, just before one lunch break, between Oban solicitor, John Stevenson and a solicitor in Glasgow.

'What do you do for lunch?' John asked.

'Oh, I suppose I shall just have to fight my way through the crowds, stand in a long queue, wait for a sandwich and bring it back to my office. By that time the hour will be up. And what about you?'

'Well, it's a beautiful day here,' said John. 'I think I'll have a trip round the Bay on my water skis. There will be plenty of time before two o'clock.'

I was never sure of how good a water skier John was or whether he skied at all, but at least it illustrated a different way of life.

On another occasion John was comparing notes with a partner of a large Edinburgh firm with a huge staff.

'Do you have any staff problems, Mr Stevenson,' asked the Edinburgh lawer.

'Unfortunately, I do,' replied John. 'Fifty per cent of my staff are off ill just now.'

'Good heavens, is there an epidemic in Oban?'

'Not exactly, Yvonne's got 'flu.'

The coming of large supermarkets has led to huge changes, which include the closing down of various local grocery shops. The power of such massive organizations is worrying and they continue to threaten other local businesses. That will further reduce the choices we have and the kind of service we enjoyed from local shops. I remember my butcher friend, Alastair Jackson, telling me of a phone call he had received at home one Saturday night. It went something like this: 'I am cooking my evening meal and I got this nice steak from Tesco this afternoon. I am not sure how I should best cook it. Can you help me?'

Another change is that visitors are now coming here at all times of the year, which is to be welcomed. At one time, when I was first in Oban, I used to take a holiday in September. By the time I got back after a two-week break, Oban was a totally different town with only a few people around. Now tourists and tour buses can be seen at any time of the year.

Sadly, we no longer hear the bells from the Carmelite Monastery, which used to be a regular reminder of serenity and decency. It may have been one of the nuns who told me the lovely story of the wee boy in one of the poorer parts of the world, walking home from school in the middle of a violent thunder storm. His mother, anxious for his safety, set out in search of him. She saw him coming casually across the field, apparently unconcerned. Indeed, after each flash of lightning, he stopped, looked up to the skies, patted his hair back into place and smiled. 'Hurry on home before you are struck,' called out his mother. 'What on earth are you doing?'

'God keeps taking my photo,' came the reply, 'and I want to look my best for him.'

I can sometimes be accused of dwelling on gloomy and morbid things. But they are a natural part of life and there can be lessons to be learned from how other people have managed to survive some of life's least welcome changes. Being myself a natural pessimist, I have a dread of how I would cope if faced with severe physical or emotional pain. Drawing on other people's experiences, which I have often found inspiring, can help with some of life's difficulties. It is worth remembering that 'life is not a rehearsal'.

I see the courage of others almost every day, whether it is those who have lost their loved ones; those who are being constantly bullied and demeaned in the work place but who still, day by day, force themselves out of their homes and in to work; those whose children have gone off the rails, sometimes through drugs, and are committing all kinds of dishonest and violent acts in their homes and in the homes of neighbours and friends; those whose partners, often but not always because of drink, have become violent and abusive to them on a regular basis, but who frequently, because of the children and the lack of a real alternative, stay at home night after night nervously awaiting the abuser's return; those about to lose their jobs or their businesses with no prospect of other employment; those in danger of being thrown out of their homes; those who have had terminal illnesses diagnosed; those who have returned home at the end of a normal day to find that their partners have gone off with the children, because they have found someone else who they think might be better.

I also think of the friend of mine who married full of love and confidence and who then had the experience, only a few months later, of having her twenty-one-year-old husband diagnosed with schizophrenia, of which there had been no previous signs of any kind. Very soon his unintended violence became too dangerous for his wife and newborn son and he had to spend the rest of his life in a home before dying of a heart attack aged fifty.

All those sadly common experiences obviously bring about monumental changes in the lives of those affected. Friends of mine had to draw on all their strengths of optimism and courage when a son went off to college, did not find time to buy a promised new helmet for his pedal bike and was then the wholly innocent victim of a road accident which left him in intensive care for three months, fighting for his life. Recovery – but not quite complete – was eventually made but many lives had changed.

A young lady client and friend was raped by a bogus taxi driver and naturally wanted to put the incident out of her mind and well behind her. At the same time, it was vital that she gave evidence to ensure that the attacker was not allowed to continue roaming the streets. Freakishly, she had to give evidence twice because the first judge took ill and the trial had to begin all over again, with the victim once more having to spend hours giving details of her awful experience to a second jury. I was not at the trial but I think it safe to say that the legal system must have let her down by allowing the cross-examination to go on so long – three days and two days. Apart from the continuing trauma, that friend's life has been irreversibly changed because she will never again be able to earn her living in the licensed trade business, where work finishes in the early hours.

Remembering other peoples' experiences, without dwelling on them unnecessarily, should help the more fortunate of us to appreciate just how lucky we are and to hold on to what we have. I once read: 'If you have never experienced the danger of battle, the loneliness of imprisonment, the agony of torture or the pangs of starvation, you are ahead of 500 million people in the world.' It is always worth remembering individual acts of courage. Malcolm Michie's close friend, Donnie MacLeod, went to see him at a time when Malcolm's end was near, after a long cancer illness. Donnie was greatly upset to see him at home, lying on the settee, hardly able to move and seemingly not much more than skin and bones. He went back to his own home in a state of distress, but as he entered the phone was ringing. It was Malcolm.

'It's me. I was just wondering if you wanted to go out for a spot of lunch.'

A few years later, Donnie was himself being treated for cancer. I was told that his spirit was so great that some of the other patients thought that he had been brought into hospital just to keep them cheerful and did not realize that he was himself a patient. Could Malcolm's example have been an influence?

It has been said before that we ignore the lessons of history at our peril. I think also that we ignore the lessons from other people's day-to-day experiences at our peril. That is one of the main reasons for this book. When we are young we often think history is totally unimportant and boring but it is encouraging when there are signs that young people have learned the experiences of the past. I remember a friend of mine showing me a poem written by her twelve-year-old son about the First World War, seventy years after that ghastly event. Her boy wrote:

In the First World War people died.
Soldiers in trenches made by mud
Soldiers lying wounded on the ground
In pain with wounds and blood
The surroundings with gas and smoke
The weapons, guns and knives
People dying for their country
Giving up their lives.

I once met a man who, on the battlefields of the First World War, had had his leg sawn off without an anaesthetic. I could not bear to think of it but it reminded me, not just of the ghastly realities of war, but also of the fact that everyone has a tale to tell. Sadly we don't always have time to listen. I like to think young people will learn the futility of war and try to make sure it never happens again, but that still seems to be a forlorn hope.

Keeping in mind the lessons from history does not mean that anyone should dwell in the past – especially any unpleasant parts of it. I recently read of a man, Alfred Anderson, who celebrated his 106th birthday by unveiling a memorial at the Black Watch Headquarters in Perth. Eighty-nine years before, he had joined the Black Watch as a seventeen-year-old and, like many others, had had horrible experiences in the fields of battle during the war. After the ceremony he commented: 'We lived for each day during the war. At 106 I do much the same again. If I dwelled on what happened during those terrible times, I would never have lived to see 106. It's over, it's past. It is today that matters and a better tomorrow.'

On a happy note, I once overheard two jazz man talking about music and composition. One asked the other:

'Do you ever wake up in the middle of the night with a marvellous new tune in your head and find by the morning that you have forgotten how it went and you lost it all.'

'Yes,' replied the other, 'I do and it happened to me just the other night, but it was such a beautiful new melody that I decided to go downstairs, even although it was the middle of the night, and write down the music before I forgot. Unfortunately, when I got up in the morning I found that I had written the notes for "Stardust".'

That was a tune written by Hoagy Carmichael back in the 1920s and until the Beatles came on the scene, 'Stardust' sold the most copies of any music in history. So what was the music being played on the radio when I came into my house after writing part of this book in my gazebo – 'Stardust'? No. it was the Beatles. And what was it they were singing?

'Paperback Writer'.